Also by IRVING KOLODIN

The Guide to Long Playing Records: Orchestral Music
The Musical Life
The Story of the Metropolitan Opera: 1883–1950
The Metropolitan Opera: 1883–1966
The Continuity of Music: A History of Influence

These are Borzoi Books published in New York by Alfred A. Knopf

The Interior Beethoven

IRVING KOLODIN

The Interior Beethoven

A BIOGRAPHY OF THE MUSIC

ALFRED·A·KNOPF New York
1975

THIS IS A BORZOI BOOK

PUBLISHED BY ALFRED A. KNOPF, INC.

Library of Congress Cataloging in Publication Data:
Kolodin, Irving, (date)
The interior Beethoven.
1. Beethoven, Ludwig van, 1770–1827. Works.
I. Title
ML410.B42K64   780'.92'4   74–7741
ISBN 0–394–46626–6

Manufactured in the United States of America

FIRST EDITION

To Alfred

*for publishing books that taught us
not only what to read
but how to write*

INTERIOR *Belonging to the mental or spiritual life; not bodily or worldly.*

(Webster's New International Dictionary, Second Edition)

CONTENTS

ACKNOWLEDGMENTS

MY THANKS on behalf of the content of *The Interior Beethoven* are directed in homage to a unique breed of interpreters I have encountered during a lifetime of listening. They are the ones who illuminate as they communicate and enlighten as they invigorate. Among them the late Artur Schnabel was the standard-bearer, but the number who marched behind him was legion.

I owe a special, personal debt to Dr. Joseph Braunstein, who read the manuscript with a scholar's eye. In addition, unsolicited and from the generosity of his heart, he contributed several invaluable instances from the Beethoven literature that are pertinent to the thesis of this book. They are separately identified as they occur.

I.K.

FOREWORD

O N ONE OF THOSE RESTLESS NIGHTS that beset those who over-extend their mental capacities, I was visited by a spectral being inquiring: "And how is Beethoven?" As nearly as I can recall, my reply was: "To borrow a current phrase, Beethoven is alive and well and living on Mount Parnassus. He has a villa (the biggest around, for that is how things are run in the Afterworld) down the street from Mozart's and, naturally, a little higher up on the hill than Wagner's. This is a source of some irritation to Wagner, who does not claim that he should have a bigger villa than Beethoven's, but grumbles about not having one as big . . . *Meistersinger*, you know? And *Tristan?* And *Parsifal?* Not to mention the *Ring*. But the last time it was taken up with the Parnassus Housing Committee, even Wagner had to admit that, in pure elapsed time, the nine symphonies, the thirty-two piano sonatas, sixteen quartets, and innumerable other works gave Beethoven a distinctive edge. Quality, I may add, is never discussed in the Afterworld. The mere fact that you are living on Mount Parnassus is evidence that you have passed the qualifications for entry. As for changes of status, or reassignment, it is recognized that somebody who is *in* this century (like Vivaldi) might well go back down again in the 2020s. So the Committee takes the long view and doesn't jump to hasty reassignments. Beethoven, of course, did not turn up at the hearings. Besides, like Bach, Haydn, and Mozart, when they meet for a beer, he always says: 'These newcomers had it easy—they knew everything we had done, before they even *started* as composers. It wasn't like that in *our* time.' "

It was out of such considerations that the realization crystallized that any words addressed at this time to Beethoven should deal less with the temporal being of the composer—that obsessed, crabbed, cursed, and most exalted of men, whose life is a model of nothing but endeavor—than with its indestructible product. Even though the staggering mass of music he produced is more familiar to the present generation than to any previous one, it continues to absorb, to challenge, and in some final aspects, to baffle the imagination. It shares with some other inexhaustible subjects the ever-enticing fascination that the more one knows it, the more one wants to know about it.

It is a further enticement that the more one knows about it, the more one finds to know about it. One can enjoy, even venerate, two great masterpieces for much of a lifetime without perceiving any specific link between them. Then, in a flash of re-awakened attention, the inner relationship may become so strongly manifest that they may be comprehended as products of the same impulse, differently articulated. This relates not only to the obvious hallmarks of Beethoven's rigorously controlled technical procedures, or the benchmarks by which he measured, and rejected, results that would have made the reputation of almost any other composer. It refers to deeper manifestations of the creative will than even he knew to exist.

One cannot even allude to such a concept as the "deeper manifestation of the creative will" without paying tribute to the late Ernest Newman. The re-publication, during the duplecentennial year, of his notable brief on *The Unconscious Beethoven*[1] marks a deserved endorsement of the insights it contains and the glimpses they provide into the composer's creative processes. It is a cardinal virtue of Newman's treatment that it focuses attention, as I have written, not only on "what Beethoven was, but where he was—at a historical junction of musical forces."

Newman's signboard to the future comprehension of such creativity points directions, defines highroads—as opposed to byroads—in a way which will well serve any who can read as they run. Fundamentally, any journey undertaken into so uncharted, non-finite, and enticing a territory as "the deeper manifestation of the creative will" must, inevitably, be self-conducted. There is no Cook's Tour to Interior Beethoven, as there may be even to Outer Mongolia. Any such quest into the heart of darkness that is every artist's "creative will" must be an individual enterprise.

[1] Ernest Newman: *The Unconscious Beethoven*, with an Introduction by Irving Kolodin (New York: Alfred A. Knopf; 1970). Originally published by Knopf, New York, in 1927.

What follows is this individual's venture into Interior Beethoven, or Basic Beethoven, or what may be termed the Upper Congo of the Intellect. Its remote sources continue even today to irrigate the lowlands and highlands through which the stream of Beethoven's thought flows majestically to the sea of uncharted musical possibilities.

I.K.

October 1, 1974

The Interior
Beethoven

I

Thus Knocks Fate
at the Door
(Again, and Again, and Again)

I

AMONG THE BASICS of Interior Beethoven, none are more fundamental than the thoughts, emotions, and impulses aroused by the rhythmic-melodic formulation ♪♪♪|♩ . It is a phrase known to countless thousands as the germ cell from which he evolved the C-minor Symphony (No. 5), the most widely performed of all orchestral works. Countless more, who have knowledge of little else associated with its creator, recall it as the V for Victory symbol which forged a common bond among men around the world during the most costly war ever waged. The coincidence that its rhythmic pattern paralleled the telegraphic dots and dash • • • — of V in the International Code, made the four notes intelligible to men who had no other common language.

In his pioneering and enduringly informative volume on the symphonies,[1] Sir George Grove observed decades ago: "The earliest sketches of the work [Symphony No. 5] are in a collection of sheets which also contain sketches for the G major piano concerto. . . . The

[1] George Grove: *Beethoven and His Nine Symphonies* (London: Novello and Company, Ltd.; 1896, preface dating from February 29, 1896), p. 141.

opening is probably the most famous theme in the world, and Beethoven's first memorandum of it is textually as follows":

"The theme is merely the four notes; but here[2] we have the manner in which Beethoven first proposed to develop them."

The scheme of presentation (statement in the treble, answer in the bass) that Beethoven utilized as the first movement developed is clearly defined. There are also rudimentary suggestions of the climbing, straining, surging dynamic power with which Beethoven would drive his thematic nail into the consciousness of the musical world. But the nail itself would have to be hand-forged on the hammer-and-anvil of Beethoven's mind before it would suit his purpose. That would take time.

Search as one may through the earlier sketchbooks—the repository of Beethoven's random thoughts and transient impulses—which he began to keep systematically[3] in 1800 and continued through his life, no prior notation of the ♪♪♪|♪ pattern can be turned up. Thus the entry of 1803 is all that Sir George says it is: The earliest written occurrence of such a sketch. But this is not to say that it is the earliest utilization by Beethoven of such a rhythmic pattern. Its occurrence

[2] Gustav Nottebohm: *Beethoveniana: Aufsätze und Mittheilungen* (New York and London: Johnson Reprint Corporation; 1970), p. 10. Originally published by Verlag von C. F. Peters, Leipzig, 1872.

[3] The so-called "Kafka Sketchbooks" (in Ludwig van Beethoven: *Autograph Miscellany from Circa 1786 to 1799*, 2 vols. ed. Joseph Kerman [London: Trustees of The British Museum; 1970 and New York: Columbia University Press; 1970], are much more "sketchy" and, valuable as they are, in no sense systematic.

may not always be immediately apparent to the eye, but the ear is harder to deceive.

For listeners of today (whether casual or intensive), access to almost any note Beethoven ever wrote, played on the instrument for which he wrote it, is a commonplace. Perhaps Sir George dreamed that the invention, during his lifetime, of sound-reproducing devices (by Edison and others) might one day afford such a convenience. But he did not live to know it. He had, by visual recognition alone, given voice to a profound insight in demonstrating that two works of greatly different character might emerge from a single musical cell. One can take no exception to his statement that, widely different as the famously forceful symphony (No. 5) and the infinitely beguiling concerto (No. 4) are, "the rhythm of the subject is the same in each."[4]

Grove has furthermore alerted the prospector for intellectual treasure not to discard a softer substance because it lacks the shape or weight of the diamond in the rough for which he is seeking. The cutting edge might, after all, be buried within a coarser covering. Nor is it inevitable that a theme destined for use in a concerto be invented with that purpose in mind. Above all, Grove has posed the possibility that the creator himself might not be a volitional participant in a chain of events outside his conscious awareness.

Given the greater operational facilities of our time, Grove could conceivably have extended his discoveries into quartets and sonatas, trios and overtures as well as symphonies and concertos. That is to say, a listener-prospector of today, interested in tracking such a phrase as ♪♪♪|♩ to its earliest occurrence, may command an aural review not merely of almost every note Beethoven ever wrote, but in the sequence in which it was written. This is, of course, repeatedly dissimilar to the sequence in which the works were published. In my own experience with the seventy-five disks[5] of the twelve Deutsche Grammophon Gesellschaft albums, which move systematically from pre–Opus 1 to post–Opus 135, such a review can be accomplished in seven or eight weeks of concentrated listening.

---

[4] Grove: *Beethoven and His Nine Symphonies*, p. 142.
[5] Such addenda as folk songs arranged by Beethoven for the English publisher George Thomson continue to accumulate.

The net of it is that, had such a possibility presented itself to Sir George, he would, in all probability, have abandoned wholly any trust in one of the most familiar anecdotes in the lore of music. It is the one to which Anton Schindler, the composer's sometimes irritating factotum and more often inaccurate biographer, gave circulation in the 1860s.[6]

Of the C-minor Symphony, Schindler says: "The composer himself provided a key when, one day in this author's presence, he pointed to the beginning of the first movement [♪♪♪|♩] and expressed in these words the fundamental idea of the work: 'Thus knocks fate at the door.'"

If this was indeed Beethoven's own statement, one would have to charge him with forgetfulness (at the least), for Fate had been knocking at his door without a conscious response for some time previously. Sir George Grove could have heard it, as I have heard it, in a work which predates the entry in the 1803 sketchbook by at least half a dozen years. I refer to the finale of the C-minor Piano Sonata (Opus 10, No. 1) which begins:[7]

As Beethoven applies himself to the elaboration and amplification of this material (in the development section) it is converted, at a climactic point, into:

---

[6] Anton Felix Schindler: *Beethoven as I Knew Him*, ed. Donald W. McArdle and trans. Constance S. Jolly (Chapel Hill: University of North Carolina Press; 1966—also London: Faber and Faber; 1966), p. 147.

[7] The form in which the beginning of the finale is printed, without the eighth rest necessary to complete the first figure of the first measures, follows the *Urtext* (unedited). Kalmus edition, I, 88.

One, two, three, four, five statements of the seemingly insignificant phrase and, in the space of two and a fraction measures, it has come and gone. Nor does it reappear in the remaining seventy measures of the movement. But it is "gone" only from the forefront of the creator's mind, engrossed with a particular phase of a particular work of 1796. In a way thoroughly typical of Beethoven's mental functioning it has retreated to an obscure recess of that capacious mind, neither filed nor forgotten, awaiting an appropriate moment to surface for reconsideration. In the instance of ♫♫♩|♩, half a dozen years passed before it began to clamor for such reconsideration and fulfillment. In a manner characteristic of the recurrence and reuse of other thematic or harmonic or rhythmic cells, when the fulfillment was finally achieved on a sufficiently monumental scale, Beethoven's preoccupation with it ended. Some other urgent problem was always at hand to be seized upon, or for Beethoven to be seized by.

In his comprehensive and masterly consideration of the string quartets Joseph Kerman says, apropos of the B-flat Quartet (Opus 130) of the final five: "This cadence [in the *poco scherzoso*] recalls the Allegretto Scherzando of the Eighth Symphony, the movement based on his joke about the Mälzel metronome."[8] (A friend and admirer of the man who devised the tick-tock instrument for marking musical time, Beethoven simulated its insistent beat in the second movement of his Eighth Symphony.) Continues Kerman: "Beethoven had a way of realizing his unfulfilled conceptions. The quartet [of 1825] helped clarify what, in 1812, had been dimly and much less beautifully present in his mind." My extension of Kerman's statement—and the premise on which this book is founded—would be: "Beethoven had an obsession with realizing his unfulfilled conceptions." It was out of this tenacity and this absorption with the shaping and spacing of musical materials that Beethoven created the reservoir of thought, the seed bank of idea that nourished the musical community of Europe for decades.

Should one be so disposed, hints of the ♫♫♩|♩ pattern can be isolated in works even earlier than the C-minor Sonata of Opus 10 (see p. 41). In the main they prove—on closer, visual inspection—to be wrong signals to the ear. Such an instance may be found in the introductory Marcia of the Serenade for String Trio (Opus 8). The passage begins in measure 4, with the violin and viola in tandem, the

---

[8] Joseph Kerman: *The Beethoven Quartets* (New York: Alfred A. Knopf; 1967), p. 317. Mälzel's instrument of 1812 (when the Eighth Symphony was written) was a predecessor of the now well-known "metronome" he produced in 1816.

cello answering in the low register. The usage suggests the later, antiphonal (statement and response) pattern to which ♪♪♩|♩ was predisposed. On investigation we find a conventional triplet and quarter— ♩♩♩ ♩—lacking the bite, the force, and the impact of ♪♪♩|♩. As a foil, in some later works, to ♪♪♩|♩, ♩♩♩ ♩ has its own kind of utility. On its own, however, all the triplet form has to offer is an even succession of accents over two beats, rather than the staggered succession of emphasis in ♪♪♩|♩. The latter is not only spread over three beats, but *across* a barline, which provides for a major accent and a sustained downbeat.

It is of considerable significance to me that the first authentic statement of ♪♪♩|♩ emerges from a heated musical discourse rather than in a flash of inspiration. It was *attained* by Beethoven's own kind of diligence and application rather than being *received* as a gift through some form of divine intercession later composers have called an *Einfall*.[9] And in the heat of that discourse it attained at once the craggy spareness of outline, without harmony or supporting chords, that was to characterize its final, famous form.

In the years before it moved from the remote wings of Beethoven's thinking to stage center, ♪♪♩|♩ did not disappear from his vocabulary. As one may repeatedly find in the broad span of his literature, a nuclear idea occurs and reoccurs in gradually widening spheres of influence. Finally it ceases to be an incidental element, subordinate to some other impulse, and emerges as the generative force of a whole on its own.

A meaningful intermediate reference occurs about halfway between the completion of the sonata to which it is altogether incidental and the beginning of the symphony in which it is fiercely elemental. As if divinely ordained, the work is one which shares the key of C minor with the sonata and the symphony. Documentation of the hypnotic influence that keys and positions on the scale (high or low, bass, middle, and treble) exercised on composers of the eighteenth and nineteenth centuries is too limited for generalizations to be permissible. But an infinity of evidence leaves little doubt that such an influence did exist.

Only four years separate the C-minor Sonata from the C-minor Concerto of 1800. But the expansion of Beethoven's musical concepts, as well as of the means to realize them, was enormous. No longer obliged to pursue the paths of others, striking out ever more boldly into

---

[9] Paul Hindemith: *A Composer's World* (Garden City, N.Y.: Doubleday; 1961), p. 68.

hitherto unexplored territory, Beethoven was clearing ground toward
a high road of his own. It would, in time, become a path for others to
follow—as far as they could.

In the C-minor Concerto (No. 3)—the first which is clearly, unmistakably Beethoven—the outline of the tonic chord provides the
basis for an opening statement by the orchestral strings (in unison):

At measure 25, Beethoven launches a ♫♩|♩ pattern, which be-
comes at measure 86 ♩♩♩♩. After various permutations, the rhythmic
pattern evolves into ♫♩♪, alternating with ♫♩|♩. At measure 489,
the propulsive force behind the final thrust by the piano is ♫♩♪.

The compulsion to logic and organic unity that prompted Beethoven to tie the movements of a large work ever more closely together
—by eliminating air space for applause and building themes from interrelated elements—has one of its earliest expressions in the finale of the
Third Concerto. Its underlying thought is

The initial motif of six notes (♪|♫♫♩|♩) not only carries forward the
♫♩♪ pulse established in the first movement, it ensures, as surely as
the signature to the work is Beethoven's, fragmentation into ♫♩|♩. In
the final scampering Presto, there is a sequence of eight measures in
which the timpani adds the insistent to the inevitable by marking the
figure—now accelerated to ♫♫|♩—four times. In each instance, the
emphasis is across the barline, pointing the way to the eruptive force
it later became.

With so close an approximation to the C-minor Symphony's
nuclear cell in being, it is mere curiosity to speculate why did it not

begin to expand at once, and, if not immediately, why in 1803? Between 1800, when Beethoven finished the Third Concerto, and 1803, when he began the Fifth Symphony, he composed at the typically tempestuous pace of his early thirties. The works completed or well under way included the Symphony No. 2; the *Creatures of Prometheus,* with its by-product, the E-flat variations of Opus 35 (and, collaterally, the finale of the *Eroica* Symphony based upon the theme utilized in those variations); a dozen sonatas, including the "Moonlight" for piano (Opus 27, No. 2) and the "Kreutzer" for piano and violin (Opus 47). None of these is in C minor save the Opus 30, No. 2, Sonata for Piano and Violin. Nothing like the ♩♩♩|♩ motive appears in it nor in any of the others.

So much for the negative. The affirmative must, inevitably, be associated with a concert of his own works which Beethoven produced in the Theater-an-der-Wien on April 5, 1803. Through the influence of Emanuel Schikaneder, who had collaborated with Mozart on *Die Zauberflöte* and was plying his trade as impresario in the "new" Theater-an-der-Wien, Beethoven had been commissioned to write an opera for its stage. Nothing came of the opera project for many months, but the arrangement provided for the composer to live in the building and to have the use of the auditorium for a concert on his own behalf.

As presented under Beethoven's direction, the program included the first two symphonies, the long-awaited premiere of the Third Concerto, and *Christus am Ölberg* (*Christ on the Mount of Olives*), an oratorio composed for the occasion. From an account of the concert left by Ignaz Ritter von Seyfried (who later conducted the first performance of *Fidelio*), we learn several things of prime interest about Beethoven's working habits.

To facilitate his performance of the solo part, Beethoven enlisted the assistance of Seyfried as page turner. The pages were mostly illegible —where the staves were not actually blank. For the main, Beethoven played the solo part from memory. This was not merely, as Seyfried later explained, because "he had not time to put it all down on paper."[10] It was at least partially intended to frustrate unauthorized appropriation of the material before it appeared in printed form. Seyfried's efforts to interpret Beethoven's nods and gestures as cues for turning the pages were more amusing to the composer than helpful to the soloist.

[10] Alexander Wheelock Thayer: *Life of Beethoven,* 2 vols., rev. and ed. Elliot Forbes (Princeton: Princeton University Press; 1964), I, 329. Hereafter cited as Thayer-Forbes (1964).

Between April and July 1803, Beethoven prepared a fair copy of the piano part for a performance he conducted, with his pupil Ferdinand Ries as soloist. The publication project was then well advanced, and Ries assisted Beethoven in proofreading the printed sheets. Did this fresh involvement with the idiom, the force, and the provocative possibilities of ♫♫|♩ germinate its subsequent growth in Beethoven's mind? To me, the sequence of events is less speculative than conclusive.

It is in no way conjectural that once the pounding rhythm of ♫♫|♩ was at large in Beethoven's mind it remained an obsession until the creation of the jubilant finale of the Fifth Symphony *five years later* gave him ultimate fulfillment. In addition to its softer echo in the G-major Concerto, noted by Grove, it is a frenetic force in the F-minor Piano Sonata, Opus 57, a creation of 1804. It is heard as a hammering in the bass within the first eleven measures of the first movement, and is a combative element in the spiritual turmoil that has caused this work to be known as the "Appassionata":

A passage in the first movement of the C-major (Triple) Concerto, Opus 56, created during 1803 and 1804, finds the solo violin and cello converging—measure 276—in contrary motion on a figure with much the same engulfing impulse. It may also be found in the thirty-two variations in C minor for piano (finished in 1806 and published without opus number), as well as in both the 1805 and 1806 versions of *Fidelio*. Much the same impetus erupts in each of the *Razumovsky* Quartets of Opus 59 (1806): in movement one of the first (measure 290), in the slow movement of the second (measure 129), and in the trio of the minuetto of No. 3. In several instances, including the Opus 57 sonata, the gravitation to the final form inevitably follows.

In each of these, the true connection with the basic pattern is esablished not so much in the repeated notes as in the flow of accent *across* the beat, most often across the barline. In the first act of *Fidelio*, where a ¾ meter prevails, it comes and goes in such a figuration as ♪♫ ♩ (*within* the bar), but the energizing effect is much the same.

As a final phenomenon, it may be noted that the exhalation of the full force of ♫♫♩|♩ that impels the C-minor Symphony to an unprecedented level of exaltation leaves room for no afterthoughts, no unfulfilled impulse. When the ultimate pulsation has been achieved, not merely in a recurrent rhythm but in a pervasive heartbeat present at the beginning, the middle, and the end of the whole work, it all but ceased to exist for Beethoven. Now and then the pattern recurs, but in a way neither obsessive nor possessive. It had moved toward, on, and off center stage, giving way to one or another in the long list of problems awaiting Beethoven's attention, to be grappled with, subjugated, and sublimated.

2

CONSPICUOUS AMONG THEM is a pillar of the Beethoven superstructure as well known to musicians as ♫♫♩|♩, if not as broadly associated with nonmusical values. As the musical counterpart of Schiller's "Freude, schöner Götterfunken, Tochter aus Elysium," on which Beethoven constructed the choral finale of his Ninth Symphony, it has its share of special identity on at least one day in each three hundred and sixty-five. That is the twenty-fourth of October, the date on which the United Nations commemorates its founding in 1945, by a concert including the *Ode to Joy*, as a symbol of man's struggle for universal brotherhood. Thus, of all the composers who ever lived, Beethoven has the unique distinction of creating one motif (♫♫♩|♩) that became a rallying call in a world struggle against oppression and another (♩ ♩ ♩ ♩ ♩ ♩ ♩ ♩) that conveys mankind's yearning for an understanding transcending self-interest.

The first thought of putting Schiller's *Ode* to music came to Beethoven in 1793, only a few years after its creation in 1785.[11] Whether this was implemented by so much as a musical sketch is unknown; none has

---

[11] Grove: *Beethoven and His Nine Symphonies*, p. 322.

survived. It was not until nearly thirty years later that the words and the tune came together. This was not for lack of impulse, for the idea keeps recurring among Beethoven's reminders to himself of future projects. But the foreordained conjunction of music and words long eluded him.

For an organic link to exist between these two most famous groups of notes created by Beethoven would be an act of divine dispensation almost too fortuitous to contemplate. That such a link can be demonstrated to exist is further to the premise that Beethoven was frequently motivated by impulses outside his conscious control.

A point of beginning may be derived from Grove's observation (see p. 5) that the rhythmic cell from which the C-minor Symphony grew also set in motion the G-major Concerto for piano and orchestra (♫♫|♩, as the progenitor of ♩ ♪♫♫|♩). From the momentum thus generated came the famous dialogue between orchestra and piano in the concerto's Adagio (likened by Liszt to the confrontation between Orpheus and the Furies). From the power of music to subdue even the most adamant resistance emerged the resolution of differences joyously affirmed in the concerto's finale.

Good feeling and common respect are crowned, at measure 80, with this lovable phrase (first stated by the piano):

It can be heard and enjoyed a hundred times for the sublimely beautiful thing it is without secondary associations of any sort. But the hundred and first time, it may suddenly be apprehended as a direct predecessor of a phrase described by Grove[12] as the "most pregnant passage" from which Beethoven gave birth to the music for Schiller's *Ode*:

Finale

Freu-de, schö- ner Göt-ter Funk-en Toch- ter aus E - li - si- um.

Some may seize on the discrepancy of key signatures between the concerto and the symphony to dispute the claim of "identity"; but the difference is apparent, not real. At the point of introducing the second theme of the concerto's finale, Beethoven had moved from the basic G major to its dominant, D. That is, of course, the equivalent of the sketch cited above. The reality is that the two ideas are situated at identical points on the staff, and are basically responsive to the same melodic formulation. The evolutionary progression is also Beethoven-perfect in reducing a more complex design to a simpler one.

Indeed, if the tones underlined in the concerto excerpt are isolated from those around them, the outcome is:

or, seven of the fourteen notes in the excerpt from the sketchbook of 1822 previously quoted by Grove. Should a previous F-sharp (bracketed in the concerto excerpt) be added, the identity becomes almost complete.

As projected in the concerto excerpt, part of the "chorale" theme is embodied in the bridge between the two halves of the finale's second subject. But the instrumental coloration Beethoven selected as a background to the piano phrase also flashes a signal to the attentive ear. It is a bassoon-clarinet-oboe-flute mixture almost identical with that utilized by Beethoven at the first appearance of the "Freude" theme in the Ninth Symphony (Allegro assai, p. 246, Penguin miniature score). As the phrase comes and goes in the succeeding phases of the finale it literally *grows* extensions and additions ever more subtly indicative of things to come—once one is aware what *DID* come and the source of its seeds.

In tracing the emergence of Beethoven's involvement with Schiller's words, Grove presents an illuminating series of sketches dated 1798,

12 Ibid., p. 328.

1811, and early 1822. None bears even the slightest resemblance to the eventual form cited above (see p. 14). Meanwhile, the predestined partner to Schiller's words was pursuing a musical life of its own in Beethoven's mind. It may be found at its most primitive in the song of 1794–95 entitled "Seufzer eines Ungeliebten und Gegenliebe." "Seufzer eines Ungeliebten" is an Andantino preface to the livelier (Allegretto) "Gegenliebe." The latter begins:

but the young composer does not follow through with anything more than sequential statements.

Once the formulation surfaced again in the finale of the G-major Concerto, it became—as ♫♩♩ had previously—obsessive with Beethoven and would not leave him alone. It may be recognized in the C-major Choral Fantasia (Opus 80) of 1808, at the beginning of the Meno allegro:

Two years later, in a setting of Goethe's "Mit einem gemalten Band" (Opus 83), it becomes:

In the seldom-heard *König Stephan* Overture (Op. 117, first performed in Budapest in 1812), Beethoven is writing a peroration of the Ninth's finale even before he had completed the Eighth:

The oddly fascinating fact about these premonitions, prognostications, and probings is that each has a *share* of the final form, but none comes out quite the same way. The one from the Choral Fantasia doesn't begin altogether in the way that "Freude" does, but it ends rather like it. The setting of the Goethe song begins in much the same way that Beethoven deemed proper for Schiller, but doesn't follow through.

Most remarkable of all is the excerpt from the *König Stephan* Overture. Here we are presented with the extraordinary spectacle of Beethoven's mind leapfrogging all manner of in-between details—not to mention a time period of ten years—to project the way in which he would use a *fragment* of a theme before the theme itself ("Freude") had been brought from the mystic recesses of his mind into the context of a totality. There is, indeed, very little difference between the *König Stephan* passage and the dramatically fugal stretto in the finale of the Ninth Symphony, which begins:

Thus may be traced, through one celebrated creation, a whole cycle of artistic generation and crossbreeding. It dramatically demonstrates the manner in which words in search of a musical fulfillment are, at length, brought together with a musical thought whose nature *demands* a verbal counterpart. The oddity of all oddities is that it was, in essence, a *completed* idea—in the finale of the G-major Concerto—which gave rise, through some form of artistic parthenogenesis, to another idea altogether.

This is a process related, although not wholly akin, to another manifestation of Beethoven's tenacious pursuit of meaning. I refer to one in which he returned to the original form of an idea he had either discarded or so altered as to be unrecognizable. A single instance may be mentioned here as precedent to several others to come. In an article devoted to data contained in Nottebohm's *Beethoveniana* when it first appeared, the English scholar J. B. Shedlock cites[13] the early form of an idea from which emerged the Andante of the C-minor Symphony.

It has its share of interest, as almost every early form of a finally famous
Beethoven invention does. It is, in effect, the unlovely cocoon

from which emerged the beautifully colored butterfly:

But the special fascination it holds for me is embodied in a whole
range of secondary thoughts, suggestive of a butterfly of quite a different
coloration, or, perhaps, a pair of winged beings habituated to another
kind of space. Traced to their place in the marvelous aviary inhabited
by Beethoven's flights of fancy, the quest ends on a branch of thought
fully twenty years in the future. Here, clearly, is the first dim shadow of
what would become a poignant moment in the C-sharp-minor Quartet,
Opus 131. A product of very nearly Beethoven's last year, it is a work
whose total of poignant moments has few close competitors by anyone.

The usual citation of a "movement" as the location of a specific
segment of a musical work has little utility in this quartet, which moves
through peaks and valleys of expression with scarcely an interruption.
In what Beethoven has designated No. 4, at measure 99, is the marking
Andante moderato e lusinghiero ("At a moderate pace and in a coax-
ing manner"), at which a spurt of energy subsides into a moment of
sober reflection. And here, one might say, is the long-delayed moment
of fulfillment for an idea cited by Nottebohm and reproduced by Shed-

lock as the source for the slow movement of the C-minor Symphony.

As repossessed by Beethoven for a second cycle of life, it begins with a pattern of imitation initiated by the cello and echoed by the viola:

(The passage has been rewritten on the conventional bass [C] and treble [G] clefs to facilitate reading.)

The two parts thus overlap each other, canonically. In either case, the musical action is almost identical with that imagined by Beethoven twenty years before, now turned to another purpose to suit a different need. Of that, there is no doubt.

My only question is: Did Beethoven retrieve the earlier form from some deep freeze of mental semen for purposes of later artistic impregnation, or was it deliberately sought in the sketchbook itself? My own conclusion does not incline to the image of Beethoven, the impulsive *begeistert* creator, thumbing through dusty scrapbooks for an unfulfilled, still-fertile kernel of thought. Indeed, Dr. Joseph Braunstein, to whose careful, creative reading of this text I owe more than the debt already expressed in the Acknowledgments, cites a source much more contemporary with Opus 131 as his choice for this thought's predecessor (see p. 302).

Whatever power of recollection may be invoked, it has nothing to do with the ordinary kind of memory. Schindler makes note[14] that in 1822 Beethoven could not recollect the details of a tour he made to Berlin in 1796, saying, "His memory of events of the past was always extremely poor."

[14] Schindler: *Beethoven as I Knew Him*, p. 63.

On the other hand, Beethoven said more than once (see p. 176) that when a musical idea had entered his mind he never forgot it. Had he possessed Mozart's fluency or Schubert's happy contentment with the inspiration of a moment, he would certainly have had a less arduous creative life. But he would not have been *Beethoven*, nor would the dual product of a single seedling have given cause for such an inquiry as this into musical botany, tonal horticulture, and aesthetic cross-breeding.

II

Beethoven's First, Forgotten, Masterpiece

S UCH CROSSCURRENTS and interior relationships in the works of the continuously maturing Beethoven are enlightening but hardly unexpected for a musician with the *Eroica* Symphony of 1803 behind him. But what is one to say of the Beethoven not yet settled in Vienna, and with the *Eroica* a dozen years in the future, who was capable of producing music on the level of his greatest to come? On the level, that is, of *Fidelio?*

The proper comment—after an incredulous rejection of the idea altogether—would be: "It must be embodied in some work generally unknown and in very restricted circulation." This would be in accordance with the common view of Beethoven's pre-Vienna compositions summarized by one of his more musically perceptive biographers: "Before 1792, the year he settled in Vienna, Ludwig did not compose anything particularly noteworthy."[1]

As of the date of Schauffler's statement, both conditions stated above were true: the work was generally unknown and in very restricted circulation. Thus, the observation may be attributed to lack of information rather than a lapse of judgment. Had Schauffler been provided the opportunity for hearing Beethoven's *Cantata on the Death of Emperor*

---

[1] Robert Haven Schauffler: *Beethoven: The Man Who Freed Music* (New York: Outlook Company; 1929), p. 19.

Joseph II, now instantly accessible, he might have concluded otherwise. It contains pages of music not only transcending the merely noteworthy, but capable of generating one of the most memorable moments in all of Beethoven.

In Thayer's unsurpassed source work on the composer,[2] a footnote by its first editor, Henry E. Krehbiel, makes mention of a performance of the cantata in New York in March 1920. There is no known identification of another until the performances conducted by Thomas Schippers with the New York Philharmonic in 1965. Doubtless these were related to the publication the year before of a new edition of the work by G. Schirmer, Inc. (New York). From these circumstances emerged its first recording (CBS 32 11 0039). It is performed in a Latin text commissioned by the publisher rather than in the original German.

The circumstances bearing on the work's creation were set forth in a prefatory note by Elliot Forbes, who edited the most recent edition of Thayer's *Beethoven*, published by the Princeton University Press in 1964:

> On February 20th, 1790, Emperor Joseph II, the great Reformer, passed away. The news took four days to travel from Vienna to Bonn where his brother, Max Franz, was Elector. To express the sorrow felt at Bonn, the Lesegesellschaft, a literary society, planned a memorial celebration to take place on March 19th. In the minutes of the society's meeting on February 28th the wish is expressed "that either before or after the speech something musical would be performed: a cantata will make a splendid effect: a local young poet has submitted a text today, which is certainly worthy of the collaboration of a master; thus it is up to one of the excellent composers who are members of our society or else an outside composer to take the trouble to make music."[3]

Among the composers who could have been identified as "members of our society" was Christian Gottlob Neefe, court organist to Elector Maximilian Friedrich from 1781 to 1784, and thereafter to his successor, Max Franz. Almost since his arrival in Bonn, he had been a wise counsellor to Beethoven, and would remain so until the departure of his prize pupil for studies in Vienna. The statement extolling the text as "worthy of the collaboration of a master" came to have an unintentionally prophetic significance. The capable Neefe did not, for whatever

---

[2] Alexander Wheelock Thayer: *The Life of Ludwig van Beethoven*, 3 vols., ed. Henry E. Krehbiel (New York: G. Schirmer; 1921), I, 130. Hereafter cited as Thayer-Krehbiel (1921).

[3] Ludwig Schiedermair: *Der Junge Beethoven* (Bonn: F. Dümmler; 1951), pp. 219–20.

reason, respond, but the master-to-be, then a young member of the Bonn orchestra, did.

For the creation of a conventionally ceremonious work by a member of the Lesegesellschaft, a month would doubtless have been sufficient time. But the circumstances, and the text by Severin Averdonk, stirred something in Beethoven that transcended both the conventional and the merely ceremonious. It was his first encounter, artistically, with man's mortality; but the reality of death was not new in his personal life. The supreme zenith of happiness in his early life, the visit to Vienna in 1787 during which he met Mozart, had been cut short by news from Bonn that his mother, aged only forty, was desperately ill. He set about the return journey immediately, but arrived in Bonn only in time to be at her bedside when she died. It thus became the responsibility of Beethoven, at seventeen (and believing himself to be a year younger), to be the man of the family for his two younger brothers. His father, as is well known, was intemperate and irresponsible. At his death, in 1792, Beethoven became head of the little family in name as well as in fact.

It is also a possibility that Beethoven's heartfelt reaction to Joseph's death might have had a closer, more personal cause. Thayer, basing his statement on a recollection of Schindler's, speculates that Beethoven might have met the Emperor during the same visit to Vienna in which he met Mozart. Schindler attributes this statement, "he then met two men who deeply and indelibly impressed themselves on the sixteen-year-old boy's mind: the Emperor Joseph and Mozart" to "the testimony of the young composer's friends."[4]

In the most recent version of Schindler's text one may also read: "Mozart's prophetic words about the young musician's future, pronounced after Beethoven had improvised a fugue on a theme that Mozart had given him, 'This young man will make a name for himself in the world,' have been repeated in substance again and again, but we do not know exactly when and where the 'Monarch of Music' said them. Some claim it was when the Emperor, on the recommendation of the Elector Max Franz, summoned Beethoven to his apartments and listened to him in the presence of Mozart."[5]

MacArdle, editor of the Schindler text quoted above, considers such a visit improbable, noting that Beethoven's stay in April 1787 overlapped Joseph's presence in Vienna by only four days. But if Beethoven did

[4] Schindler: *Beethoven as I Knew Him*, p. 46.
[5] Ibid.

bear a recommendation from Joseph's brother, the Elector of Cologne, and his credentials were sufficient to earn an audience with Mozart, why could not the two happenings have been interrelated, especially as the music-loving Joseph and Mozart were well acquainted?[6]

However speculative the possibility of such a meeting, it cannot be dismissed as impossible or even unlikely. Often enough, a well-founded speculation can be closer to the mark than an apparent truth. It was, for an example, a generally accepted "truth" for much of the nineteenth century that the very cantata herein under discussion was irretrievably gone, lost, most likely destroyed as an adolescent folly by Beethoven himself. But, writes Schindler in the text of 1860, "Such drastic self-criticism is indeed surprising, since he preserved other experiments in composition."[7] Its reappearance at an auction of 1884 (when the bookseller who had acquired the manuscript from the estate of Johann Nepomuk Hummel offered it for sale) proved Schindler's well-reasoned speculation to have been correct.

Even had Joseph not received the young Beethoven in April 1787, it is possible that he had—at the instigation of his brother—arranged the meeting with Mozart. In any case, whether awed by the dead sovereign's lofty stature, responsive to the description of him in Averdonk's text as "der Vater unsterblichen Thaten" ("the father of immortal endeavors"), or vicariously reliving in sorrowful recollection the death of his mother, Beethoven's creative impulse struck chords deeper than he knew he possessed. He became so absorbed in the task that time was the least of his concerns. The minutes of the Society reported two days before the scheduled performance that "for various reasons the proposed cantata cannot be performed."

Some have surmised that the work was not finished in time, others that it contained technical difficulties beyond the ability of the Bonn orchestra's personnel. Very likely, as the reference is to "various reasons," the causes for the postponement were multiple. Beethoven's faith in the worth of what he had written is clear from his efforts to arrange a performance later in 1790. This was in Mergentheim, a town upriver on the Rhine to Frankfurt and then on the Main (where it is situated). Nikolaus Simrock, whose rise to prominence as a publisher was greatly aided by an early association with Beethoven, was then a young horn player in the Bonn orchestra. He recalled many years later that "all the

---

[6] Joseph is commonly credited with having recalled to Mozart and da Ponte the anecdote on which they based *Così fan tutte*.

[7] Schindler: *Beethoven as I Knew Him*, p. 42.

figures in the Cantata were completely unusual, therein lay the difficulty." In today's view of the score, there is little to be considered complicated. But Bonn in 1790 was not, for musical accomplishment, Berlin of 1970.

As a link to Beethoven's future, the cantata may very well have been the instrument of his removal from Bonn to Vienna in fall 1792. During Christmastime 1790, Joseph Haydn passed through Bonn en route to London for the first of his visits at the invitation of Johann Peter Salomon. He was royally received, but there is nothing to indicate that Beethoven was among those invited to meet the visiting celebrity. On his return journey to Vienna in late June 1792, Haydn once again broke his journey in Bonn, and this time he did meet Beethoven. He consented to look at some of his compositions, and several sources are in agreement that the *Trauerkantate* was among them. Furthermore, at least one of them asserts that it "aroused Haydn's interest."[8] It was, certainly, among the evidences of talent that prompted Haydn to suggest a period of study in Vienna for Beethoven, inferentially under the master's own supervision.

For all of Beethoven's pride in the work, and Haydn's (presumably) high regard for it, no evidence exists of a performance of the cantata during Beethoven's lifetime. However that is far from saying that none of the music in it was heard during his lifetime. Two portions of it became vital parts of the first version of *Fidelio* (1805). They survived all the alterations the score underwent (Beethoven evolved the final form in 1814) and are heard whenever *Fidelio* is given today.

Identification of them will leave no doubt with anyone who cherishes *Fidelio* that Beethoven's enduring attachment was justified. From the solemn opening of the cantata, in which the grief of Joseph's subjects at his death is proclaimed,

---

[8] *Grove's Dictionary of Music and Musicians*, 5th edn., ed. Eric Blom (New York: St. Martin's Press; 1954), see Beethoven article by William McNaught, Vol. I, p. 534.

Beethoven retrieved the musical tone as well as the spiritual gloom to depict the dungeon in which Florestan is imprisoned as the curtain rises for Act II of *Fidelio*:

And for the moment of exaltation when the chains on Florestan's hands are removed by the Minister of Justice, Beethoven turned to the aria for soprano (section three of the cantata) extolling Joseph's appeal to his people. From it he evolved one of the most affecting passages in all of *Fidelio*, which is to say, in all of Beethoven.

Rather than being merely a point of departure for something to follow (as could be said of the chords for the opening of the dungeon scene), it is a moment of catharsis in itself. It is built into an embodiment of the emotion of not a single performer alone, but of all those present—principals and chorus, and orchestra as well.

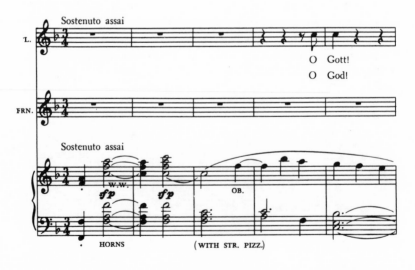

(*continued*)

A comparison with the form it first possessed in the cantata,

(*continued*)

shows that Beethoven's treatment of 1805 is less a transformation than an elaboration of his spontaneous impulse of 1790. And its qualifications to bear comparison with the material he added to the score as late as 1814 (see p. 192) are simple testimony to the enduring eloquence of the work he was doing well before he left Bonn for Vienna.

Considered comparatively, the values in the two segments of the cantata which the older Beethoven deemed acceptable for *Fidelio* might be summarized thus: The opening chords, strong and simple, are admirably suited to the purpose they serve—a purpose which such chords, or their equivalents, had served similarly in the works of others, especially in works of Gluck. But the arching, sinuous figure in F sung by the soprano, and expressive of the people's esteem for Joseph ("Then uprose all mankind"), speaks in accents not associated with any predecessor.

It is a phrase of great melodic distinction as well as of striking originality, an invention which, of itself, provides justification for calling this cantata "Beethoven's first, forgotten, masterpiece." It emerges from the young mind's questing sense of beauty, and his lifelong search for new expressions of it. It is, in other words, an early instance of the imaginative thinking that set aside the better works of Beethoven not only from the inferior ones of others, but also from the inferior ones of his own.

Its recurrence in *Fidelio* occurs on page 140 of the piano score (p. 167 of the Eulenburg miniature orchestral score). As the two citations show, its reuse in 1805 follows in every essential detail the outline Beethoven had set forth in 1790, even to the key (F major), the basic harmonization, and the use of the oboe to bear the melodic outline. The climax is delayed, however, as the Beethoven of 1805, exercising the supervisory judgment of thirty-five on the invention of his twenty-year-old self, extends the episode marked Sostenuto assai over six pages of vocal writing. This intensification of expression is altogether in keeping with the heightened urgency of emotion, from a funeral tribute to a dead monarch to the celebration of renewed life for a liberated prisoner. As Beethoven converts the rejoicing into six pages of celestially intertwined vocal writing, a new musical resource comes to birth.

It is out of this episode that were born the means for Wagner to convey the introspective thoughts of Sachs, Walther, Eva, Magdalene, and David in the great quintet in the Workshop Scene (Act III) of *Die Meistersinger*. By extension, the Beethoven-Wagner example gave rise to the intertwining of voices and orchestra with which Strauss enthralls the listener to the third-act trio of the Marschallin, Sophie, and Octavian in *Der Rosenkavalier*. The six pages, in other words, are absorbing not only for the power of the utterance they embody, but also for the response they generated in the minds of two later masters—both celebrated for their devotion to, as well as interpretations of, *Fidelio*.

What makes a melody great, or greater, is, per se, difficult to verbalize. Were it otherwise, the effect of a beautifully proportioned melodic sequence, with reach and return, arching line and sinuous curve, all delicately poised on a harmonic pedestal, could be as well achieved in words as in tones. But there may be a circumstance in which the composer's choice of a *demonstrably* uncommon note at a daringly unexpected place points to the crux of his thought and localizes a specific aspect of its appeal.

Such a place in the F-major melodic line common to Joseph II and Leonore is undoubtedly the high B-flat (fourth note in the sequence) with which the young Beethoven piques aural attention and gives a hint of many similar, unexpected delights to come.

Why the citation of this particular instance? Because it violates a principle of melodic construction held in high regard by all the rule-givers of the time in going *outside* the chordal structure (of F) to settle on what was, as of 1790, a "foreign" tone. Even worse, it is a seventh (discord!) above the C with which the phrase began. What confirms it as an element of delight rather than dissonance is the logic with which Beethoven retrieves his moment of waywardness. He leads the line directly down, first to the expected (but delayed) A, then straight to the C from which the emotional impulse emanated. This is an early instance of many similar strokes of daring by which the deviations of Beethoven became the accepted practice of others. Even at twenty, Beethoven possessed the invaluable attribute of knowing just how far to go too far.

With Brahms this kind of arching curve to a dangerously unexpected melodic crux and return to a point of origin resulted in a formulation now considered distinctively his own. An early instance may be cited from the F-minor Sonata, Opus 5, whose slow movement begins Andante espressivo:

Relocated in the key of Beethoven's cantata, or the *Fidelio* elaboration, it is recognizably an expression within the same range of intervals from C to B-flat—the outline of a dominant seventh chord.

It is out of this soil that Brahms bred such melodic blossoms as the one which bears the words "Wie Melodien zieht es mir," one of his most memorable songs:

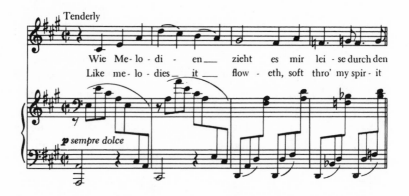

Here the thrust is beyond the seventh to the ninth as the crest of the melody (on "Melodien" no less!), a typical instance of a pioneering thought breaking ground for an even wider deviation from prior custom.

It was, perhaps, out of such internal identity with his great predecessor (filtered through the additional identities of Schumann and Schubert) that Brahms declared, when the cantata was reborn at its Vienna premiere in 1884: "Even if there was no name on the title page none other could be conjectured—it is Beethoven through and through! The beautiful and noble pathos, sublime in its feeling and imagination, the intensity, perhaps violent in its expression, moreover the voice leading and declamation, and in the two outside sections, all the characteristics which we may observe and associate with his later works . . ."[9]

[9] Thayer-Forbes (1964), I, 120.

In thus asserting, as of his twentieth year, an ability to produce music of a quality characteristic of him at thirty-five, Beethoven clearly back-dated considerably the time at which he is commonly assumed to have attained a musical identity of his own. The cantata also clearly defines the difference between Beethoven's gifts and those of the "Monarch of Music" to whom Schindler referred. He was not a young Mozart, compounding incredibly facile likenesses of the work being done when he was eight, ten, or fourteen, but a burgeoning Beethoven, projecting through impulsive ineptitude the dim, provocative intimations of things to come.

Together, these considerations invite review and reappraisal of all the sizable works written by Beethoven in Bonn, as well as a close investigation of the conditioning which provided him with the musical means to achieve an expression on the order of the cantata before he was twenty.

Buried therein may, or may not, be evidence bearing on the two major impulses that relate works from one period of Beethoven to those of another: intentional, volitional reuse of material he had invented and used previously; and unintentional, nonvolitional extension and expansion of ideas which continued to mature and grow within him until they achieved maximum fulfillment. Answers may be elusive; but the quest itself cannot fail to be absorbing.

III

Beginnings in Bonn

I

THE CIRCUMSTANCES OF 1792 which brought about Beethoven's removal from provincial Bonn to cosmopolitan Vienna were as dramatic as they were unexpected. It may even be that the involvement of the eminent Haydn has caused them to be assessed at a higher point of importance than they merit. The four days' journey from the Rhine to the Danube doubtless had a profound psychological effect on Beethoven. He had been granted a singular recognition, which could hardly fail to feed the strong strain of superiority already incubating within him.

The relocation might, indeed, have affected him even more personally than it did musically. It certainly did not make him greatly more a composer in 1795, when his official Opus 1 was published, than he had been in 1793 or 1792, or, as has already been demonstrated, in 1790. Thus the disposition to make a cleavage between Beethoven's "preparation" in Bonn and his "fulfillment" in Vienna is not merely to overstate the facts, but to promote a wrong assessment of Beethoven's own nature.

He was continuously in a state of preparation for further fulfillment of his extraordinary abilities: this went on throughout his life. Even at the end, when the body could no longer combat infection or throw off debilitation, his musical resources were gushing new ideas. It was, indeed, the French invasion of the Rhineland in 1794 that made permanent the residence in Vienna that was intended to be only an interlude in Beethoven's service in Bonn. With the court scattered and Elector Max

Franz himself in flight, Beethoven's obligation to Bonn was no longer operative. He was thus at liberty to pursue the opportunities of Vienna after its nominal "educational advantages" had run their course.

In the context of a continuous development from birth to death, there can be little doubt that the half decade between 1785 and 1790 was of crucial importance in Beethoven's life. On one side was a lad of fifteen misled by his father's exploitation of his possibilities as a prodigy to believe he was younger than he really was.[1] On the other side was a self-assured young man whose reputation as a master of the keyboard was challenged only by his achievements as a composer.

Squarely in the middle of the half decade was the first visit to Vienna in 1787, with its long-cherished memories of meetings with Mozart and possibly Emperor Joseph II. In the aftermath of his hasty return to Bonn because of his mother's fatal illness, he left behind his infancy as a composer. It would not be long before he would, as guardian of his younger brothers, also leave behind his boyhood and adolescence.

For lack of so-called durable products, that infancy has rarely received the attention it deserves, for all that it is an indivisible part of Beethoven's total evolution. Not unlike Alexander Pope's mature recollection of a childish self who "lisp'd in numbers, for the numbers come," Beethoven lisped in music because the music came. Though seldom heard today as Beethoven then cast them, some salient ideas persist, for the same reason that parts of the *Cantata on the Death of Joseph II* reappeared in *Fidelio*. They had, by Beethoven's later taste and judgment, merits worth preserving.

A conspicuous instance is provided by the three quartets for piano and strings written in 1785 (they were posthumously published as "Opus 152" but are more properly designated today in the WoO category as WoO 36[2]). No clue remains to Beethoven's choice of the piano-violin-viola-cello combination rather than the more customary piano-violin-cello trio. One thinks instinctively of the Mozart piano quartets as prototypes, but there is no creditable explanation for Beethoven's knowledge of the earliest (in G minor, K.478, completed October 16, 1785) almost before it was written (see pp. 46–47).

---

[1] In March 1778, Ludwig gave a concert in Cologne at which he was billed by Johann Beethoven as "his little son of six years." He was then well past seven "going on" eight. See Maynard Solomon's essay, "Beethoven's Birth Year," in Paul Henry Lang, ed.: *The Creative World of Beethoven* (New York: W. W. Norton; 1970).

[2] WoO is the designation for the Werke ohne Opuszahl, or Works Without Opus Numbers, pioneered by Nottebohm in his catalogue, and greatly expanded in its later version by Georg Kinsky.

Whatever the impulse that prompted their creation, the two bearing No. 1 (in E-flat) and No. 2 (in D) arouse admiration primarily for the youthful ease with which Beethoven achieves his ensemble purpose. The C-major (identified as No. 3, though it was the first to be written) has a ring of familiarity as well. The reason for this is simple. The second theme of its first movement was good enough to be utilized at the same point in the third of his published piano sonatas (Opus 2, No. 3). The opening of the slow movement served him as the beginning point for the Adagio of his first sonata (Opus 2, No. 1). To the public that greeted the publication of the three sonatas in 1796, the material of 1785 was an acceptable representation of Beethoven in his mid-twenties.

Even earlier is a Piano Concerto in E-flat, dated 1784. No complete score of the concerto has been preserved, but a reconstruction by Willy Hess has, for me, the ring of conviction. (To Beethoven in his fourteenth calendar year, "orchestra" meant strings plus pairs of horns and flutes.) Awkward as this early effort is in some harmonic respects, and primitive as it is in form, its themes nevertheless flow and sing. Indeed, at times it has the fresh-from-the-heart, birdlike quality of the music Mozart was creating in the early days of his marriage to Constanze.

It is dangerous to read overmuch into so limited an expression, but the intimations of things to come may be found repeatedly in phraseologies and preferences which recur, in bolder relief, as Beethoven matures. They include his way with inner voices, the running, assertive ascending figures against the running, staunchly opposing descending figures, devices for freshening the contours of the so-called Alberti bass, a fondness for *sforzandi*, abrupt accents, and similar devices for searching out the aural equivalents of light and shade.

One of the more conspicuous instances of such a preference or predilection is the following, at measure 15 of the first movement of the E-flat Concerto:

In a later (but not very much later) phraseology, it emerges in the opening Allegro con brio of the C-major Concerto (published as No. 1, though it was written in 1797, after the B-flat, published as No. 2) as

As might be expected, one of the musicologists who paid properly close attention to the early works of Beethoven was Donald Francis Tovey. In his discussion entitled "The Larger Tonality"[3] Tovey observes: "The remoter key-relations always have directly impressive effects when used by a master who does not squander them. No amount of squandering by later masters or crowding out by later resources can alter their value in their proper place. Beethoven had penetrated to the root of the matter before he was fifteen."

The provocation for Tovey's provocative statement is to be found not only in the early piano quartet mentioned previously, but even more pointedly in the third Bagatelle of Opus 33. Says Tovey: "The Bagatelles, op. 33, were published in 1802,[4] and Beethoven had certainly by that time polished them to perfection. It is, therefore, unfortunate for their reputation that the autograph bears, in a scrawl indistinguishable from Beethoven's, the date 1783." The sonata sequence, as reproduced from the early quartet, shows Beethoven moving from G minor (in succeeding measures) through D major, G, C minor, A major, D minor, all by means of a descending chromatic line in the bass. In the Bagatelle, it is the substitution of D major—after a beginning in F major—for the expected D *minor* that Tovey likens to such a verbal phraseology as "Three children sliding on the ice" followed by the

---

[3] Donald Francis Tovey: *Beethoven* (London: Oxford University Press; 1945), p. 34.

[4] They were first advertised for sale in May 1803.

unexpected "all on a summer's day." The return to F (by a simple sub-stitution of F-natural for F-sharp) is characterized by Tovey as "an authentic word of power from Beethoven."

Still to be explored and accounted for are the earliest of Beethoven's compositions to be preserved in published form. In most texts in which they are mentioned, the three sonatas are not explored . . . a reasonable consequence of their inscription to "The most noble Archbishop and Elector of Cologne Maximilian Friedrich, my most gracious master" from "Ludwig van Beethoven aged eleven years."

For one who takes the trouble to seek them out in the complete works of Beethoven the results are not merely rewarding—they are startling.

Here, for example, in the opening measures of Sonata No. 2, in F minor, is the first solo work by Beethoven for piano to begin with a slow introduction. Its first eight measures are as follows:

Beethoven did not return to this "old-fashioned" way of starting a piano sonata until the eighth in the formal succession of thirty-two. That sonata is, of course, the universally known Opus 13, in C minor

("Pathétique"), of which the early measures, with their steady upward surge of chromatics, are among the most prophetic in all of Beethoven, early or late:

(*continued*)

What has only been implied in the work of 1783, with its tentatively daring upward progression (F–G-flat–G-flat–A-natural), is boldly spelled out in the sequence of 1798 which begins on the same F (measure 6) and climbs relentlessly through a full octave before starting its downward plunge.

The next in a sequence of extraordinary links between the Beethoven of 1783 and 1798 erupts in measure 2 of the early F-minor's Allegro assai:

which, with organ point rumbling in the bass and an angry thought rising in the treble, is clearly a first, incomplete form of the "Pathétique's" Allegro di molto e con brio:

If this may be dismissed as a mere shadowy resemblance, consider the manner in which the barely teen-aged Beethoven makes a phrase out of what is essentially an outburst:

It is nothing less than the rise and fall of the "Pathétique's"

repeated by the young, leonine Beethoven of 1798 for drama, and concluding:

(continued)

Throughout the beginner's work, other indications of the restless, questing spirit of the Beethoven-to-come strain at the bonds of technical limitation to reveal just what was burning in the youthful breast. To pursue them in detail would be only to burden the reader with redundancies supporting the essential truth of Kerman's statement that "Beethoven had a way of realizing his unfulfilled conceptions" (see p. 7). His point of departure was a work of Beethoven's mid-forties; but if the child is truly father to the man, the outcome was thirty years in the making.

With these instances of precocity to alert the attention, what could one hope to find further in the early Elector sonatas? The "Hammerklavier"? The "Waldstein"? The "Appassionata"? Who chooses to look may find any, or all, according to his reading of the runes. I am content to make note (in the fifth measure of Sonata No. 1, in E-flat) of the

figure and to observe that in the development section, at measure 11, it is converted into

The antiphonal pattern of statement and response passes from one hand to the other, but the infant resources of Beethoven are able, only, to put the ♪♪♩|♩ pattern away in a conventional box (cadence). There it would slumber, and grow, and grow, until the time came for it to escape its confinement and assert itself.

2

LATENT IN THE BACKGROUND of all these early works was a heredity of music and a family conditioning that all but predetermined Beethoven's career from birth. Among the several generations of musicians who shared the surname were Johann Beethoven, a father to whom Ludwig was neither devoted nor attached; and the grandfather, also Ludwig, whose portrait in the elegant attire suitable for a Kapellmeister of the

Elector's court from 1761[5] till his death in 1773 was a prized possession of the composer through all the years of his life in Vienna.

The suggestion of a Dutch or Flemish strain in Beethoven can be read in the older Ludwig's roundish face and slightly pursed lips. It can also be verified in researches establishing Ludwig I as a native of Antwerp, Belgium. Born in 1712 and educated in a choir school from which he went on to study organ and the realization (interpretation) of figured bass, Ludwig senior came to Bonn in 1733 at the invitation of Elector Clemens August. Of the several children born to the wife he soon married, the only survivor beyond infancy was Johann, born in 1739 or 1740.

Unlike Ludwig senior, whose talent and diligence earned him rank as Kapellmeister after nearly thirty years of valued service to the Elector, Johann was less talented and not nearly as diligent. His fondness for drinking not only affected his execution of a court musician's duties, but doubtless had a part in the deterioration of his tenor voice while he was in his early forties. This, in turn, lessened his usefulness to the Elector, diminished his earning powers, and resulted in more drinking. It also put on his firstborn, Ludwig, the burden of contributing to the family income before he was into his teens.

In a conversation reported much later by Schindler, Beethoven is reputed to have said that Mozart's genius had been fully realized largely because of the "consistent instruction of his father."[6] Mozart doubtless had an enormous asset in a father not merely able to perceive the magnitude of his son's genius but to participate in its flowering for nearly thirty years (1756–87). But one may wonder whether better teachers than were available to Beethoven in Bonn during the first ten years of his life would have greatly accelerated his development. He could, of course, have done very well without the kind of "instruction" that began at midnight when he was roused by his tippling father and a drunken companion, and kept at the clavier or violin till dawn.

Nevertheless, by innate talent, Beethoven had progressed sufficiently to fill the duties of second court organist at the age of eleven. Before the E-flat Concerto was born in 1783, he was cembalo player in the orchestra and sometimes deputy for its absent leader. By 1784, when his father's annual wage was 315 florins (after twenty-eight years' service), Ludwig was adding nearly half as much (150 florins) to the family's income.[7]

---

[5] Thayer-Forbes (1964), I, 42, 44, 46.
[6] Ibid., p. 79.
[7] Ibid., p. 78.

The "absent leader" for whom Beethoven deputized at twelve was Christian Gottlob Neefe, perhaps the most influential musical force the boy encountered while he remained in Bonn. Born in Chemnitz, Saxony, in 1748, Neefe became court organist to the Elector of Cologne in 1781. It was soon apparent that he was better qualified to be Beethoven's mentor than any person previously available in Bonn. Within the year they formed an association that endured for a decade. In effect, the otherwise obscure Neefe was the intermediary who delivered the unknown Beethoven to the doorstep of the eminent, world-famous Haydn.

By 1783, Neefe declared in print (Cramer's *Magazin der Musik*): "This young genius deserves every subsidy. He should be allowed to travel. He certainly might become another Wolfgang Amadeus Mozart, if he will continue the way he started out." This first, formal linking of the Rhinelander's name to that of Mozart may well have related to his completion at about that time of the three "Electoral" sonatas. Unlike some prodigies, who feel abused by their teachers, Beethoven cherished Neefe in later life as he did then.

It has been said, and can bear re-saying, that Neefe made a monumental contribution to his pupil's future, at an early point in their association, by directing his attention to Bach's *Well-Tempered Clavier*. Very likely Neefe came by his esteem for J. S. Bach (at a time when J. C., K. P. E., W. F., and other sons were "the" Bachs to their contemporaries) during the period (1769–76) he spent in Leipzig. (Even Mozart, it might be noted, did not have Beethoven's early knowledge of the "48.") Not only was this indoctrination of enormous influence on the sophistication of Beethoven's taste and judgment, it opened many doors that might otherwise have been closed when he migrated to Vienna in the early 1790s.

In either case, there tends to be some confusion between instruction and education. The former depends on teachers and their qualifications. The latter derives from exposure to subject matter. Had Beethoven the benefits of residence in Vienna and Mozart's influence, his rate of progress between 1784 and 1791 might have been accelerated. But Bonn without Mozart had its advantages for Beethoven nevertheless.

When competent instruction was combined with such exposure to subject matter as Neefe's enthusiasm for the *Well-Tempered Clavier* provided, it became educational. When Beethoven's employment as organist, cembalist, and eventually violist in the court orchestra brought him into close contact with many of the newest works being written in Europe between 1780 and 1792, that, too, was educational, in a completely professional context.

In 1781, for example, André Grétry's *Le Jugement de Midas* was given in Bonn,[8] only three years after its premiere in Paris. Whatever the merits of the stage performance by a company that divided its time among such communities as Frankfurt, Cologne, and Kassel, it provided Bonn's musical community with an opportunity to hear the pathbreaking overture. This is a section so unlike other operatic *sinfonias* being written in 1778, when it was new, that Raymond Leppard declares it "abandons all the old formulas and sets out, in Grétry's own words, to describe the dawn, a shepherd playing his pipe, and a storm during which Apollo 'est précipité du ciel'; moreover we are instructed not to begin this overture before the curtain has risen."[9] The implication is that Grétry was determined that his music be heard rather than blanketed by the chatter an opera audience considers permissible any-time the curtain is down—during overtures, interludes, entr'actes, or whatever. Finally, says Leppard: "This overture must be the first of its kind, even antedating and perhaps influencing Gluck's *Iphigénie en Tauride*."

In other respects, Bonn's share of the company's playing time was, as befitted the seat of the Elector's winter residence, considerable. In 1781–82 there were performances of plays and musical pieces (operas, operettas, or their eighteenth-century equivalent) from September to June, when the Elector transferred the seat of government to Münster.

In later years of the decade, the pattern of activity varied according to the resources of the company and the amount of money the Elector allocated to its support. But in the thirteen months during which Beethoven was a member of the orchestra's viola section[10] he took part in performances of Mozart's *Die Entführung aus dem Serail, Don Giovanni,* and *Le Nozze di Figaro* (in German); Paisiello's *Il Barbiere di Siviglia,* Gluck's *Die Pilgrimme von Mekka*; Cimarosa's *Der Schmaus (Il Convito)*; plus less well-known works of the indispensable Grétry and such other notables of the time as Salieri, Dittersdorf, and Sacchini. In earlier years of the decade, visiting companies provided Beethoven with an indoctrination in the choicest works of the Gluck literature. In

---

[8] Ibid., I, 31.

[9] In the annotation for Philips stereo disk PHS 900–235 on which he conducts and performs on the harpsichord in the performance by the New Philharmonia Orchestra.

[10] His service began on January 3, 1789, and was terminated on February 23, 1790, when the death of Joseph II in Vienna caused his brother Maximilian to suspend Bonn's theatrical activities.

the carnival season of 1785, for example, Bonn heard performances of *Orfeo ed Euridice* and *Alceste*, four operas of Salieri, five of Paisiello, and more still of Grétry.[11] In a winter season that provided performances three times a week during January and February, the emphasis was on spoken comedy and *opéra-comique*. In the latter category, works of Grétry, Pergolesi, Gossec, Philidor, and the Schwarzendorf called Martini predominated. In the carnival season of 1787, Bonn heard more of the repertory with which it was already familiar. From time to time, Neefe organized stage performances utilizing local talent, for which Beethoven was the rehearsal pianist.

From 1778 until his departure for Vienna—which is to say, a period of four years—Beethoven was a viola player in both the opera orchestra and the chapel orchestra. Among Beethoven's young colleagues who served under Franz Ries as concertmaster were such men of later merit as Bernhard Romberg, whose manual of cello playing became the instrument's standard early in the nineteenth century; the horn-playing publisher-to-be Simrock; and flutist-composer Anton Reicha who eventually succeeded François-Adrien Boieldieu in the Institut de France. Taken together, this group of thirty-one players constituted, in Thayer's opinion, "a school for instrumental music such as Handel, Bach, Mozart and Haydn had not enjoyed in their youth."[12]

Lest this seem overweighted on the side of opera for a musician whose interest in the theater was not all-consuming, mention may be made of the statement by Thayer that "From 1784 on, [Beethoven] was in a position to become acquainted almost at once with Mozart's latest major works."[13] This unelaborated, abundantly tantalizing comment might seem speculative or based on hearsay were it not that 1784 marked the beginning of Maximilian Franz's tenure as Elector of Cologne and his residence in Bonn, with all its subsequent Beethoven associations. A music lover by heredity (his mother was the celebrated Empress Maria Theresa, whose broad interests included all the arts), Maximilian's connection with Mozart can be traced to 1775. It was on the occasion of Maximilian's visit to Salzburg in 1775 that Mozart created *Il Re Pastore*, with its beautiful "L'amerò, sarò costante" for soprano with violin obbligato. They met again in 1782 when the Elector-to-be crossed Mozart's path in Vienna, and some conversation ensued[14]

[11] Thayer-Forbes (1964), I, 80–1.
[12] Ibid., p. 96.
[13] Ibid., p. 67.
[14] Emily Anderson: *The Letters of Mozart*, 3 vols. (London: Macmillan and Co.; 1938). Volume III, p. 1,184, contains a report of such a conversation from Mozart to his father in a letter dated January 23, 1782.

of the composer coming to Bonn when Maximilian's appointment was confirmed. When the time finally arrived, the post was occupied and Mozart was absorbed with plans for *Le Nozze di Figaro* in Vienna.

The implied possibility that Beethoven, despite the lack of external evidence, may indeed have been abreast of what Mozart was doing between 1784 and 1791 cannot be verified in any source known to me bearing on Bonn. But there is a collateral commentary from Vienna which may, at this late date, contain an answer to the riddle. By 1784, Mozart had been in the Austrian capital for three years, and was enjoying one of his occasional periods of financial advantage as well as artistic productivity.

The possibility that his artistic fertility might be exploited to produce a more than occasional period of financial advantage prompted Mozart to suggest an ingenious arrangement to his father. The idea was for Mozart senior to act as agent (in Salzburg) on behalf of various music-loving princes of the German states whereby they would acquire, for their exclusive enjoyment, handwritten copies of Mozart's newest scores. Such a service would be restricted to "reliable" customers who could be counted on to hold their acquisitions in confidence. This was designed to bypass the usual practice by which the composer would accept a small sum for an engraving of a new work which a purchaser or a purchaser's friend would pass on to another engraver in Germany or France. He could copy and sell the work without income of any kind for the composer.

On his son's behalf, Leopold Mozart wrote a letter, dated April 3, 1784,[15] to Prince von Fürstenberg at Donaueschingen. It describes the work, for piano, as one "no one knows about" and thus meet for a monarch's delectation (like a virgin being purchased for a harem).

In a later letter (August 8, 1786) Mozart corresponds, in much the same vein, directly with Sebastian Winter, a Salzburger who had risen to the eminence of being the Prince von Fürstenberg's major domo.

This resulted in a "sale" by which, on September 30, Mozart dispatched three concertos and three symphonies. He assured the recipient that they should not be confused with any other works in general circulation, that they were drawn from "compositions which I keep for myself or for a small circle of music lovers and connoisseurs (who promise not to let them out of their hands)." Further, he guaranteed they "cannot possibly be known elsewhere, as they are not even known in Vienna. And that is the case with the three concertos which I have the honor

15 Ibid., p. 1,301.

of sending to His Highness. But here I have been obliged to add to the cost of copying a small additional fee of six ducats for each concerto; and I must ask His Highness not to let them out of his hands."[16]

If the Mozart Distribution-to-Royalty Service ventured as far from Vienna and Salzburg as Donaueschingen, there would seem little reason to doubt that it was available to such a confirmed Mozartian as Maximilian in Bonn. It might even account for Beethoven's production of piano quartets in the year of Mozart's first composition for such an ensemble (see p. 33) despite the lack of any publication which could serve as a connecting link. The coincidence of 1784 as the year of Mozart's letter to his father *and* of Thayer's undeveloped reference leaves no uncertainty in my mind. The conclusion is in order that Thayer was aware of such circulation of Mozart's new works and that Bonn was on the list of the "small circle of music lovers and connoisseurs" favored.

Taking into account all the possible opportunities for self-education Bonn provided, Beethoven's creation of the *Cantata on the Death of Emperor Joseph II* in 1790 must be recognized not as the product of random chance, but as the culmination of a series of interrelated events. Neefe's instruction had schooled him well for the clavier, and he was also proficient as an organist. Through his command of a string instrument (the viola), he participated in the operatic and orchestral literature performed in Bonn in the later years of the 1780s. The scarcity of completed compositions in the period following his return from the Vienna visit of 1787 may well have been a consequence of the effort he expended on behalf of his younger brothers after the death of their mother. But the cantata of 1790 certified Beethoven as neither a pianist-composer nor a violist-composer but, at the very least, as a composer-pianist whose creative work was to be taken seriously.

Such recognition is evident from the range and variety of works Beethoven wrote thereafter. When a cantata was required for the services commemorating the accession of Leopold II (another of Maria Theresa's sixteen children, five of them male) to Joseph's "Imperial Dignity" as Holy Roman Emperor, it was Beethoven who wrote it. After the turn of the year (1791) came the deliberately simplistic *Ritterballet* (long believed to have been the creation of his patron, Count Waldstein), followed by the highly proficient example of *tafelmusik* Beethoven called a "Parthie." By the time it was published, years later (with the incongruously high opus number of 103), the partita and

[16] Ibid., p. 1,340.

everything associated with it had fallen out of fashion, so it was dubbed Octet for Wind Instruments instead.

When Beethoven departed for Vienna in late 1792 he may have taken with him one of the trios which, as Opus 1, would introduce him to the musical world. This would, in all probability, have been Opus 1, No. 1, in E-flat. Kerman's comment on the material published as the "Kafka" sketchbook[17] points to the origin of themes for Opus 1, No. 2, among student work done by Beethoven *after* his arrival in Vienna, likewise ideas that were utilized in Opus 1, No. 3. On the other hand, the blazing fire that lights the *prestissimo* finale of Opus 1, No. 3,

is shown to have orginated in an earlier piano piece, marked *andante*. It is one of the earliest instances of Beethoven's attraction to a *pattern* of notes to which he would later impart a *character* hardly imaginable from its first form:

[17] Beethoven: *Autograph Miscellany* . . . , II, 276.

Another kind of dilemma surrounds the trio in E-flat, published in 1796 as Opus 3. Clearly modeled on the great E-flat Divertimento of Mozart (K.563, written in 1788), whose number and sequence of movements (as well as key) it duplicates, the year of creation was long associated with 1792.

The "documentation" for this supposition was contained in the memoirs of an English author-musician, published in 1847. But the painstaking Forbes[18] convincingly demonstrates that occurrences assigned by William Gardiner to 1792 could not have happened prior to 1794. This includes so pivotal an event as the evacuation from Bonn of Maximilian Franz and his retinue under the pressure of the advancing French army. The handwritten copy of the Beethoven trio which Gardiner took back to England might have been made from a holograph sent by the composer to Maximilian as an *envoi* of his faring in Vienna (see p. 55).

This leaves still unclarified the circumstances in which Beethoven became acquainted with the original. Was it one of those "circulated" by Mozart to favored customers, or did Beethoven make its acquaintance in Vienna, where it was published in 1792?

The later possibility has two lines of descent to commend it:

1. The divertimento was published by Artaria and Co., which found it so much to the public taste in *Hausmusik* that a version for violin and piano was brought out in 1794.

2. Artaria was also the first publisher of Beethoven, including the E-flat String Trio, issued as Opus 3. Beethoven might have been im-

---

[18] Thayer-Forbes (1964), I, 166–7.

pelled, on his own, to follow Mozart's example, or Artaria might have been inspired by the success of his first publication to ask the talented young provincial to "write me another like it."

Should this imply that Beethoven prostituted his talent—a thought unthinkable to some—it may be suggested that such opportunities were among the "educational advantages" previously cited (see p. 33). Such an awareness is crucial to an understanding of Beethoven's functioning for many years to come, and to the impulses that prompted minor as well as major projects. It is also indicative of the vast transformation in Beethoven's fortunes between the creation of the unperformed, unpublished *Trauerkantate* of 1790 and the readily marketable string trio of 1794.

IV

From the Rhine
to the Danube

I

THE BEETHOVEN LITERATURE is burdened, even overburdened, with quotations, documents, and reminiscences bearing on many obscure happenings. But there is absolutely nothing at all to illuminate one of its most important episodes: What, really, prompted Haydn to suggest that a course of study in Vienna (inferentially, under his supervision) would be of considerable benefit to the young man? By common consent, it was the *Cantata on the Death of Emperor Joseph II* that made the crucial impression. Haydn hardly remained in Bonn long enough on his return journey from London in early summer 1792 to examine a wide range of shorter works. But anything like a quotation, a remark, a written word, is lacking.

As of fall, then, the image in Haydn's mind of the young composer newly arrived in Vienna was formed, in all probability, on the "first, forgotten, masterpiece." Looked at through the ears and eyes of Haydn, what does the score tell us about its creator? The very last word in the question is, almost, the first word in the answer:

1. It *was* the work of a creator, of a young man capable of imagining something of his own, not merely of a compiler, however assiduous, of ideas already in existence.

2. Its creator had a sense of shape, balance, contrast, and climax—even of form. This was attested by the reappearance, at the end, of the

stark, dark atmosphere of the opening, rounded off and led to a conclusion by a closing commentary.

3. His compositional means were in no way a match for his creative impulses.

Putting oneself in the position of Haydn, nearly sixty years old, preeminent in a world of music still mourning the death of the brilliant young Mozart only months before (December 1791), one might speculate upon a possible conversation in Bonn, in which his *vis-à-vis* would be Neefe. In it, Haydn might undertake to find answers to such questions as: What kind of training had the young man had? What exercises had he written? To what disciplines had he been exposed? Alluding to the score of the cantata before him, Haydn might remark upon the obvious evidences of talent, even genius, that it contained. But he could scarcely overlook the limited use of contrapuntal devices to enrich the good, basic content.

Neefe's reference to his pupil's knowledge of Bach's preludes and fugues doubtless would have met with Haydn's approval. Such knowledge was a useful basis for keyboard performance and provided an insight into the contrapuntal practices of a great (if "outmoded") master. But in all these works in sonata form to which Neefe referred—the piano quartets, the little concerto, the early sonatas—where among them, and the many freely embellished variations, were evidences to his indoctrination in canon, fugue, imitation at the fifth, double counterpoint, and other prerequisites for compositional discipline? Neefe would have to agree that they were, for one of Haydn's respect for such indispensables, in very limited supply.

The supposed conversation is, of course, invented, as is the probe into Beethoven's background. But the diagnosis of a brilliantly gifted, insufficiently equipped aspirant to the career of a composer may be read in the prescription for growth and development drafted by "Dr." Haydn when the twenty-two-year-old arrived in Vienna at the beginning of November 1792. Inasmuch as Haydn left that city on January 19, 1794, for his second visit to London, the maximum period of their possible association would have been fourteen months. By the time Haydn's return to Vienna was celebrated, on December 16, 1795, with a "grand musical concert" including "three grand symphonies, not yet heard, which the Chapelmaster composed during his last sojourn in London," the erstwhile pupil was present not only to celebrate his twenty-fifth birthday but to perform "a piano concerto of his own composing."[1]

---

[1] Thayer-Krehbiel (1921), I, 188.

All the schooling, counseling, or tutorial influence to which Beethoven was exposed in Vienna was thus confined to a three-year period.
Eager and attentive at the outset to Haydn's guidance, then exasperated
by its intermittent character, and finally apprehensive that his master's
interest was casual rather than profound, Beethoven soon turned to
others for assistance. A little-known but important link in the chain
of influence was Johann Schenk,[2] to whom Beethoven had been introduced by a mutual friend. After glancing at some exercises based on J. J.
Fux's *Gradus ad Parnassum*, in which errors in Beethoven's handwriting
had remained uncorrected by Haydn, Schenk offered to help him. He
specified, however, that his relationship with Beethoven would have to
be confidential—doubtless to avoid a confrontation with so powerful
a personality as Haydn. This has led to the allegation that Beethoven
"went behind Haydn's back"[3] to seek Schenk's assistance. It is quite clear
that Beethoven worked with *both* men in the early months of 1793 until,
in June, he accompanied Haydn to the summer home of the Esterházys
at Eisenstadt.

The major document bearing directly on Beethoven's studies in
Vienna is a letter dated November 23, 1793, from Haydn to Maximilian
Franz at Bonn in support of Beethoven's request for a larger allowance.
It begins:

> I am taking the liberty of sending to your Reverence in all humility
> a few pieces of music, a quintet, an eight-voiced "Parthie," an oboe
> concerto, a set of variations for the piano and a fugue composed
> by my dear pupil Beethoven who was so graciously entrusted to me.
> They will, I flatter myself, be graciously accepted by your Reverence
> as evidence of his diligence beyond the scope of his own studies. On
> the basis of these pieces, expert and amateur alike cannot but admit
> that Beethoven will in time become one of the greatest musical
> artists in Europe, and I shall be proud to call myself his teacher.
> I only wish that he might remain with me for some time. . . .

It concludes:

> In the hope that your Reverence will graciously accept this request
> of mine in behalf of my dear pupil, I am, with deepest respect,
> your Reverence's most humble and obedient servant,
>
> JOSEPH HAYDN
> *Esterházy*[4]
> *Kapellmeister of Prince Nicholas*

---

[2] Thayer-Forbes (1964), I, 141. Schenk was the composer of operas much
favored by the Viennese, especially *Der Dorfbarbier* (1796).

[3] Joseph Schmidt-Görg and Hans Schmidt: *Ludwig van Beethoven* (New
York: Praeger; 1970), p. 17.

[4] Thayer-Forbes (1964), I, 144.

This scarcely suggests a man wary of a pupil who went behind Haydn's back to seek the assistance of another. On the other hand, it hardly supports an estimate of Haydn as a worldly-wise, appropriately sophisticated individual. Princes, no more than others, are not disposed to have their generosity questioned, especially in a plea for *greater* generosity. Maximilian Franz not merely rejected the request, he pointed his refusal with these terse words to Haydn:

> The music of young Beethoven which you sent me I received with your letter. Since, however, this music, with the exception of the fugue, was composed and performed *here in Bonn* [italics added] before he departed on his second journey to Vienna, I cannot regard it as progress . . .
>
> I am wondering whether he had not better come back here in order to resume his work. For I very much doubt that he has made any important progress in composition and in the development of his musical taste during his present stay, and I fear that, as in the case of his first journey to Vienna, he will bring back nothing but debts.
>
> *December 23, 1793*[5]

The first inclination is to blame Beethoven for having misled Haydn; but there is a possibility that Haydn selected, from a variety of scores by Beethoven in his possession, those that he thought best represented his pupil. It was, in any case, the penalty of having a musically literate prince who could distinguish between what he knew and what was new.

One may also read a subtle warning in the Elector's speculation that the time might have come for Beethoven to return to Bonn. He did not suggest that Beethoven's studies might be more profitably pursued in Bonn. He was to be recalled in order "to resume his work," perhaps as successor to Neefe.

In a recent essay on Beethoven's studies with Haydn, Alfred Mann makes the assertion that "The Elector . . . visited Vienna shortly before Haydn's departure"[6] for London, without giving further documentation of an incident not to be found in most Beethoven biographies. Mann also suggests that it was Haydn who "probably" brought Beethoven and J. G. Albrechtsberger together. Albrechtsberger was a close colleague of Haydn's as well as the most pedagogic proponent of counterpoint available in Vienna. In any case, Beethoven began a course of study with

[5] Ibid., p. 145.
[6] Lang: *The Creative World of Beethoven*, see Alfred Mann's essay, "Beethoven's Contrapuntal Studies with Haydn," p. 220.

Albrechtsberger after Haydn's departure for London on January 19, 1794. He also arranged for a three-times-a-week brush-up study of the violin with Ignaz Schuppanzigh. Only nineteen, but already giving strong evidence of the musicianship that was to dominate the famous quartet bearing his name, Schuppanzigh remained a close friend as well as a favored interpreter of Beethoven's ensemble works until the composer's death thirty years later.

Conceivably, this burst of diligence might have followed a meeting in Vienna at which the Elector and Beethoven were present. It might also have prompted the composition of the string trio attributed to 1794, and of which Gardiner obtained a copy in Bonn (see p. 49). However, Beethoven's tie to Bonn was permanently severed before the end of the year. The pressures of war that had caused Maximilian to evacuate his court from Bonn between October 22, 1792, and April 21, 1793, were again weighing heavily upon him. By October 1794, he was again a fugitive and this time there was no reprieve.

Concurrently, Beethoven's affairs were maturing in a way that made a return to Bonn highly unlikely in any case. During 1794 and the early months of 1795 he exploited the opportunities that presented themselves to him in a widening circle of acquaintances in Vienna. From the scanty data bearing on Beethoven's faring in Vienna at this time, one can piece together a fairly detailed picture of an able, ambitious, and energetic young man forging steadily ahead on a chosen path.

For the earliest details, one must turn to Bonn for written evidence of the reports that had begun to filter back from Vienna. One is contained in a letter dated January 26, 1793, or four months after Beethoven's arrival in Vienna, from Bartolomäus Ludwig Fischenich, a jurist and professor of law at the University of Bonn, to Charlotte von Schiller, wife of the poet-playwright, at Jena. He enclosed a copy of a setting by Beethoven of a poem by Sophie Mereau-Brentano with the words:

> It is composed by a local young man whose musical talent is generally praised and who has been sent recently to Haydn in Vienna by the Elector. He will also compose Schiller's Freude, each stanza separately. I am expecting something perfect, as he is only interested in great and sublime matters. Haydn has written to Bonn that he wants to commission great operas to the young man and is afraid he will quit composing. . . .[7]

In a response dated February 11, Charlotte Schiller (whose musical qualifications were those of the average, cultivated young lady of the

[7] Paul Nettl: *Beethoven Encyclopaedia* (New York: Philosophical Library; 1956), p. 57.

time) wrote: "The composition of 'Feuerfarb' is very good; I am expecting a lot of the artist and am looking forward to his composition of 'Freude.' " The former Charlotte von Lengefeld's perceptions were beyond criticism, but she would had to have been farsighted indeed to witness the fulfillment of her expectations for the Schiller *Ode*. However, she might well have participated in Beethoven's glorious fulfillment when the Ninth Symphony was introduced to the world two years before her death in 1826.[8]

This famous first indication of the young Beethoven's intention *vis-à-vis* the Schiller *Ode* (see p. 12) has the double interest of defining Beethoven's lofty musical objectives and conveying Haydn's satisfaction with his pupil's progress during the first months of their Viennese experiment. Those acquainted with Haydn's jocularity will read the reference to "commissioning great operas" and being "afraid he will quit composing" as the same kind of humorous enlargement of Beethoven's prodigious promise as his later query, when their ways had parted, to a mutual friend: "How goes it with our Great Mogul?"[9] Supporting evidence for the Fischenich letter is contained in a dispatch to the *Berliner Musik-Zeitung* in which Neefe reported that "this L.v.B. [Beethoven's full name had been mentioned previously] . . . is said to be making great progress in art . . ."[10]

Perhaps the most illuminating evidence of the progress Beethoven had made during his first year's residence in musical Vienna is contained in a brief entry in an account book he was keeping in fall 1793, just about the time Haydn was writing to Maximilian Franz: "Supped in the evening at Swieten's, 17 pourboire. To the janitor 4 x for opening the door." Of unidentified date, addressed to Beethoven at Alserstrasse, No. 45, is a message from the same Swieten, reading: "If there is nothing to hinder next Wednesday I should be glad to see you at my home at half past 8 with your nightcap in your bag. Give me an immediate answer."

2

THE APPEARANCE in Beethoven's life of Gottfried van Swieten may be likened to theme C in a rondo on historic motives (Mozart, Haydn, Swieten). A native of Leyden, Holland, where he was born in 1733,

---

[8] Friedrich Schiller: *William Tell*, Introduction by Gilbert J. Jordan (New York: Bobbs-Merrill; 1964).
[9] Thayer-Forbes (1964), I, 240.
[10] Ibid., p. 113.

Swieten migrated to Vienna in 1745 when his father, Gerhard,[11] became the personal physician to Empress Maria Theresa. In his own right, Gottfried van Swieten matured to serve as Austrian ambassador to Brussels, Paris, Warsaw, and Berlin before becoming director of the Imperial Library in 1777. He was also charged with the direction of the Austrian education department, a post in which he was credited with bringing about results of historic importance.

However distinguished these achievements of his official career, they must take second place to the even more lasting consequences of his unofficial career as music lover *in excelsis* and connoisseur *par excellence.* Swieten was particularly responsive to the influence he encountered during his tour of duty in Berlin, where K. P. E. Bach flourished and neither his father nor Handel were forgotten. When Mozart settled in Vienna in 1781, Swieten, who had already met Haydn in Berlin, was one of the first to befriend him. They became closely acquainted in 1782, with results recorded in a letter of April 10, from Mozart to his father: "I have been intending to ask you, when you return the rondo, to enclose with it Handel's six fugues and Eberlin's toccatas and fugues. I go every Sunday to Baron von Swieten, where nothing is played but Handel and Bach . . ."[12]

It was Swieten who persuaded Mozart to add instrumental parts to Handel's scoring for *Acis and Galatea, Messiah,* the *Ode for St. Cecilia's Day,* and *Alexander's Feast.* On Swieten's behalf, Mozart also scored for strings a C-minor fugue originally written for two pianos. In the new form it includes a prefatory adagio (K.546).

When subject to translation by those who knew Swieten's habits and locution, the message cited above would read: "I am having a musicale on Wednesday evening to which you are invited. Come and play some of the 48 you learned in Bonn, and be prepared to stay the night." The imperious "Give me an immediate answer" is the verbal equivalent of the haughty manner in which Swieten would rise to his feet and silently stare down people whose conversation disturbed his concentration at a musicale.

Though his passion was indeed music, he was not so warmly disposed to musicians. Wealthy and unmarried, he might have assisted Mozart financially in his time of need, but he never did.[13] If, as reputed,

[11] Otto Jahn: *Life of Mozart,* 3 vols., trans. Pauline D. Townsend, Preface by George Grove (London: Novello, Ewer and Co.; 1882), II, 374.

[12] Anderson: *The Letters of Mozart, III,* 1,192.

[13] Jahn: *Life of Mozart,* II, 385.

he paid for the pauper's funeral[14] which closed the troubled, almost overproductive life of Mozart, it was all too little, and much too late.

Idiosyncrasies and affectations aside, Swieten's favor was of inestimable value in furthering Beethoven's penetration to the inner circle of Vienna's musical life. Such sponsorship is of signal service to the young and talented in almost any community at any time. In the Vienna of the 1790s, it was all but indispensable. Public concerts were rarities, save as benefits or when organized on behalf of a reigning favorite, such as Haydn; a musical "press" hardly existed; most music was made in homes, palaces, or at such musicales as Swieten's.

Soon enough, the polar temperaments of the patrician and the provincial came into conflict. Schindler, who wrote his biography out of some personal experience with Beethoven's temper (see pp. 272-3), observes "Even Swieten's discreet advice often went unheeded, and, although he had been the one to introduce Beethoven into the high circles of society, he had no recourse but to feel gratified when his headstrong and independent young protégé consented to be present at his musical soirées."[15]

Ultimately, Beethoven valued Swieten's part in his life at the high esteem of inscribing the First Symphony to him when it was published in 1801—a lordly gesture from the self-made nobleman. Doubtless it filled Swieten's cup to overflowing, for 1801 was the year in which he collaborated actively with Haydn on *Die Jahreszeiten* (*The Seasons*) as he had previously on *Die Schöpfung* (*The Creation*). In both instances he not only exerted the power of persuasion required for Haydn to undertake such large projects, but provided him with texts, in German, from English sources.

Not without interest is the address—Alserstrasse, No. 45—to which Swieten dispatched his message of 1793 to Beethoven. It was the residence of Prince Karl Lichnowsky, to whom Beethoven inscribed the three trios of his Opus 1 when they were published in 1795. According to the custom of the time, a favored plebeian could be given lodgings on the lower floor of a domicile otherwise occupied in suitable splendor by its owner. This arrangement began for Beethoven early in 1793 (to judge by Forbes' statement that it was "soon" after his arrival in Vienna[16]) and endured until 1795 when Beethoven felt sufficiently established to find quarters of his own.

---

[14] Nettl: *Beethoven Encyclopaedia*, p. 255.
[15] Schindler: *Beethoven as I Knew Him*, p. 50.
[16] Thayer-Forbes (1964), II, 1,109.

For a while, the successive steps of becoming "established" went hand in hand with his course of study with Albrechtsberger. Even before it began, Beethoven had broken his "maiden," in the long run of publishing, with the appearance of his variations on "Se vuol ballare" (from Mozart's *Le Nozze di Figaro*) in July 1793. The engraving of them by Artaria reflected less Beethoven's opinion of their worth than "the request of others" and a desire to protect his claim to whatever originality they contained against "the rival pianists of Vienna," whose habit of pilfering the unpublished innovations of others was well known.[17]

Though already a published composer and publicly esteemed as a pianist, Beethoven resumed his status of student with Albrechtsberger. Three times a week he presented himself at his mentor's dwelling with exercises to be reviewed and corrected. The material they covered began with studies on two *canti firmi* (the elaboration of melodies over a fixed bass) and went on to contrapuntal examples of free writing, in imitation, in two-, three-, and four-part fugue, triple counterpoint, and canon. Despite his reputation for being self-willed (*selbstwollend*) and unable to get along with a teacher,[18] Beethoven applied himself with absolute seriousness to his studies, an attitude that was appreciated as well as reciprocated by Albrechtsberger. If, in the aesthetic cliché, rules are made to be broken, Beethoven was sufficiently mature at twenty-four to differentiate between exercises and aesthetics. All the indications are that he was the kind of serious craftsman who wanted to know thoroughly the rules he might be impelled to break.

The course of study with Albrechtsberger has been estimated to have covered about fifteen months, from March 1794 to May 1795.[19] Although no date of termination is recorded, drafts of some of the most advanced exercises are to be found among sketches for compositions known to have originated in May 1795. This is the presumption for belief that the lessons soon afterward ran their course.

Gustav Nottebohm, who pursued this phase of Beethoven's career in exhaustive detail, summarized the outcome of his work with Albrechtsberger as follows: "The voices acquired greater melodic flow and independence. A certain opacity took the place of the former transparency in the musical fabric. Out of a homophonic polyphony of two or more voices, there grew a polyphony that was real. The earlier obbligato accom-

---

[17] Ibid., I, 165.
[18] Thayer-Krehbiel (1921), I, 168.
[19] Thayer-Forbes (1964), I, 148.

paniment gave way to an obbligato style of writing which depended to a greater extent on counterpoint. Beethoven has accepted the principle of polyphony; his part-writing has became purer and it is noteworthy that the compositions written immediately after the lessons are among the purest that Beethoven ever composed."[20]

3

On the days of the week when Beethoven was not visiting Albrechtsberger or Schuppanzigh, he steadily, systematically applied himself to enlarging the beachhead established in Vienna with the assistance of Lichnowsky and Swieten. By August 1794, he was begging indulgence from his old Bonn friend Simrock, who had completed his transition from horn player to publisher, for failure to answer a letter more promptly. Stated cause: "an accumulation of business affairs."[21] This was but a prelude to a harvest of happenings reaped from the seeds planted during two full years in Vienna which made 1795 historic in his life.

Among the most conspicuous of them was his first public appearance in Vienna as a pianist, in a concert at the Burgtheater on March 29 for the benefit of the widows of musicians. He appeared as a soloist in his own B-flat Concerto (played with the later discarded finale) and, in a return engagement on the following evening, as an improvisor. At a third event, on March 31, Beethoven appeared as soloist in a piano concerto of Mozart, between the first and second parts of a performance of *La Clemenza di Tito* sponsored by the composer's widow. It is commonly believed to have been the D-minor (K.466), of which Beethoven was particularly fond, and for which he composed two cadenzas that are still preferred by some performers.

In this watershed year, May could be described as the time the dam broke. In a rising tide, the first wave came with the announcement on May 16 inviting subscriptions to the soon-to-be-published trios, Opus 1. He soon thereafter drifted away from Albrechtsberger on a course all his own. And at the end of the month Beethoven severed his ties with Lichnowsky and acquired quarters of his own on the Kreuzgasse.

In his dealings with another publisher at about this time, Beethoven boasted of the "handsome fee" which Artaria paid him on the

[20] Ibid.
[21] Emily Anderson: *The Letters of Beethoven*, 3 vols. (New York: St. Martin's Press; 1961), I, 17.

publication of the "Se vuol ballare" variations. It would be ironic if his decision to leave the Lichnowsky residence had been made possible by a similar fee from Artaria for the rights to the Opus 1 trios. Many years later Artaria's son told an early Beethoven biographer, Ludwig Nohl, that his father "got the money to pay Beethoven [for the publication of the trios] without the composer's knowledge from Prince Lichnowsky."[22]

So much of consequence would have made the year memorable for Beethoven. But, as the months of the year were less than half over, so too were the happenings. On August 20, Haydn returned from his second London visit, and was soon afterward a guest at one of Lichnowsky's Friday morning musicales. Beethoven's contribution to Haydn's homecoming was the first performance of the three Opus 2 piano sonatas, dedicated to his former mentor and now senior colleague. It was the order of this Lichnowsky day for music to begin early and continue for several hours, following which the musicians were invited to share the host's table at 4 p.m. for dinner. One of the known reasons for Beethoven's desire to have quarters of his own was to avoid Lichnowsky's four o'clock dinners to which, as a house guest, he was welcome at any time. A friend quotes the composer as saying, ". . . it is desired that every day I shall be home at half-past 3, put on better clothes, care for my beard, etc.—I can't stand that!"[23]

With the Opus 1 trios in print and the Opus 2 sonatas ready for the engraver, the transitional year was all but bursting with portents for the future. Still to come was the concert of December 16 (see p. 52) in which he performed a work of his own in conjunction with three symphonies of Haydn not previously heard in Vienna. By then, he was no longer "the pupil Beethoven" but a possessor of "the master hand." That, in any case, is the way in which he was described in an advertisement for the annual ball (November 22) sponsored in the Redoutensaal by the Gesellschaft der bildenen Künstler.[24] The event had originated in 1792, and it was Haydn, as Vienna's reigning master, who had been invited to write twelve minuets and twelve German dances to commemorate the occasion. In 1793, the privilege was extended to Royal Imperial Composer Koželuch; in 1704 to the eminent Dittersdorf.

For the expanded ball of 1795, the announcement proclaimed: "The music for the Minuets and German Dances for this ball is an

[22] Thayer-Krehbiel (1921), I, 185 *n.*
[23] Thayer-Forbes (1964), I, 172.
[24] Ibid., p. 177.

entirely new arrangement. For the larger room they were written by Royal Imperial Kapellmeister Süssmayr; for the smaller room by the master hand of Hr. Ludwig van Beethoven out of love for the artistic fraternity."[25] It was an extraordinary transition in artistic estate for the young man from Bonn who had come to Vienna not much more than three years before. He was not only succeeding, in part at least, to an honor previously bestowed on Haydn. He was collaborating with the musician chosen to complete Mozart's last earthly endeavor, the Requiem he left unfinished at his death the year before Beethoven came to Vienna.

[25] Ibid., p. 177.

V

Beethoven in Clavierland

I

POSSIBLY THE MOST COMPREHENSIVE and certainly the most personal description of musical life in Vienna during the last quarter of the eighteenth century is contained in a text not designed to be either—Mozart's letters to his father in Salzburg. The earliest in the sequence, dated March 17, 1781, describes Wolfgang A. Mozart's arrival, as an employee of the Archbishop of Salzburg, in the city that was destined to become home for the rest of his life. It proceeds with the account of his dismissal for insubordination, booted (literally) from the antechamber with a "kick on the arse" by the chamberlain Count Arco.[1] Through trials and triumphs, the letters spell out in detail the tastes of the moneyed Viennese, their fanaticism and their fickleness. The sequence terminates all too regrettably on April 4, 1787, with the beginning of the illness that resulted in Leopold Mozart's death at the end of May. The subsequent letters to others are much less revealing, musically, than those which passed between son and father.

In his first flush of enthusiasm at liberation from irksome service to the Archbishop, Mozart wrote to his father (April 4, 1781): "I assure you this is a splendid place and for my *métier* the best one in the world."[2]

---

[1] Anderson: *The Letters of Mozart*, III, 1,102. The words of Mozart to his father in the German text are "einen tritt im arsch."

[2] Ibid., pp. 1,071–2.

With the passage of time and the upsurge of confidence that came from some immediate successes as composer as well as performer (teaching was as yet an untapped resource because it was coming on summer and the wealthy had departed to their country places), Mozart's eloquence soared to new heights. By June 2 he was proclaiming: "Hier ist doch gewiss das Clavierland" ("Here indeed is the land of the clavier"),[3] and making plans to exploit it to his purpose.

In the very first of the letters, Mozart announces: "Well, I must close this letter which I shall hand in at the post office on the way, for I must be off to Prince Galitzin's." There follows a parade of names which came to be associated as much with Beethoven as with Mozart. The Ambassador from Russia to Austria did not endure to become the patron of the same name to whom the great quartets of Opus 127 (E-flat), Opus 130 (B-flat), and Opus 132 (A minor) are dedicated. But he endowed the name with associations that prompted another bearer of it to seek out the aging, ailing *meister* and turn his mind to quartet writing after a lapse from 1810 to 1824. One such impulse could assure a patron a place in Paradise.

Among the other names which come and go in the Mozart chronicle are those of the Count and Countess Maria Thun (the former, the patron for whom Mozart created the *Linz* Symphony; the latter, a celebrated devotee of the art). Together they reared the daughters who became regal wives for two of Beethoven's greatest benefactors: Elisabeth, who married Prince Razumovsky; and Christiane, whose husband was Prince Karl Lichnowsky. The Baron van Swieten is early identified (see p. 57); soon after comes Antonio Salieri, with whom Beethoven studied vocal composition, and Christoph von Gluck. All were part of the scene before the turn of the season and the resumption of urban life in the fall of 1781.

Much of Mozart's time in the early months of 1782 was devoted to the composition of *Die Entführung aus dem Serail*, his first great success[4] in Vienna. On its favor was built the reclame which served him

---

[3] Wilhelm A. Bauer and Otto Erich Deutsch: *Mozarts Briefe und Aufzeichnungen*, 3 vols. (Kassel: Barenreiter; 1963), III, 125.

[4] Alfred Loewenberg: *Annals of Opera, 1597–1940* (Cambridge, Eng.: W. Heffer and Sons; 1943), p. 195. The author puts at thirty-four the number of performances of *Die Entführung* in Vienna between 1782 and 1788, when the "National Singspiel" at the Burgtheater came to an end. Of collateral interest is the identity of Bonn as the first German town to hear it (in 1783, preceded only by Prague). Sixteen other communities heard it by 1785, and ten more by the end of the decade. Indeed, had Mozart retained an earning interest from but *four* of his operas—*Die Entführung, Le Nozze di Figaro, Don Giovanni,* and *Die Zauberflöte*—he would not have suffered the indignity of "starvation amid plenty" that hastened his death.

so well in the immediate aftermath of its premiere on July 16, 1782. Steadily the names in the letters grow more familiar: the Archduke Maximilian (not yet the Elector of Cologne), Esterházy, Clementi. By 1784, when Mozart had improved his position in Clavierland to the point at which he could risk a series of concerts on his own, the gamble was hedged by a list of subscribers whose names comprised a *Who's Who* of aristocratic Vienna (letter of March 20, 1784).

In a list including more than one hundred and fifty names, to which admission was available to anyone with the price, it is understandable that a majority of those represented have no identity two hundred years later. But it is also remarkable that it included many names which are, either by official position or personal association, highly meaningful still. Among them are:[5]

L'Ambassadeur d'Espagne
Comte de Würm
b) Baron von Swieten
Comte Charles d'Auersperg
b) Comtesse Staremberg
née Neiperg
b) Comte Nep d'Herberstein
b) Prince Joseph Lobkowitz
b) Névery
b) Le Comte Fries
de Puthon[6]
b) Comtesse Thun
née d'Ulfeld
b) Joseph Palfy
b) Comtesse Esterházy
b) Comte Jean Esterházy
b) Joseph Dietrichstein
b) Prince Louis Lichtenstein

de Meyenberg
Comte de Kuffstein
b) Bar: de Braun
Prince Gallitzin
b) Comte Ladislaus d'Erdödy
b) Comte Czernin
b) Comte Etienne Zitchi
b) Princess Lignowsky
[Lichnowsky]
b) Comte Waldstein
Comte George Waldstein
b) Le Comte Harrach l'ainé
b) Comtesse Waldstein
née d'Ulfeld
b) Prince de Schwarzenberg
b) Comtesse Apumoni [Apponyi?]
Prince de Meklenbourg
b) Comtesse de Hazfeld
Comte Montecuculi

A perusal of this list, side by side with that of the subscribers to Beethoven's Opus 1 trios in 1795, leaves little doubt that the Vienna in which Mozart flourished and failed was, in many respects, the Vienna in which Beethoven mounted his first campaign for public favor a dozen

[5] The list is given, excerpted, as reproduced on pages 1,297–9 and 1,300 of Anderson: *The Letters of Mozart*, III, in the spellings Mozart provided in a communiqué of March 20, 1784, to his father. In a footnote Miss Anderson mentions: "The first page of the autograph is a torn sheet. The beginning of the letter has been lost." It is not unreasonable to assume that the whole list included the First Fifty of Vienna's cultural, as well as social, aristocracy.

[6] A baron of this same aristocratic banking family was the principal officer of the Salzburg Festival when it was reorganized in the 1950s, after the lapse during World War II.

years later. (The letter b beside the names in the Mozart listing above identifies those who were also subscribers to the Beethoven trios.) The essence of the community condition was summarized by the unspeakable Count Arco (see p. 63) when Mozart was petitioning, through him, for release from the Archbishop of Salzburg's service: "Believe me, you allow yourself to be far too easily dazzled in Vienna. At first, it's true, you are overwhelmed with praises and make a great deal of money into the bargain—but how long does it last? After a few months the Viennese want something new."[7]

If Arco's words were not known to Beethoven, the legendary volatility of the Viennese unquestionably was. The dependence of Mozart's widow and children on such charity as he himself extended (in the benefit concert at Burgtheater) was a steady reminder of the overwork and undernourishment which had ended Mozart's life at thirty-five. If Beethoven were to escape a comparable disaster, his relationship with the public, especially the moneyed public, of Vienna would have to be different.

Beethoven did not then, or ever, assume the burden of family life which kept Mozart at the writing table far into the night. Also, he was made of tougher mental as well as physical fiber. But he eventually became as obsessed with his nephew Karl as Mozart was with his family, and the toughest character can be eroded by the abrasive effects of poor judgment or imprudence.

Providentially for Beethoven, the likeness of his musical genius to Mozart's was not duplicated in their conditioning for earthly existence. It has already been noted (see p. 42) that Beethoven considered himself disadvantaged in not having a father with Leopold Mozart's musical acuity to guide his development. But if Leopold educated his son magnificently for a musical career, he restricted and constricted him socially by constant remonstrations about right and wrong, good and bad, provident and improvident in his day-to-day conduct. One senses, from their letters, a perpetual sense of immaturity in Mozart's dealing with the world because he was conditioned by his father to live by standards that applied to an earlier generation.

For Leopold, being "in service" was virtually the only way for a musician to subsist. The worthy objective was to be "in service" to an Emperor rather than an Archbishop because the job paid better. In consequence, Mozart realized all too little of the earning power his genius might have brought him. Moreover, until his break with the Arch-

<hr />

[7] Anderson: *The Letters of Mozart*, III, 1,099.

bishop, he accepted a position of indecent servility. He was even re-strained from discussing his situation frankly in letters to his father, for fear that they might be read by hostile eyes and affect Leopold's situation in Salzburg.

If Johann Beethoven neglected his son's musical education, he did —if only by forfeit—spare him from social conformism and a reverence for his "betters." A wage-earner at fourteen and the guiding spirit to his younger brothers soon after, Beethoven was conditioned to self-improvement not merely as a way of life but as a condition of survival. From such lack of options emerged a resolute belief in self-determination of his own destiny. Mozart's acceptance of his mother's death as "God's will" when, at nineteen he had to report the harsh news from Paris to his father in Salzburg, had little part in Beethoven's thinking. It was eminently appropriate that the Revolution which swept Europe in the 1790s swept away the court in Bonn to which he was attached. One doubts that Beethoven would have returned to it in any case.

As a proponent of the social inequities denounced by Beaumarchais, Mozart projected, through *Le Nozze di Figaro*, a message of independence for his audience which he was never able to practice productively himself. Even the scheme conceived in 1784 for selling, privately, a concerto or a symphony to a nobleman, did not go far enough. When, a few years later, Beethoven had a product in which a member of the Fürstenberg family[8] might be interested, he flattered the Princess von Liechtenstein (née Landgravine Fürstenberg) more and profited in greater measure himself by dedicating his Sonata in E-flat, Opus 27, No. 1, to her, rather than soliciting a "subscription."

Bit by bit, year by year, eventually work by work, Beethoven man-aged to erode the master-servant relationship to which most of his predecessors had been abjectly servile. For one Handel, who found both a monarch and a market in London, there were a hundred others who labored for a meager subsistence while creating products that could not be duplicated at any price. It took time and aggressive action for Beethoven to reverse the customary relationship, but he initiated a mode of dealing both with patrons and publishers which became the profitable way of life for many who followed.

That is not to say that he didn't appreciate the importance of royalty; but he managed, eventually, to use them rather than be used by them. Some of the time he applied to his relationship with Archduke Rudolph doubtless could have been utilized more productively

[8] They were Mozart's princely customers in Donaueschingen (see p. 46).

at the writing desk. But, more and more, writing "to order" meant writing to an "order" which served his ends rather than those of others.

2

FOR THE WHILE, these projections for the future were still some distance in the future. The present, for Beethoven—as at the end of the spectacularly successful year of 1795—was to a large extent still under the shadow of Mozart. This, paradoxically, grew longer as the time of Mozart's mortal life receded.[9] Individuals who had known and patronized him (not to his advantage) were present on every side. In the aftermath of his mortifying death, the impulse was to do better by the next such "immortal" with whom they might be confronted. If by 1795, both Prince Lichnowsky and Baron van Swieten had reason to rate Beethoven as a headstrong and self-willed fellow, they nevertheless were ready to acclaim him, musically, with the highest praise they could command—"another Mozart."

Disposed to do the best he could by Beethoven's talent, though he had early warnings of the young man's cantankerous character, was Lichnowsky himself. An exact contemporary of Mozart, having also been born in 1756, Lichnowsky's musical competence was sufficient to earn not only Mozart's appreciation as a patron, but also his consideration as a pupil. Doubtless his musical interests, as well as his rank, commended him to the Count and Countess Thun, whose household he entered through marriage to their daughter Maria Christiane.

Among the evidences of Lichnowsky's goodwill toward Mozart was a tour he sponsored in 1789, the objective of which was the court of the music-loving Friedrich Wilhelm II in Berlin. As may be read in the massive biography of Mozart by Otto Jahn:

[9] During Mozart's productive lifetime—which covered more than twenty of his thirty-five years—144 of his works were published. This seemingly substantial total was, however, heavily weighted on the side of individual piano sonatas (twenty-nine), sonatas and variations for violin and piano (thirty-three), trios and quartets (twenty-two), and dances (sixteen) for a total of exactly one hundred. Of larger works, the catalogue included but one opera (*Die Entführung*), three symphonies (No. 31, *Paris*, in D; No. 33, in B-flat; and No. 35, *Haffner*, in D) and six concertos (all for clavier: No. 5, in D; No. 11, in F; No. 12, in A; No. 13, in C; No. 16, in D; No. 17, in G; and No. 27, in B-flat). In addition to *Die Entführung*, which was published complete, there were "selections" available from *Bastien und Bastienne*, *Le Nozze di Figaro*, *Don Giovanni*, *Così fan tutte*, and *Die Zauberflöte*. But, says A. Hyatt King (from whose *Mozart in Retrospect* [London: Oxford University Press; 1955], pp. 9–10, the preceding figures were taken), "within little more than a decade after his death his music was to be printed in a flood unprecedented in the musical history of any age or country." J. P. Spehr of Brunswick announced a complete edition in 1797, and by 1860 Breitkopf und Härtel had seventeen volumes of its own edition in print.

Mozart's unsatisfactory position in Vienna, both from a pecuniary and a professional point of view, doubtless inclined him to a professional tour, to which the immediate inducement was an invitation from Prince Karl Lichnowsky. . . . His estates in Schleswig[10] and his position in the Prussian army necessitated his residence from time to time in Berlin; and, being on the point of repairing thither in the spring of 1789, he invited Mozart to accompany him. The musical taste and liberality [of the monarch] augured well for the expedition, and Lichnowsky's support was likely to prove a valuable aid. Accordingly, on April 8, they set out. . . .[11]

In 1796, older by seven years but not appreciably wiser in the ways of genius, Prince Lichnowsky extended his hospitality and his entrée at the court of Friedrich Wilhelm II once again. Though Beethoven had previously relinquished the Princely bed and board, Lichnowsky's continuing interest embraced the composer's personal as well as professional well-being. Theirs, indeed, was the kind of relationship that endured despite causes for recrimination on both sides. It included one period during which Lichnowsky again accommodated Beethoven as a house guest though, because of some fancied slight, the composer was not talking to him at the time.[12]

No doubt with some thought of the historic adventure with Mozart,[13] Lichnowsky invited Beethoven to accompany him on a similar tour, beginning in mid-February 1796. They reached Prague together, but Beethoven found the natives so friendly and the business prospects so good that he lingered, as Lichnowsky went on alone. This is detailed in a letter Beethoven wrote to his brother Nikolaus Johann, who had recently arrived in Vienna from Bonn. It is dated February 19, and reads, in part: "First of all, I am well, very well. My art is winning me friends and renown, and what more do I want? And this time I shall make a good deal of money. I shall remain here for a few weeks longer and then travel to Dresden, Leipzig and Berlin [thus repeating Mozart's itinerary]. . . . P. Lichnowsky will soon be on his way back to Vienna. He had already left Prague. . . ."[14]

Eventually Beethoven did get to Berlin (late May is the indicated

[10] The reference to Schleswig should read Schlesien (Silesia), which is located much farther south.

[11] Jahn: *Life of Mozart*, III, 226.

[12] Nettl: *Beethoven Encyclopaedia*, p. 120.

[13] Mozart finally returned to Vienna by way of Prague–Dresden–Leipzig–Berlin on June 4, 1789, having forewarned his wife, Constanze, that she would have to rejoice at his safe return rather at the size of the earnings he was bringing back. His principal purse from the tour was one hundred friedrichsdors from Friedrich Wilhelm II, minus expenses and one hundred florins he had "lent" to a friend whose need Mozart reckoned as greater than his own. Jahn: *Life of Mozart*, III, 236.

[14] Anderson: *The Letters of Beethoven*, I, 23.

but undocumented date), where his ability as a pianist confirmed everything that Lichnowsky had promised. He also pleased Friedrich Wilhelm II by composing for him the two cello and piano sonatas published as Opus 5. The cello-playing monarch's[15] regard for Beethoven was conveyed not merely by a gift of a hundred louis d'or, but also by the suggestion that he join his court as Kapellmeister. Nothing ever came of this proposal, but Beethoven long cherished the snuffbox in which the gold coins were contained. It was, he was fond of saying, "no ordinary box, but one of the kind which are presented to Ambassadors.[16]

If the young man started on the Lichnowsky-sponsored tour as "another Mozart," he ended it quite like the one and only Beethoven. As well as bidding his noble traveling companion—and benefactor—farewell as soon as it suited his convenience, Beethoven left little doubt that he could make the rest of the journey on his own. It was an action typical both of Beethoven's growing self-involvement and his belief that his art assured him any position to which he aspired.

Typical too of Beethoven's practicality was the manner in which he converted a conventional royal dedication into an unconventional dividend. When Mozart returned to Vienna with what was left of Friedrich Wilhelm's one hundred friedrichsdors, he spent much time in writing a string quartet for which the monarch paid him another hundred friedrichsdors.[17] He did not, however, have any further income from the composition. Beethoven gave the same monarch two sonatas written on the spot in return for one hundred louis d'or (a more valuable coin)[18] and also retained rights for the publication and sale of the rights to Artaria.

This transaction forecast the manner in which Beethoven would convert to personal advantage the new technologies of printing and publishing as they emerged during his lifetime. Most productive of all was the development of lithography, a speedier, cheaper technique than engraving. The procedure, created in large part by Alois Senefelder,

[15] He was the nephew of, as well as successor to, Frederick the Great, whose fondness for playing the flute is legendary.

[16] H. C. Robbins Landon: *Beethoven* (New York: Macmillan; 1970), p. 92. The quotation is ascribed to Beethoven's pupil and friend, Ries.

[17] Jahn: *Life of Mozart*, III, 237.

[18] Anderson: *The Letters of Beethoven*, I, xi and xii, contains a table of conversion values by which, as of Beethoven's time in Berlin, the friedrichsdor was valued at sixteen shillings and the louis d'or at twenty shillings in British exchange, or 25 percent more. The hundred louis d'or would thus have had the value of a hundred pounds, or something more than five hundred dollars. In today's purchasing power, the sum for the two sonatas would have been several thousand dollars.

accelerated the production of printed music in Germany and Austria, especially for making it available for home use at a few pennies a page. Giovanni Ricordi was one of those who was attracted to learn Senefelder's methods in Leipzig, and to found a flourishing business in his native city, Milan.

Eventually Beethoven would utilize his great repute and massive prestige to sell the rights to the *Missa Solemnis* to several publishers simultaneously while soliciting, from kings and kaisers, princes and a czar, subscriptions to "handwritten copies" of a work of which "no others will ever be published." The work was, of course, dedicated to Archduke Rudolph. For the while, Beethoven busied himself to take advantage of the brisk demand for his *Hausmusik* by writing a variety of works which had no overwhelming importance as self-expression. The approach of the publication date would often be heralded by an advertisement in the Viennese press, much as one might advertise the recording of a popular "musical" today.

The writer in Grove's *Dictionary*[19] who asserts that "Beethoven did no hackwork" may have had his own, narrow sense of the term to justify its blanket application. (He does allow that the setting of folk songs Beethoven made in quantity between 1810 and 1819 for his English publisher "might be so regarded.") Others, however, would have to conclude that Beethoven turned his hand not only regularly but systematically to tasks for which the only motivation was monetary or honorific. In this particular period of 1796–98, during which he had been liberated from scholastic disciplines and freed from the nagging threat of a return to Bonn, Beethoven made no conspicuous progress in musical idiom. By the measure of some earlier works, it remained either stationary or retrogressed.

In the year of the tour to Prague, Dresden, Leipzig, and Berlin, Beethoven produced a minimal number of durable or even enterprising works. Among projects begun in 1795 and finished in 1796 were a recomposition for string quintet of the octet written in Bonn half a dozen years before (the second dedication brings the name of Apponyi into the lexicon of Beethoven sponsors for the first time); a serenade (eventually published as Opus 25) which adds the flute to the list of home-favored instruments also favored by Beethoven; and two works for solo voice, "Adélaïde" and "Ah, perfido!", which demonstrate his command

[19] *Grove's Dictionary of Music and Musicians*, 5th edn., Beethoven article by William McNaught, Vol. I, p. 534.

of conventional German sentiment and traditional Italian drama.

During 1796 Beethoven originated and completed the cello sonatas dedicated to Friedrich Wilhelm II; the uncomplicated quintet for piano and winds published as Opus 16; one of two "easy" sonatas which were eventually published together as Opus 49; several sets of piano variations; and a song for a patriotic occasion. The first of the Opus 10 sonatas and the C-major Concerto were probably sketched. Also products of 1796 were the unadventurous sonata for piano four hands (Opus 6), a serenade for string trio (Opus 8), a set of variations based on an air from Grétry's *Richard, Coeur de Lion,* and several movements for mandolin, alone and with cembalo.

The most enterprising effort of the year was the E-flat Piano Sonata dedicated to Countess Anna-Luisa-Barbara (Babette) de Keglevics when it was published as Opus 7 by Artaria in 1797. In the latter year Beethoven began the string trios of Opus 9 and presumably pushed ahead with the Opus 10 piano sonatas, also beginning the sonatas for piano with obbligato violin (Opus 12). But the sole completed work was another patriotic song (Austria was at war with the French in this period) titled "Kriegslied der Österreicher" and dated April 14, 1797. It was not much heard, then or later.

Aside from the piano sonatas and the C-major Concerto, this is scant production, even less imposing aspiration, for the young man who had announced his identity with the three trios of Opus 1, the three piano sonatas of Opus 2, and the string trio of Opus 3. Indeed, much of the work he was doing in 1796 and 1797 was surprisingly acquiescent in tone for one already marked as a rebel and hothead. Virtually every instrumental work—whether titled divertimento or trio, parthie or octet, serenade or quintet—accommodated itself to eighteenth-century models, in several instances[20] to specific examples by Mozart and Haydn.

Perhaps a part of the explanation may be found in the dedication of the Opus 9 trios to Count (Johann George von) Browne, an officer of the Russian court based in Vienna, but of Irish descent. It is both lengthy and effusive, designating Brown as "my first Maecenas" (Lichnowsky, poor man, apparently did not qualify). Both Browne and his wife were music lovers, and Beethoven dedicated to the piano-playing Countess his twelve variations on a Danse Russe (WoO 71, a product of 1786). In return, Beethoven received a handsome saddle

20 Those bearing Opus numbers 3, 8, 9, 16, and 25.

horse, which he never could learn to ride. He discovered, to his considerable cost somewhat later, that a servant in his employ had been stabling and feeding the animal at Beethoven's expense, retaining for himself the money he obtained for the horse's hire. He disposed of both horse and servant immediately.

The implication of all this would not be how well Beethoven was faring financially in Vienna barely half a dozen years after his arrival, but how his objectives had altered. Rather than pressing on with the urgent impulses Haydn had found censurable in the C-minor trio of Opus 1, Beethoven had all but turned aside from his own direction and true character to gratify the taste of those who made Vienna the *Clavierland* that Mozart termed it.

To the roughhewn provincial, the notion, as of 1792, of stabling a horse and employing a servant would have aroused as much laughter as the pomposity of Swieten or Haydn's peruke. And the same Rhinelander who preferred rough clothes and the common food of a tavern to the approved attire and the amenities of Lichnowsky's table might have looked with scorn on the decorum and tractability that characterize many of the works in this period bearing Beethoven's name.

It could, of course, have been the price he was willing to pay for "staying in favor" in Vienna, against Count Arco's cynical contention (see p. 66) that "a man's reputation here lasts but a short time. . . . After a few months the Viennese want something new." If so, the cost was too high. On the other hand, it might have been a by-product of applying too well the lessons learned from Albrechtsberger. As quoted earlier (see p. 60), Nottebohm commended the works "written immediately after the lessons" as "among the purest Beethoven ever composed."

One need not quarrel with Nottebohm's conception of "purity" as an objective good. But one may doubt that looking out for such "objectives" was true to Beethoven's character as a creative spirit going his own untrammeled way.

3

FORTUNATELY, the inner ferment and intellectual restlessness which were Beethoven's birthright were neither forgotten nor forsworn, merely suppressed. Across the weeks and months of this period—1796–97, and part of 1798—they surface now and then in works Beethoven created specifically for his own use, most particularly for his own instrument, the piano. Where that involvement led him in the C-minor Sonata of Opus 10 has already been dealt with at some length (see pp. 6–7). The Opus 7 Sonata strikes me as an effort to extend the scope of his expression without enlarging the range of his vocabulary. Like much else written at this time, the C-major Concerto (performed in 1798, but not published until 1800) is designed primarily for entertainment rather than self-expression.

Amid all its desire to please, the concerto now designated as No. 1 (though its composition *followed* the B-flat bearing No. 2) does give intimations of things to come, beginning with the extended orchestral introduction to the first movement. This serves the dual function of stimulating the listener's attention and arousing interest in the music to come, two arts in which Mozart was challenged only by Haydn, who devised its master plan. The introduction announces the advent of a new contender for mastery, especially when the far from uncommon swing between major and minor leads Beethoven to this formulation:

In context, this passage serves the momentary function of moving the music from one place on the circle of keys to another. But it lingers in Beethoven's mind as a likely device for utilization (in an expanded form) at a similar point in his next concerto, No. 3, in C minor:

(This reduced version preserves the harmonic motion as it occurs in the strings, omitting the complementary writing in the woodwinds and the sustained tones in the horns.)

Out of these combined impulses—the major-minor interchange, in a sighing formulation of half steps, and the syncopated figuration at the point marked A—emerges something of the even greater Beethoven. That is, a vivid tonal stroke in the dramatic portraiture which makes the *Coriolanus* Overture (of 1807) the extraordinarily innovative thing it is.

Seemingly an insignificant link among the many stronger, more conspicuous ones that form the chain connecting early- to middle-period Beethoven, and middle to late, the sequence depicted on page 74 shares one major characteristic with many other instances. A formulation initially *incidental* to another line of thought eventually emerges as consequential, and that which has been recessive becomes dominant. The E-flat–C-minor syndrome is particularly productive of such growths and developments.

A further characteristic of such seedlings is that they need not originate in a conspicuous context. The attentive ear soon discovers that some of Beethoven's most forward-looking, germinal thoughts occurred to him in works which were, as a totality, not of first quality or major importance.

Among the sonatas of Opus 2, for example, No. 1, with its staunch F-minor opening and expressive slow movement, and No. 2, with its A-major playfulness alternating with ardor and intensity—a characteristic Beethoven polarity—are more often performed and more greatly admired than No. 3, in C. But it is in No. 3 that one discerns the composer of the mid-1790s moving out of the immediate expressive context in the direction of means *beyond* his ability to exploit. Like the ♫♫|♩ eruption in Opus 10, No. 1, they are not lost, only set aside awaiting the time when the composer has grown up to their management as well as to their imagining.

On page seven of the first movement of Opus 2, No. 3, for example, the uneven rhythmic pattern created by the action-reaction between the two hands of

Allegro con brio

will be brooded upon, nurtured, and matured until it emerges, a dozen years later, as

the urgent, pulsating passage which Beethoven preserved through other alterations as the climax to his several *Leonore* overtures (the quoted example is a reduction of its occurrence in the *Leonore* No. 2).

More often than not, such an idea is, at the outset, essentially a physical outline lacking emotional character. One can imagine it being filed in a mental music bank until Beethoven found the artistic means to evoke an inner substance and dramatic substance appropriate to it— as, for example, when he eventually found the match of form and purpose for the words and music of Schiller's "Freude, schöner Götterfunken."

Reverting to the same sonata (No. 3 of Opus 2), one finds another aural alert in the slow movement. This is the kind that signals, to the receptive mind, the first flash of an idea, in the unpromising usage by one composer of a stylistic trait of another, later composer.

In the Beethoven sonata (measures 11–16 of the second movement) it is

(*continued*)

In the Schubert B-minor Symphony (*Unfinished*) it comes to attention (measure 66 of the second movement) as:

It moves considerably closer to the prototype in Beethoven when Schubert relocates the moving figure in the bass (in measure 96):

Here it is at the *bottom* of the harmonic structure (as Beethoven had it originally) where it can govern the shifting harmonic colorations above in Schubert's own uniquely resourceful way . . . including, especially, the *en*harmonic.

It is not the duplication of Beethoven's intervals which makes the cited passage worthy of mention. It is rather the fertilization of Schubert's imagination by Beethoven's initiative, and the distinctive results that were born as a result, that are consequential.

Within the same four-movement structure one can discern other evidences of ferment. The potion is brewed, innocently enough, in a moment of the Scherzo (A) which evolves into a closing statement for this segment of the movement (B):

(*continued*)

Both phases of the thought, thus casually disposed of, persisted in Beethoven's thinking to have a generative part in the later Scherzo (beginning at measure 25), on a heroically larger scale, of the Symphony No. 7:

(*continued*)

The dynamics of rhythm and accent are, of course, a propulsive part of the force that Beethoven develops in the measures to come.

Such instances of organic growth across the decades of Beethoven's output are not only recurrent but typical of the tenacity with which he pursued his own line of musical thought to its ultimate fulfillment. Contradictory though it may seem for obscure early works to contain means that became ends in later, celebrated masterpieces, the underlying reason is simple.

The "greater works" of such a composer as Beethoven are, by inspection, those in which the musical content has been so compacted into an expressive unity that no "waste" or surplus is left over for other use, by Beethoven or anyone else. It is in the lesser works, those in which the material has not been crushed, mauled, and hammered into a solid mass, that unexploited possibilities and unfulfilled opportunities may be discerned.

VI

Finding His Way

I

HOWEVER MUCH ONE MIGHT, for intellectual reasons, wish to separate the creator's body from the body of his creations, it is impossible wholly to do so. The Beethoven who spent part of 1796 on travels to Prague, Dresden, Leipzig, and Berlin was hardly the youth who had lodged with Lichnowsky shortly after his arrival from Bonn nearly five years before. Nor was he yet the man he would be a few years later. There was much new with which he had to familiarize himself. Not the least was worldly success.

How much the need for such self-awareness was responsible for the different, even indifferent, character of much of the music Beethoven wrote in this period is not a subject to invite dogmatic opinion. For many months, in 1796 and 1797, one cannot even reconstruct a reasonable chronology of his activities or establish just when he was at work on one score or another. In 1796 the blank period is between June (following his return from Berlin) and November. In 1797 it falls in much the same period (between May and October).

Most Beethoven biographers assume it was during one or both of these undocumented intervals that Beethoven suffered a serious illness, or illnesses. It is alluded to by one of the earliest of the biographers, Joseph Fischoff. However, Fischoff was not born until 1804 and did not begin his work until nearly the end of the composer's life. He was thus dependent on others (including Beethoven's nephew, Karl, who was two years younger than Fischoff) for details of Beethoven's early life. The sentences in Fischoff's manuscript bearing on "a dangerous illness" Beethoven suffered in 1796 read: ". . . on a hot summer day, [Beethoven] became greatly overheated in his home, threw open doors and windows, disrobed down to his trousers and cooled himself in a draft at the open window. The consequence was a dangerous illness, which, on his convalescence, settled in his organs of hearing, and from this time on his deafness steadily increased."[1]

The attribution of such an illness to 1796 is disputed by Forbes on the reasonable premise that the tours undertaken by Beethoven in the fall of that year hardly suggest the venture of a man recently recovered from a serious illness, one severe enough to affect his hearing. That the year was 1797 rather than 1796 has greater credibility; or still more probably, that Fischoff compressed the events of two years into a single incident. On May 29, 1797, Beethoven wrote to his boyhood friend Franz Gerhard Wegeler, in Bonn: "I am well and I may say that my health is steadily improving."[2] This is indicative of some distress, but hardly of the magnitude described by Fischoff nearly a quarter of a century later. Nor is the season of the year suggestive of intense heat, a draft, and its aftermath.

References to matters of health are of more than casual interest in Beethoven's letters to Wegeler, an avid student of medicine who became a distinguished physician. It is in a later letter to Wegeler, written on June 29, 1801, that the beginning of a chronology of the ailment's onset and development can be based. In addition to bearing the trust of a doctor-patient relationship, Wegeler was a devoted friend in whose discretion Beethoven could repose any confidence with full assurance of secrecy.

One can imagine the distress with which Wegeler read such words as: "For two years now I have ceased to attend any social function for I cannot bring myself to tell people 'I am deaf.'"[3] This is one sentence in an extraordinarily long communication. It is invaluable for pinpointing 1799 as the year in which Beethoven's deafness first began to intrude upon his daily life.

This is not to say that 1799 was the year in which impaired hearing first began to affect Beethoven's functioning as a composer. This would, in the nature of things, precede the time when his social relations with others began to be disturbed. As much is confirmed in another statement in the same text: "For the past three years my hearing has been growing

---

[1] Thayer-Forbes (1964), I, 187–8.
[2] Anderson: *The Letters of Beethoven*, I, 27.
[3] Ibid., p. 60.

constantly weaker."[4] This would require an adjustment to 1798 as the year in which Beethoven first became aware that, beyond the normal difficulties of composing, he would have to deal with an abnormal one.

In another letter of only a few days later, he confided to another friend, Karl Amenda, much the same alarming information: "Let me tell you that my most prized possession, my *hearing*, has greatly deteriorated. When you were still with me, I felt the symptoms."[5] That would have been in 1799, after which Amenda left Vienna to return to his home in Courland.[6] Thus the two letters corroborate 1799 as the time when Beethoven's affliction began to affect his social, as well as professional, life.

Presumably Wegeler responded to Beethoven in a letter or letters not now known to exist. Beethoven's reply, in November, described for his medical friend the kind of treatment that had been prescribed, and, in fact, reported that the "humming and buzzing" ("*Sausen und Brausen*") in his ears was "slightly less than it used to be." He writes ruefully of his hope of getting married but, whether this or other prospects of happiness are fulfilled, he vows to "seize Fate by the throat: it shall certainly not bend and crush me completely. . . ."[7]

The culmination of these confidences was the curious, heartrending document of fall 1802 known, after the suburb of Vienna where it was written, as the Heiligenstadt Testament. By now Beethoven was convinced that he would soon die. To assure equitable distribution of his property among his relatives, he wrote out an emotionally overwrought statement of his will. The document never served its primary purpose, for it did not become known until after his death, twenty-five years later. But it contained insights into his mental state, as of 1802, that can be derived from no other written source:

> For six years now I have been afflicted with an incurable condition made worse by incompetent physicians. . . . I am obliged—when only in my twenty-eighth year—to become a philosopher, and that is not easy, and for an artist it is harder than for any other. . . . I go to meet death joyfully. . . . If it comes before I have had the opportunity to fulfill my artistic destiny, despite my hard fate, it shall have come too soon, and I shall wish that it had come later.[8]

[4] Ibid., p. 59.
[5] Ibid., p. 63.
[6] Courland is a coastal region of what is now Latvia (U.S.S.R.).
[7] Anderson: *The Letters of Beethoven*, I, 66.
[8] Landon: *Beethoven*, pp. 145–6.

By almost all ordinary reckoning, the "twenty-eighth year" of a man born in 1770 would be 1798. However, ordinary reckoning cannot be invoked in any circumstance relating to Beethoven, even his belief in his own birthdate. It has already been noted that, as of 1783, the dedication of the three sonatas to the Elector Maximilian Friedrich identified the composer as eleven, when he was very close to thirteen. One would have assumed that this childish misconception would have been corrected long before he reached twenty-eight, but the evidence is otherwise.[9] As late as 1810, Beethoven insisted that he was born in 1772, that another infant also given the name of Ludwig was born in 1770, but lived only a few months. It is also confusing that his birthday, coming as it did in December, introduced a further ambiguity into a statement of his "twenty-eighth year." By this reckoning, Beethoven would have been in his "twenty-eighth year" all the time he was twenty-seven, or until December 16, 1800.

A chronological arrangement of all the data bearing on Beethoven's deafness would yield the following sequence (key—H.T., Heiligenstadt Testament; W., letters to Wegeler):

1796—The onset of what became "an incurable condition" (H.T.).

1797—An illness, from which he was "steadily improving" (W., 1797).

1798—His hearing is "growing constantly weaker" (W., 1801).

1799—He ceases to attend "any social function" (The equivalent in a letter to Amenda) (W., 1801).

1800—Forced to become "a philosopher" (H.T.).

1801—Vows to "seize Fate by the throat" (W., 1801).

1801—Deplores the little time he has "to fulfill my artistic destiny"; determines to do his best (H.T.).

Amid all the confusion of dates and uncertainty of occurrences, one area of clarity and certainty remains: the music Beethoven was creating in this time period. Is there anything in it that bears witness, directly or indirectly, to the distress recorded by Fischoff and confirmed in Beethoven's letters? To suppose that every passing fluctuation of health leaves its traces in the work being done by an artist would be to misread the history of art and misjudge the nature of man. But to contend, as some do, that no art *ever* reflects the conditions of the

[9] Lang: *The Creative World of Beethoven,* see Maynard Solomon's essay, "Beethoven's Birth Year," p. 205.

artist would be to misread, equally, the explosive interaction of art and man, in the face of a dire dilemma.

In the music identified with 1796 and 1797, there is little to contradict a concept of Beethoven as a man in prime health, secure in the possession of prizable assets, pursuing a path of his own choice. Most of this writing is outgoing and affirmative, and that which is neither is a boisterous reflection of his rough vitality and exuberant humor. If the slow movement of the Sonata in D, Opus 10, No. 3, probes deeper and mirrors a greater introspection than any prior Largo, this may be related to its occurrence in early 1798 (the three works of Opus 10 were published together in the fall of 1798).

If 1798 was indeed the year—as Beethoven's words to Wegeler in 1801 would imply—and summer the time, then the work of the young Beethoven that carries the heavy burden of gravity in the face of "a dire dilemma," rebellion against Fate, depression, resentment, and, finally, determination to struggle on against all odds, is precisely where it ought to be. It is the C-minor Sonata, Opus 13, to which Beethoven himself gave the name of "Pathétique" when it was published in 1799.

2

THE C-MINOR SONATA suits the circumstances attributed to it not merely because of a suggestive title, emotional intensity of an uncommon kind, and the musical originality with which it is infused, but because of all these things, and one thing more. It dares to breach the eighteenth-century convention that art is a rarefied form of intellectual expression concerned primarily with technique, manner, style, and perhaps a small share of personal participation, and to broach the nineteenth-century conviction that art is above all autobiographical, that its inner core and marrow derive from the visceral being of the man who creates it.

There are, to be sure, expressions in this vein (some of them famous) in works by Vivaldi, Bach, Mozart, Haydn, and Handel. On occasion, one or the other indulged himself in an extended expression of a personal character. In a brief retrospect, one could cite Bach's "Capriccio on the Departure of a Beloved Brother," the *Farewell* Symphony of Haydn, the G-minor Quintet and Symphony No. 40 (K.550) of Mozart. They are, however, deviations from a norm rather than established procedure.

For Beethoven, the step that carried him across the threshold of the "Pathétique" was neither tentative nor indecisive, taken with a mental reservation of, perhaps, turning back. It was motivated by inner forces sufficiently urgent to rupture surface equanimity, to cleave a break with the past that gradually widened from a crack to a chasm. That the "Pathétique" fulfills this description intimately is beyond question: its singularity is subject not only to affirmation but to exposition. That the seeds of it were sown as far back as the F-minor of the Electoral trinity (see pp. 36–37) would leave no doubt with the musical psychiatrist that the crisis with which Beethoven was confronted shook him out of all the complacency engendered by his Viennese success and returned him to the kind of determination that makes a child (of the proper sort) convinced that he can move mountains.

But there was, along with the child's determination, a youth's talent and a maturing man's craftsmanship. By my reckoning, the "Pathétique" is the first wholly personal work—conditioned by no consideration of impressing a patron, pleasing a purchaser, or propitiating a learned elder—Beethoven had written since the *Cantata on the Death of Emperor Joseph II* in 1790. In his first encounter with the reality of death, the Beethoven of the cantata had drawn music from previously unapproached depths; in his first encounter with the reality of life, the Beethoven of the "Pathétique" rediscovered these depths and marked them for his own through all the years to come.

One might make much or little of Beethoven's reversion, in the "Pathétique," not only to certain formulations of the early F-minor (*Elector*) Sonata, but also to the use of a slow introductory section for the first time in fifteen years. It comes and goes, at several points thereafter, in obedience to a historical practice not observed in his seven previously published sonatas.

So much is readily apparent to the unaided, all-but-untutored eye. What these and other details reveal to the expert eye[10] is of such dramatic importance in the unfolding life drama of Beethoven's music that more than passing attention is mandatory. Viewed through Rudolph Réti's particularly expert eye, this sometimes denigrated "early work" may be seen to contain a veritable card index to the procedures, inner relationships, and structural details that recur, in ever more subtle and sophisticated ways, through the whole panorama of works to come.

From Réti one may glean the important awareness that the opening Grave is no mere introductory "preluding," but a prefatory statement of much that is germinal in the movement that follows. As different as the portentous opening chords of the Grave:

---

[10] Rudolph Réti: *Thematic Patterns in the Sonatas of Beethoven* (New York: Macmillan; 1967), pp. 17–94.

are from the impetuous opening of the Allegro:

Réti demonstrates beyond contradiction that they are basically the same idea, taken at different rates of speed and spread out over longer or shorter time spans. The alteration from minor (Introduction) to major (Allegro) conforms to an interchange of mode common to many nineteenth-century composers and works.

It is but a step from this disclosure of identity to Réti's citation of what he terms the "prime cells" of the "Pathétique," those terse formulations which are, in his words, "the core of its structural life." To the interval C–E-flat, imbedded in the first three notes of the Grave,

Réti gives the name "prime cell." The drop from A-flat (below "high" C) to D (above middle C), coming to rest a half step higher on E-flat, he calls the "concluding motif":

Out of these cells, their inversions and transpositions, emerge many of the phrases and figures closely associated with this powerful, forthright work.

How they complement one another, contest for supremacy, or combine in triumph is far too complex a demonstration to be excerpted or paraphrased. Réti's exposition leaves no doubt with me that the "Pathétique" is the work of an artist not merely in supreme control of his material, but also responsive to *motivations he may not so much understand as obey*. The analysis demonstrates convincingly the unerring logic of what Beethoven did; it cannot tell us *why* he did it, or which part of it was volitional, which part nonvolitional (unconsciously motivated). My resolution of this uncertainty would be: It was not because Beethoven responded as he did to these stimuli that he was a great artist; it is, rather, a measure of his artistry that he grasped every latent implication of the self-created cells and motifs, and, whether or not he recognized them as such, pursued them relentlessly to the outcome with which we are all familiar.

No one can prove or disprove the extent to which Beethoven pursued these concepts consciously. Certainly it is possible to call a sequence of notes a "prime cell" when one has, ready at hand, the utilization that made it "prime." How it *became* "prime" I would relate more to aesthetic judgment, artistic discrimination, and innate taste than I would to analytic power or creative logic. The "Pathétique" is a greater outburst of communicative power and rather more a homophonic work than those post-Albrechtsberger writings commended by Nottebohm (see pp. 59–60) for "purer" part-writing and "real" polyphony.

If this spells a liberation from pedagogical shackles, it is hardly too soon. So far as I can observe, the "Pathétique" has no "impure" part-writing, a matter of minor consequence in any case. It is a great and enduring expression not because of the absence or presence of such minutiae, but because it embodies a liberation from theory and a release from emotional inhibitions under the pressure of stresses and strains too great to ignore or repress. It is not the "whole" Beethoven of the "Appassionata" any more than the Beethoven of the "Appassionata" is the "whole" Beethoven of the "Hammerklavier," Opus 106. But it is the "whole" Beethoven of 1798 as he was capable of realizing it.

Being more concerned with structure than with content in his commentary, Réti does not dwell on the rising tide of chromaticism in the Grave, which laps ever closer to the Wagnerian shores of Cornwall and *Tristan* before receding. But it is plain to see, as well as to hear, that it grew out of the C–E-flat cell, with its tortuous, toiling, uphill climb, answered by the searching, seeking, declining line of the bass performing the opposite, or retrograde, pattern of the cell, in inversion.

As addendum, attention may be directed to the phraseology I have employed (all unconsciously) in describing this set of musical circumstances and their chromatic character. It is but a relatively brief stride down the highway of musical history to the juncture at which "retrograde," "inversion," "opposite" became indispensable to the exposition of another kind of chromaticism: serial writing.

3

IT WAS, OF COURSE, impossible for Beethoven to write nothing but "Pathétique" sonatas, just as it was not possible for Schubert to produce only *Erlkönigs* and no *Deutsche Tänze*. The mood comes, grips, wrenches, and claims its toll. It then dissipates, and another humor takes its place. It is in the nature of genius to be prolific, mercurial, less rather than more predictable. Or, if one prefers another kind of characterization, to be hypersensitive, feverishly responsive, or inaccessibly withdrawn.

According to his custom, Beethoven worked during 1797–98 on several projects concurrently. Once such a project was sketched, the essential materials defined, work might go forward concurrently on several compositions of greatly diverse character (the C-minor Symphony and the G-major Concerto could serve as a classic example of such disparity). In the same period of days and months when the "Pathétique" was evolving, Beethoven was beset by a variety of other impulses. Some were embodied in musical forms sufficiently advanced to be candidates for final editing and copying; others were no more than nuclear cells, shadowy outlines to be set aside for later consideration, when they would begin to germinate and grow. Of two incipient involvements, the one that prevailed was the group of string quartets published as Opus 18; the one deferred was the Concerto No. 3, in C minor, for piano and orchestra. Growing side by side with the six quartets were the E-flat Septet (Opus 20) and the C-major Symphony (Opus 21, No. 1).

Why six quartets in Opus 18 rather than the groups of three which had sufficed for the piano trios of Opus 1, the piano sonatas of Opus 2 and Opus 10, the string trios of Opus 9, or the piano and violin sonatas of Opus 12? No reason, in all probability, other than a custom of the time, to which Boccherini and Dittersdorf, as well as Haydn and Mozart, were responsive. From Opus 1, in 1760, through those numbered 2, 3, 9, 17, 20, 33, and 50, Haydn's quartets regularly appeared in sets of six. And in 1785, when Mozart rendered his tribute to Haydn's leadership in such writing, it was with six quartets.

One might suppose that such examples of eighteenth-century practice would have lost their pertinence by the late 1790s. Perhaps they would have with Mozart's death in 1791, had not Haydn continued to live and compose quartets. During the period of Beethoven's gradual establishment in Vienna, Haydn produced the six quartets of 1793 (issued in two groups of three, with Opus numbers 71 and 73) and the six of 1799 united in the single Opus 76, in which were included such world favorites as the "Quinten" and the "Emperor."

Thus, though Beethoven was unwilling to describe himself as "a pupil of Haydn," he was not averse to learning from him, pragmatically, and emulating him, artistically. The keyboard was still a means of expression more congenial to Beethoven than the strings, and he was well aware of his limitations in challenging such a combination for the first time.

The publication of Opus 18 in 1801 was broken into two segments of three each, but no attempt was made to preserve chronology in the numbering, even within the two groupings. The most reliable sources would suggest the following:

The first to be composed, the D major, was issued as No. 3.
The second in the sequence was the F major, issued as No. 1.
The third in order of creation, in G, appeared as No. 2.
The fourth to be written, in A, was published as No. 5.
The fifth to be finished, in B-flat, appeared as No. 6.
The sixth, in C minor, began the second group as No. 4.

The rationale, if any, would appear to be that each group of three started with a "later," hence "stronger," work.

As fond as amateur quartet players are of the greatest works of Haydn and Mozart, many of them find a special attraction, a more abiding satisfaction, in the Opus 18 quartets of Beethoven. This may, in a purely psychological way, relate to their sense of participation in the actual series of events that culminated, decades later, in the peerless final five (which, for lack of technical credentials, they will never perform themselves). Not all of the first six are equal in quality, and the very best fall short of the greatest quartets of Mozart and Haydn. But Beethoven was the inheritor of their rich tradition, to which he brought his own strong brand of individuality.

Repeatedly, one hears the conversational interchanges which Mozart raised to the level of high comedy or spirited intellectuality (in the G-major [K.387] and A-major [K.464] quartets) rudely interrupted by the rough dialect of the Rhinelander. Or the leaping lines and jaunty rhythms of a Haydnesque finale jolted into new conformations by a vigor and muscularity unknown to the originator of the manner. As for the slow movements of the Opus 18 quartets, they are, already, very much Beethoven's own, shaped by the hand which had produced quantities of them in piano sonatas and smaller ensemble works bearing Opus numbers from 1 to 14. The earliest slow movements for piano (Opus 2) have suggestions of four-part writing, and the stunning slow movement of the otherwise amiable F-major Quartet (Opus 18, No. 1) has a counterpart in the eloquent Largo e mesto of the Opus 10, No. 3, Sonata (both, as it happens, in D minor).

Against all learned argument to the contrary[11] I cling to the belief that the most popular of the Opus 18 quartets—No. 4, in C minor—is also the one most typical of the composer. It is neither the most sophisticated in compositional craft nor the most elegantly formulated for the strings (No. 6, in B-flat, is superior in the first respect, the A-major, No. 5, in the second). But it has, especially in the first movement, the earnestness, directness, and determined, unswerving pursuit of an emotional objective which typify Beethoven's best at this period.

Opus 18, No. 4, is, in short, personal to Beethoven in the way that almost everything which occurred to him as "C minor" was personal to him. Here, in particularly bold relief, is the distinctly two-sided profile he presents when the key signature is three flats: the stern, harsh, embattled C-minor side and the nobler, loftier look of its relative, E-flat major. Together, the keys (which fly the banner of the same *in hoc signo vinces*) take in a larger segment of Beethoven's greatest works than any other major-minor pairing. In every instance, whether the prevailing condition is major or minor, both sides of the profile are exposed. Chronologically, the range is from the C-minor Trio of Opus 1 to the C-minor Sonata of Opus 111, from the E-flat Piano Sonata of Opus 7 to the E-flat Quartet of Opus 127, the Third and Fifth Piano concertos, the Third and Fifth symphonies (in inverted succession to the piano concertos, with E-flat preceding C-minor), the Opus 20 Septet (E-flat), the Opus 70, No. 2, Trio (also in E-flat), etc., etc.

<hr />

[11] Kerman: *The Beethoven Quartets,* p. 71.

Whether the C-minor under current consideration (Opus 18, No. 4) is, actually, the last of the group to be created can only be guessed by elimination, not established by documentation. There is general agreement that some of its material predates 1799 by more than a little. And no sketches have been preserved to indicate 1798 or 1799. As stated by Thayer (and projected in the listing of the quartets on p. 91) the chronology is as follows: "... The composition of the quartets was begun in 1798, that in D ... being the first undertaken. This was followed by that in F and soon after ... work was begun on that in G. ... He then wrote the one in A. ... The Quartets in B-flat and C-minor followed, the latter being, perhaps, the last. ..."[12]

Whatever the temporal circumstances or the chronological pattern, penetration through the screen of the familiar to the bedrock of substance shows clearly that, as well as projecting intimations of many things to come in C minor, the Quartet bearing No. 4 also foreshadows details, modes of procedure, lines of thought to be exploited by Beethoven in his E-flat phase. As an instance, attention may be directed to the buildup just before the beginning of the recapitulation, the critical point in a sonata form sequence at which the opening matter has been brought back with the hope, if not the assurance, of launching a clinching argument to solidify the original presentation.

(*continued*)

Contributing to the total impression are a mysterious fluttering figure in the middle voices, an ominous movement in the bass, and hesitant answering phrases in the first violin. Not unlike the first occurrence of the ♫♩♩ formulation in the C-minor Piano Sonata, Opus 10, No. 1, the passage does not reappear in this movement, and thus might be regarded as a mere passing fancy. But it is a fantasy that passed into a far more memorable form, assumed a greater structural function in the first movement of another work with a three-flat signature, the Third (*Eroica*) Symphony:

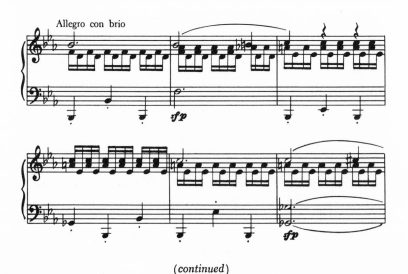

(*continued*)

Here, too, the components include a repeated figure in the middle voices, steady movement (along chordal lines) in the bass, and responsive answering phrases at the top. Now, however, Beethoven deploys their potential for arousing anticipation at two points: as in the quartet, just prior to the recapitulation of the first great E-flat theme and then, even more potently (in the form quoted above) as another linch-pin, from the recapitulation to the coda, or grand summing up. Now the design has grown to cover thirty measures, rather than the mere eight of its first form in the quartet. When the tension within the contracted, coiled spring of sound is finally released, it launches with a great, irresistible momentum those climaxing measures of the coda in which all the choirs join, gradually, in a shout of triumphal salute to the hero:

As an instance of far-reaching implications in the minor mode, one may select the curve of an inner voice which comes and goes at various points as a counter figure to the primary thematic matter. As encountered on the way back to the recapitulation (only a few measures before the first Opus 18, No. 4, example cited above, see p. 94), it has this form:

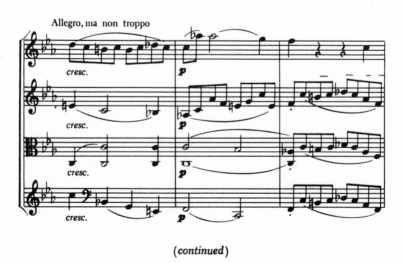

(continued)

When the idea recurred to Beethoven about a decade later (1810), it was not merely elongated in time values, but reconstructed for the new purpose it served in the *Egmont* Overture. I refer to the notes in the quartet excerpt which have lines added above them. In the overture, the pattern, in the cellos, serves as the main counter voice at measures 28, 29, 30, and 31, and becomes increasingly compulsive as the drama in Beethoven's evocation of Goethe's tragedy rises to a climax:

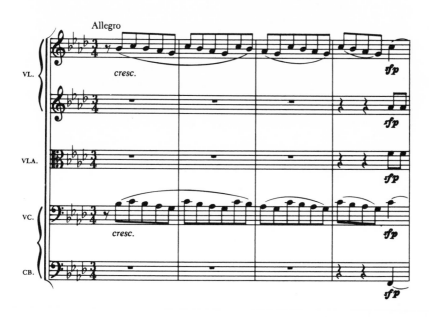

(continued)

As an instance of memory persisting not merely to reproduce but to improve on an idea, few things in the lore of Beethoven are more illuminating than the upgrading of a simple effect in the same C-minor quartet (measures 166–71 of the first movement):

to a historic innovation of color and intensity in the finale of the C-minor Symphony (No. 5) where Beethoven calls up his newfound resource of the piccolo to add its shrill, penetrating outcry not only to the same kind of trill, but actually on the same *tone* (G below "high" C, which, in this instrument, *sounds* an octave higher):

(continued)

If, as suggested (on p. 92), the C-minor quartet, and particularly its first movement, "synthesize Beethoven's best at this period," it may be not merely for the content itself, but, as demonstrated, for embodying, in relatively modest contexts, thoughts which grew to bear massively greater responsibilities in later works.

4

DESPITE THE TURMOIL and the travail by which the interior Beethoven was beset at the onset of his dismal secret, the exterior Beethoven continued to function and to flourish. Despite agonies of apprehension that his secret might be discovered, and made the subject of ridicule—or even worse, pity—Beethoven managed to sustain a social identity. "In conversation it is remarkable that there are people who have never noticed this," he mentions in the Wegeler letter of June 1801 previously cited. "Since I am often given to periods of distraction, people attribute my deafness to this. . . ."

As the first, alarmed reaction settled into stoic endurance, the palliatives and the treatments showed a measure of success that enabled him to profit from the "educational advantages" of Vienna. One was the prerogative of a well-established, highly regarded composer with the proper court connections to invite royalty, and the general public, to a concert of his newest works. Given the proper circumstances, it was reasonable for Beethoven to assume that a combination of his position and their interest would be mutually beneficial.

For the first concert in a succession that would endure for nearly a quarter of a century and eventually include the Ninth (as well as the First) Symphony, Beethoven elected the date of April 2, 1800. A Wednesday, it doubtless had some pertinence *vis-à-vis* Lent, Easter, and other factors of consequence in so Catholic a city as Vienna. The "Imperial Royal Court Theater beside the Burg" was the place stipulated in the announcement, the content of the program set forth in these words:[13]

1. A grand symphony by the late Kapellmeister Mozart[14]
2. An aria from "The Creation" by the Princely Kapellmeister Herr Haydn, sung by Mlle. Saal.
3. A grand Concerto for the pianoforte, played and composed by Herr *Ludwig van Beethoven.*
4. A Septet, most humbly and obediently dedicated to Her Majesty the Empress, and composed by Herr *Ludwig van Beethoven* for four stringed and three wind-instruments, played by Herren

[13] Ibid., p. 255.
[14] The rank appears to have been conferred on Mozart posthumously, as it was not one from which he profited during his life and death in Vienna.

Schuppanzigh, Schreiber, Schindlecker, Bär, Nickel, Matauschek and Dietzel.

5. A Duet from Haydn's "Creation," sung by Herr and Mlle. Saal.
6. Herr *Ludwig van Beethoven* will improvise on the piano forte.
7. A new grand symphony with complete orchestra, composed by Herr *Ludwig van Beethoven*.

The inclusion of "dependable" content by Mozart and Haydn was doubtless urged upon Beethoven by well-meaning friends to cushion the impact of the novelty content in his own Septet and symphony, and the uncertain outcome of the improvisation. As for the concerto, its identity has never been accurately established. The absence of the word "new" from the bill of particulars suggests to some the B-flat (No. 2), which had been played in Vienna, whereas the C-major (No. 1) had not. On the other hand, the C-major had been performed in Prague in 1798, which, technically speaking, did not qualify it to be termed "new" either. In my judgment, Beethoven would have wanted the concert to represent him at his best in every particular, and there is no doubt that, in his own estimation as well as in that of others, the C-major Concerto ranked higher.

From the composer's point of view, the truly unquestionably "new" works of this program were the E-flat Septet and the C-major Symphony, neither performed publicly before (the Septet had been heard by an invited audience at the palace of Prince Schwarzenberg). Next-door neighbors in the hierarchy of opus numbers (the Septet is Opus 20, the symphony Opus 21) each is characteristic of the thirty-year-old composer, different as each is from the other. Nor is this as paradoxical as it may appear. A child of the eighteenth century, brought up to esteem its conventions and its protocol, Beethoven was still its son, not yet its master. If, in 1799, he was still at home in this spiritual father's house, it was becoming ever more a stranger to him.

The Opus 20 Septet, despite the absence of any qualifying terminology, takes a long lingering look at the safe haven of the divertimento, to which Mozart contributed so much and with which he became so closely identified that the designation all but died with him. Beethoven's inclusion of the double bass was not without precedent, and certainly had its adherents. In his great B-flat Serenade (K.361) for Thirteen Wind Instruments Mozart included a double bass (though some contemporary performers have opted for a contrabassoon, which can hardly perform the pizzicato specified by Mozart). Beethoven's example was good enough for both Hummel and Schubert, whose "Forellen" Quintet (Opus 114) gains resonance and support from the presence—with the piano, violin, viola and cello—of the double bass.

The index to the eagerly agreeable, almost excessively inoffensive work is contained in its dedication to "der Kaiserin Maria Theresia." For those beguiled by the magical name, it is all too easy to assume that there could be only one Maria Theresa who gave new direction to Austria's destiny, bore eleven children (including Emperors Joseph II and Leopold II, Maximilan Friedrich, Elector of Cologne, and Marie-Antoinette), and is musically memorialized by Hofmannsthal's choice of her reign for the time period (1740s) of *Der Rosenkavalier*. Her imperial reign and earthly span came to an end in November 1780, however. The later inheritor of the name was the wife of Franz (a son of Leopold II, hence a grandson of the first Maria Theresa), who came to the throne of Austria in 1792.

This Maria Theresa (Beethoven's spelling [Theresia] is the correct Austrian form) was a cultivated musician, able to raise a pretty, well-disciplined soprano voice in a private performance of a Haydn aria. She was much more partial to Beethoven's music than Franz, the "Franz den Kaiser" immortalized in Haydn's imperial Austrian anthem and the "Emperor" Quartet. He was, according to a contemporary source, wary of everything associated with Beethoven's name, saying, "There is something revolutionary in that music. . . ."[15]

In the sequence of the Septet's six movements, there is little that might have disturbed even Franz, and there is much that must have pleased his wife and the court of music lovers throughout Europe whose taste paralleled hers. The menuet (based on a theme that had served a similar purpose in the G-major Sonata of the two "easy works" published as Opus 49), variations, marcia, and finale made Beethoven's a household name throughout Europe and in England. The Septet had unprecedented sales in transcriptions in a variety of versions suitable for home usage, several in combinations that had the composer's sanction.

The Septet, in fact, spread so widely and endured so persistently that it became the bane of Beethoven's later life. One may wonder whether the mature Beethoven's well-documented revulsion to the Septet's popularity was engendered by a style he felt he had outgrown. The inscription to the Empress and, inferentially, to the less sophisticated music lovers of Europe, may have lingered in Beethoven's mind as an all-too-evident reminder of a bid for royal favor, a symbol-in-being of his earlier dependence upon royalty for a good word.

In its own way, however, the Septet does look ahead directly to other works of his own (as well as indirectly to the great Octet, Opus 166,

---

[15] Robbins Landon: *Beethoven*, p. 84.

of Franz Schubert). Those are the two Romanzas (Opus 40 and Opus 50) for violin and orchestra, and even more, the Concerto in D, Opus 61. Such affectionate treatment of the violin (thirty measures before the first double bar of the Allegro con brio) as

and

in the Adagio (measures 38–40) were necessary antecedents to enlargement of the violin's expressive capacity if it were to bear the burden
of greater emotional weight that Beethoven poured into

in the first movement of the Violin Concerto and

in the slow movement.

The symphony (No. 1) inscribed to his benefactor Swieten was,
unlike the Septet, written not to please all, but to please one—himself.
At this distance, it is difficult to discern in it anything that might be
even remotely termed revolutionary. But the audacious opening of the
slow introduction to the first movement (with its unexpected, out-of-
key dominant seventh resolving not to the expected C major but to the
"remote" F major) might have irritated some only mildly placated by
the almost immediate appearance of the home key. And that unsettling,
rising scale passage that teases the attention prior to the gay excursion of
the finale—is that the sort of thing, Emperor Franz might have complained, really necessary in a symphony?

The date of April 2, 1800, though not yet the "nineteenth" century
by the reckoning of those who saluted January 1, 1801, as its proper beginning, nevertheless drew a symbolic barline across the century-separat-
ing phase of Beethoven's development. As the Septet defines Beethoven
as the man who concluded the eighteenth century, the First Symphony
identifies him as the man who projected the nineteenth. Still to come
was the Beethoven who would prophesy the music of the twentieth
century.

VII

The Youthful Abundance

I

THE BARLINE, should one accept the image, can be thought of as double and minus either *Da Capo* or repeat sign. There would hardly be a return to the pleasantries of the Septet, and each symphony in the direction ahead would be different from its neighbors. Perhaps Beethoven reckoned, Hamlet-like, that by plunging ahead into his "sea of troubles" the infirmity, or at least his obsession with it, might be ended. It would be 1810 or 1811 before he conceded that such "troubles," physical and philosophical, were to be with him as long as he lived. That was knowledge to which he would never become reconciled, let alone resigned.

With the sure sense of direction which came to his aid many times during his career, his immediate recourse was to the mode of composition most personal to him. The piano's lifelong attraction for Beethoven was neither mysterious nor unmeaningful. Writing for the piano provided him with a satisfaction that no other form of composition possibly could. It was indeed a double satisfaction, catering as it did not only to his creative but to his re-creative impulses.

In the aftermath of the creation of the Septet and First Symphony came an absorption with the piano, and its possibilities, unprecedented

—so far as I can discover—in the literature of any major composer, and paralleled later perhaps only by Chopin and Debussy. Unlike the seven firstborn piano sonatas (with Opus numbers 2, 7, and 10) or the last five (Opus numbers 101, 106, 109, 110, and 111), those between Opus 14 and Opus 31 have no extraneous identity as the earliest or the latest. Neither can they be defined as the shortest or the longest. But they do have a family feeling and, in many ways, are the ones most redolent with promise, the richest in human values as well as a singular kind of directness and communication.

Taken together, the ten works embody much that is known to a large part of the world as the "true" Beethoven. Within the series are several of such overpowering urgency that three or four have been lost to fame and popularity simply because of their proximity to even greater ones. The ten make up nearly a third of the thirty-two chapters in Beethoven's book of the piano sonata. With those that preceded, they carry to conclusion a decade in which he wrote and published more than half of all his sonatas for piano.[1]

The two of Opus 14 are something of a prologue to the main discourse. Though created at almost the same time as the "Pathétique," with its stormy protestations, they reveal a typical duality of the Beethoven-to-come, with his capacity for dealing simultaneously with works of quite different content. Both in their musical decorum and in their pianistic accessibility the sonatas numbered Opus 14, Nos. 1 and 2, embody materials and procedures of an earlier period. This may, in part, have been a consequence of their creation for the Baroness von Braun, an amateur of the instrument, whose husband had received his title both for building a fortune and disbursing substantial parts of it on behalf of the arts in Vienna.

Though designed to entice rather than to discourage a pianist of limited technique, the works nevertheless contain much that is personal to Beethoven. According to Schindler,[2] Beethoven's true intent in these works might have been better understood had he abided by his intention to provide them with descriptive titles, akin to that of the "Pathétique." He quotes Beethoven as concluding that the titles were superfluous because "everyone recognized in both Opus 14 sonatas the dispute in dialogue between two principles, without the aid of words written above the score."[3] This, in effect, endorses Liszt's interpretation of the slow

---

[1] In this total of twenty are included the two "easy" sonatas created in 1796–97 but not published until 1805, as Opus 49.
[2] Schindler: *Beethoven*, p. 406.
[3] Ibid.

movement of the G-major Piano Concerto (No. 4) as a struggle between Orpheus and the Furies, in which the gentler, more persuasive voice prevails. It also proclaims Beethoven a predecessor to Schumann in recognizing within himself the duality that the latter formulated as Florestan and Eusebius. It was, according to Schindler, in 1822 that Beethoven expressed his regret for not having provided programmatic titles for the works of Opus 14. In a backward look, twenty-five years after their creation, he concluded that "audiences were more poetic [when the works were new] than now."[4]

Despite their musical and technical restrictions, the Opus 14 sonatas are not without a share in the forward thrust of Beethoven's creative impulse. Such a passage from the end of the first movement of the E-major (No. 1) as (final fifteen measures of first movement)

(*continued*)

---

[4] Ibid.

may pass through the mind as a mere cadential detail of an "early" Beethoven sonata, but there is more to it than that. Not only does the singing bass line carry forward the impulse revealed in the Opus 2, No. 3, sonata's slow movement (see p. 77) by the introduction of neigh- boring tones which shade the harmonic coloration above, the whole scheme defines it, with its throbbing accompaniment figuration, as the breeding ground of many a German lied to come. Indeed, all it requires is the addition of a vocal line to convey the song-sound of Franz Schubert, who was just being born in Vienna, as was the sound itself, in 1797. In time, he would move that singing bass forward in his own image, to achieve even subtler shifts of harmony appropriate to the word values to which he was so keenly attuned.

2

IT IS IN THE SEQUENCE beginning with the next sonata, Opus 22, in B-flat, that Beethoven, in the applicable words of the late Igor Stravinsky, "dis- covers and sometimes maps out the different terrains of several future composers, including himself."[5] According to Beethoven, the B-flat sonata (No. 11 in the total sequence) merited the description of "eine grosse Solo Sonate,"[6] a terminology not previously encountered. The term was perhaps devised to distinguish this sonata from the duet-sonatas which he was publishing at the time. The inscription identifies the

[5] *Harper's*, CCXL (May 1970), 35.
[6] Georg Kinsky, ed.: *Das Werk Beethovens: Thematisch-bibliographisches Verzeichnis seiner sämtlichen vollendeten Kompositionen,* completed by Hans Halm (Munich and Duisburg: G. Henle Verlag; 1955), p. 57. The phrase is contained in a letter to the Leipzig publisher F. A. Hoffmeister dated December 15, 1800.

dedicatee as the Countess Browne, whose husband had been saluted by Beethoven as his "first Maecenas" not long before.

The inner circle of "piano" works to follow has no counterpart in Beethoven's literature. Between Opus 22 and Opus 36 stretches a sequence of fourteen opus numbers of which no less than a dozen have a major involvement with the piano.[7] Whether utilized alone, as in the sonatas and variations, in company with the violin (Opus numbers 23, 24, and 30), or with voice ("An die Hoffnung," Opus 32), the music then flowing from Beethoven's mind is constantly conditioned by the keyboard as the source of all variety.

But with all the variety there is little that is exhibitionistic or overtly demonstrative. Concealed by the surface stream of sound are depths of meaning more profound than Beethoven had probed previously over so lengthy a span of expression. The outcome would have been remarkable regardless of the period of time required for its realization. The compression of the whole series into a period of approximately two years makes it a reasonable validation of Beethoven's pledge (to Wegeler) that he would "seize Fate by the throat" and embrace any means required to achieve his "artistic destiny."

Crammed into each movement of nearly every work are hints of future possibilities as well as outpourings of immediate fulfillment. As a sample of map-making, in the Stravinskyan sense, one may direct attention to the first movement of the B-flat Sonata, where may be found a piece of Wagnerian territory, charted by Eric Blom. To Blom's ear it was a formulation that "must have been in Wagner's mind when he wrote Wotan's wild evocation of Erda in *Siegfried*" (measures 7–6–5–4 before the end of the first movement):[8]

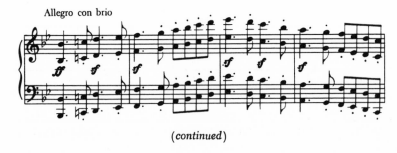

(*continued*)

[7] The exceptions in the numerical sequence are Opus 25, assigned to an early Serenade, and the String Quintet, Opus 29, also mentioned in the letter to Hoffmeister. Chronologically the composition of the *Prometheus* Ballet, though issued as Opus 43 in 1804, coincides with the B-flat Sonata, and the C-minor Concerto (No. 3, for piano and orchestra), published as Opus 37 in the same year, was likewise a product of 1800.

[8] Eric Blom: *Beethoven's Pianoforte Sonatas Discussed* (New York: Da Capo Press; 1968), p. 85.

The Wagnerian equivalent to which Blom has reference is:

A different portion of Wagner's landscape may be discerned in the Adagio, where a recurrence of the chromatic impulse of the "Pathétique" leads Beethoven over a nearly two-octave course (measures 32–34):

(continued)

Shorn of embellishments, it can be skeletonized as C-sharp, D, E-flat, E-natural, F; then (in the upper octave) C-sharp, D, E-flat, F, G, A-flat. Given the right rhythmic pattern, it is a phrase of *Tristan* in being:

Considering the interrelated Chopin-Liszt-Wagner path that led to *Tristan*, it is appropriate that Paul Bekker, one of Beethoven's most perceptive biographers, chose to describe this movement as "a nocturne before Chopin." It is also a nocturne before John Field, who is usually credited with inventing that form. He was, at the time of the work's publication in 1802, in service to Muzio Clementi, demonstrating pianos in his master's London showrooms, in exchange for instruction. His first nocturne was still a dozen years in the future.

Of the numerous ideas in the sonata which are Beethoven-to-come rather than someone-else-to-come, a pertinent one may be found in the finale, whose principal motive

(*continued*)

has more than a little in common with that of the finale of the Piano and Violin Sonata in F (Opus 24):

Searching for a way to lead the listener back from one phase of the Rondo (in Opus 22) to its first theme, Beethoven evolved the following pattern as a bridge:

(continued)

Adequate enough for its first purpose, it emerged half a dozen years later as something more than adequate for the dramatic requirements of the *Leonore* Overture No. 3:

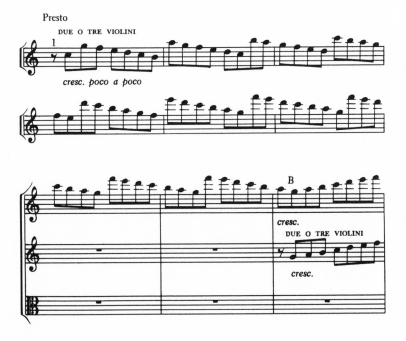

(continued)

cresc.

From the passage in the Rondo marked A surely sprang the impulse for B.

Taken together with the strong offbeat phrase first encountered in the Sonata Opus 2, No. 3 (see p. 76), it is evident that in the works of this period Beethoven was not merely discharging the accumulated tensions within him, but setting in motion forces that would assume ever more important functions in the years, and works, to come.

3

IN THE NEXT GROUP of four sonatas—each a self-contained world of aesthetic and emotional fulfillment—Beethoven moves inexorably from strength to strength. He is now in rebellion not merely against the convention of impersonality which he had shattered in the "Pathétique," but against the conventions of sonata form itself. With his sure sense of proportion and balance (where anything related to music was concerned), he had discerned that what is universally called—for want of a more explicit name—sonata form, or sonata-allegro form, is not really a *form* but a principle. Statement, elaboration, restatement are its basic divisions, but how they are arranged, balanced, compartmented, interrelated, and contrasted remains the individual composer's prerogative. It also remains his obligation, if he is concerned with a principle rather than a form, to achieve a persuasive outcome.

Despite all its rebellious impulse, the "Pathétique" remains true to fundamental sonata principles, indeed, to the form as it was practiced by Mozart and Haydn (through the use of a slow introduction). In the Opus 26, in A-flat, which begins with a slow movement, and the works of Opus numbers 27, 28, and 31 which follow, Beethoven severs such allegiances altogether. In effect he declares *his* judgment to be the scale and balance by which musical reason can be weighed. In liberating himself from the previously accepted precedents, he also liberated generations of composers to come.

Begins with a slow movement! The very words are a tocsin to alarm the purists, confound the formalists, and rejoice the spirit of those alerted to Beethoven's dependability for being undependable (in the "predictability" context).

In the "Pathétique," the Grave introduction is a command to attention, a lunge at the listener's ears and heart. The Beethoven of the A-flat's quiet Andante con variazione no longer feels any compulsion to *command* attention. He assumes its availability for whatever he feels inclined to communicate.

If the mere appearance of the Andante's printed page has a look of the future, the reason is inherent in its conception. In his elaboration of the opening idea, Beethoven moves abruptly from the old, well-worn concept of variation-by-embellishment to the new, fresh, unexploited possibilities of variation-by-transformation. The casual listener may or may not see the suggestion of the unborn Schumann's *Études Symphoniques* in the layout of the printed page, or hear a likeness of Mendelssohn along the way. But few can be unaware of Schubert's presence in the coda to the variant that brings the whole sequence to a climax:

To me, the relationship to Schubert's "An Sylvia" is not fragmen

tary, but total. The movement of the bass is, of course, Schubertian in the way this innovation of Beethoven has been identified before (see pp. 78 and 79). To it Schubert would add a divine melody from his own richness of endowment. Already, however, Beethoven has foreseen such a possibility in a limpid, interrelated malleability of musical materials which would, through Schubert's intercession and propagation, echo a century later in the *Ruhevol* of Mahler's Fourth Symphony.

In a work that begins with a slow movement and includes a funeral march, Beethoven did not see fit to provide a movement in the sonata-form discipline, or any approximation of it. Such an act of exclusion may have a precedent in Haydn or Mozart, but it is difficult to recall. Within the funeral march are both a recollection of the ruffle of drums to be heard in the second movement of Haydn's Symphony No. 100 (*Military*) and a warning of Beethoven's addition to the vocabulary of funeral music in his *Eroica* to come. The cadential figure in particular was good enough for Beethoven to carry over from its form in the sonata

to the symphony

It bears within itself a tread of feet, a sense of finality all-too-gravely appropriate to the circumstances.

Unlike some of its predecessors, the Opus 26 Sonata is a completely unified, altogether sequential expression with no movement foreign to its mood or total purpose. This may seem contradictory to those inclined to regard a sonata without a movement in sonata form as inadmissible. It may irritate others to whom the finale is inappropriately "light" to follow a funeral march. But the unity of impulse that binds the movements of Opus 26 together makes an entity of them, whether it be called a sonata or something else, and the swift-moving finale serves at least two purposes: as an alleviating contrast to what has preceded it, and as pathbreaker for the "wind over the grave" concept which Chopin whipped into an eerie chill, an even more forlorn gust, in the finale of his B-flat-minor Sonata. It hardly need be mentioned that in this work, Chopin broadened, deepened, and fulfilled Beethoven's conception of a *Marcia funebre* for piano.

Generous as Beethoven was in providing suggestions, hints, and actual motivations for others, he nevertheless exploited for his own purposes—intentionally or otherwise—more than a few ideas whose possibilities had only been hinted at when first they occurred to him. Such an instance may be found in the transformation of this sonata's (Opus 26) opening statement from

to an even more endearing form, less than a decade later, in the Allegretto ma non troppo of the E-flat Trio, Opus 70, No. 2:

(*continued*)

In the greater wisdom and compositional maturity of 1808, the theme has been stripped to essentials, the bass line reduced to its underlying elements, simplicity preferred to ornamentation. But as an affecting underpinning to purpose, the expressive anticipation in the bass (B-flat against A-flat in the treble) has been retained. This may be construed as a paraphrase in musical terms of Shakespeare's edict (in Sonnet 116):

> *Love is not love*
> *Which alters when it alteration finds.*

Or, more simply, it may be esteemed as consistency of character (Beethoven's) within a refinement of workmanship.

4

THE DEVIATION from custom which Beethoven cloaked under the defensive title of "sonata" in Opus 26 was clearly, unmistakably admitted for what it was in the two history-making works of Opus 27. Now ready to recognize that the sonata, as it had been received by him from Mozart and Haydn, was dead, gone, and dissipated, and, perhaps, convinced that the music-buying public would purchase what he wrote regardless of title, Beethoven gave to these works a title truly descriptive of them: sonatas with a fantasy character, or in the language of his choice "sonata quasi una fantasia," No. 1 and No. 2. There have been many previous fantasias (a word not unknown to Bach and Mozart) and literally uncountable sonatas. I do not know of a prior instance in which the two words are linked in a single designation.

"History-making" would thus be everybody's agreement as a reasonable designation for the C-sharp-minor, Opus 27, No. 2 (known from Vienna, where it was written, to Tokyo, where a facsimile version was produced to celebrate the bicentenary of the composer's birth, in 1970, as the "Mondschein," "Clair de lune," "Chiaro di luna," or "Moonlight"). But what of the first in E-flat? What are its claims to distinction? Many more, I would venture to say, than are recognized, or rewarded, in its status as the least performed worthy work of a great master.

As the first of the two "sonatas" which are also "fantasias," the E-flat Sonata has an automatic identity. But it is also the work of Beethoven in which the kind of writing known to us as "an Impromptu by Schubert" appears for the first time. It is conveyed by such suggestive phraseologies (end of first Allegro, first movement) as:

SCHUBERT: *Opus 90. No. 2, in E-flat, opening*:

(continued)

And in a burst of invention, as the work continues, Beethoven ex-poses a distribution of technical means—last twelve measures of the Allegro—which can only be called Schumannesque, so intimate a part did they become of the Intermezzi, the Novelletten, the Humoresques, and similar *jeux d'esprit* (to which the great romanticist gave whatever title was in favor with him at the time of composition):

Lest it be supposed that we are dealing only in pianistic guidelines, the ideational beginning of Schumann-in-Beethoven may also be noted. When Beethoven has finished the "fantasia" part of this sonata in the first three movements, he embarks on a finale which progresses from the latently contrapuntal to the rigorously fugal. Along the way (A) he scatters some musical seeds for Schumann to harvest in his C-major Toccata (Opus 7) (measures 77–79) thirty years later:

BEETHOVEN

SCHUMANN

This is the musical affirmation of the verbal allegiance Schumann was rendering in such jottings of his twenty-second year as: "Beethoven! Thou art not guide to the goal, but the goal itself!"[9]

---

[9] Gerald Abraham, ed.: *Schumann: A Symposium* (London: Oxford University Press; 1952), p. 9.

What is left to be said today of the "Moonlight" which has not already been said and resaid? To direct attention to at least two instances of the way in which its matter as well as its manner spread over musical Europe. Had Heinrich Friedrich Ludwig Rellstab (music critic and poet, some of whose verses were composed by Schubert) heard the E-minor Nocturne of John Field[10] before he heard the C-sharp-minor Sonata of Beethoven, he might have likened *its* rippling triplets in the left hand to moonlight on Lake Lucerne.[11] This, however, would have required a considerable foresight, for Beethoven's triplets

predate those of Field

[10] No. 10 in some editions, but No. 9 in the Schirmer edition (edited by Theodore Baker), from which the excerpt that follows is reproduced.

[11] Rellstab's allusion to "moonlight on Lake Lucerne" has been scoffed at as a distinction without a difference—why not moonlight on *any* waters? There is, actually, a justification for Rellstab's specification: Lake Lucerne is in a bowl of mountain sides which swirl the winds over the waters, in some circumstances, in a way that could have given him a very special image of moonlight.

by more than a decade and a half. Beethoven's line of descent could be from the Andante of Mozart's C-major Piano Concerto, K.467, which has much the same design at one point, or the first prelude of Bach's "48."

As the example indicates, it is more than a matter merely of the triplets. The melodic line gliding over their rhythmic, wavelike formation has the kind of kinship that makes an association inescapable.

If Field is present in the C-sharp-minor Sonata, can Chopin be far behind? Not much further than the finale of the same work, in which Beethoven's way of achieving a climax (last five measures of the finale)

becomes Chopin's in the Fantasie-Impromptu (measures 24–23–22–21 before the end)

Typically, Chopin rearranges the pianistic layout of the passage to suit his own technical objectives, but the sound is strikingly similar, not to mention the key (C-sharp minor) and the location of the launch pad (E in the middle register, as bass tone; E in the right hand, as top melodic note). While it is well known that Chopin was more partial, among his predecessors, to Mozart than to Beethoven, this is not to imply that he didn't know the latter's musical mind thoroughly.

Had Beethoven pursued his early impulse to attach programmatic titles to his works, *Pastorale* might have occurred to him for the D-major Sonata, Opus 28, or it might not have. In either case, it was not a likeness invented by the composer, but by the publisher August Cranz of Hamburg (for an edition he processed in 1838). Very likely the attribution relates not to the finale, as some have suggested, but to the first movement, whose character has some resemblance to the opening of the Sixth (*Pastorale*) Symphony. That is to say, it is a designation *ex post facto*, the first fact being the fame that had come to the F-major Symphony, and Cranz's appropriation of it on behalf of a work he deemed to have some relationship to it.

Its Andante establishes a plaintive A-minor mood. This has as much the character of a Mendelssohn *Song Without Words* as any composer in search of a manner of his own could acquire, without so much as "by your leave," from another. Even more, it has a specific relationship to the slow movement of Mendelssohn's A-major Symphony (No. 4, known as the *Italian*, which, by no chance at all, is also in D minor, has four beats to a measure (Beethoven's writing of his rhythmic bass as sixteenth notes makes it almost mandatory to phrase the rhythm, in an andante, as four to the bar), and employs the identical kind of running bass figure under the melody as Beethoven does. Further resemblances may be left to the reader's own initiative.

Even a nonpartisan of Beethoven would agree that the D-minor Sonata (No. 2) and the E-flat Sonata (No. 3) of those grouped in Opus 31 contain enough music to serve three works rather than two. That is just as well, for even a partisan of Beethoven, such as myself, cannot deny that the G-major, Opus 31, No. 1, is as bland and empty a work as this great man ever permitted to be published in his name. It is related to the others only in the odd circumstance that none—including the great D-minor—bears a dedication. It was published (with No. 2) in April 1803.

In the view of Eric Blom, the G-major represents "Beethoven in the unaccustomed part of a technical experimenter so taken up with the purely theoretic and mechanical considerations that he is not particularly interested in the music as such."[12] This is not only the negation of everything commonly considered characteristic of Beethoven, but, also, contrary to the values he had constantly proclaimed as music's justification and a composer's *raison d'être*.

Nothing could stand in greater contrast to this nondescript work than the resurgence of an authentic identity in the works immediately following. The sequence that began with the Opus 22 in B-flat comes not only to a glorious summation but, also, to a new proclamation of identity in sonatas Nos. 2 and 3 of Opus 31. They press to an even higher point of individuality and strength the emotional fervor of the A-flat (Opus 26), the half-seer, half-mystic vision of the C-sharp-minor (Opus 27, No. 2). Out of the personal agitation with which Beethoven was obsessed at the time of the D-minor's creation (1802), he looks forward, through the utilization of a recitative without words, to similar

---

[12] Blom: *Beethoven's Pianoforte Sonatas Discussed*, p. 125.

matter (in the identical key) of a work he would not write until more than twenty years later.

It is, musically and philosophically, akin to the recitativo of the cellos and basses that connects the third movement of the Ninth Symphony (in D minor, Opus 125) to the finale.

In the phrase marked A, the Beethoven of the D-minor Sonata was issuing a promissory note which the Beethoven of the D-minor Symphony would redeem many years later in the baritone's "O Freunde, nicht diese Töne!" (ten measures after the Presto):

In terms of the technical devices which Blom perceives in Opus 31, No. 1, none had so long a future of imitation and expropriation as the two-hand figure which launches the finale of Opus 31, No. 2. It persists through much of the movement, a *moto perpetuo* before Paganini insinuated the term into the musical vocabulary.

If the D-minor is the dynamic, brooding face of romanticism (Beethoven's affection for Mozart's concerto in that key has already been established), the E-flat Sonata (Opus 31, No. 3) is its pensive, yearning counterpart. It provides enough elements new to music in 1802 to announce, when codified and disciplined twenty years later, that a unique individuality named Robert Schumann had joined the musical board.

5

ALSO WITHIN THE COMPASS of the works grouped between Opus 22 and Opus 31 are the five works designated by Beethoven as sonatas for piano "with a violin" or "with the accompaniment of a violin" (a range of relationship rarely recognized by their string partisans of the present). Whatever the professional attitudes of those in whose keeping this repertory is today, the composer himself placed the emphasis, in his title, exactly where it is in the conception.

Purely as music, even before they are described as sonatas for piano and violin or violin and piano, the works of Opus numbers 23, 24, and 30 are vastly more ambitious in scope and content than anything previously created in the duet category. One characteristic in particular separates the earliest of the five (in F major and A minor) from their predecessors. That is, simply, that Beethoven was no longer writing *Hausmusik*, even in a nominal sense. These are sonatas which give little quarter to the professional instrumentalist and none at all to even the most gifted amateur. In both, the pianist is adversary as well as partner, amply provided with the means to protect his own interest at all times.

In the F-major (Opus 23, No. 1), the muse of Beethoven projects a smiling face in a work whose flowing conformations may support any number of affectionate nicknames, including that of *Frühling* ("Spring"), by which it is known. Even more important, it prompted many subsequent expressions in the same spirit (not excepting the Brahms sonatas in A and G major), with or without descriptive titles.

The three sonatas of Opus 30 inscribed to Alexander of Russia are esteemed by some as the best for the violin, excluding only the two even greater ones of Opus 47 and Opus 96. Of particular note is the Adagio molto espressivo of Opus 30, No. 1 (in A), in whose second strain there is more than a hint of something Verdian, something as specifically Verdian as the *Lacrymosa* of the Requiem. They are close neighbors on the staff (the Beethoven in B minor, the Verdi in B-flat minor) and even closer kin in their conformations:

BEETHOVEN

VERDI

It is well known that Verdi, in his later life, carried a pocket edition of Beethoven quartets with him to read on his travels. It is, in any case, an extraordinary instance of how one musical thread can be woven into the fabric of another, or one trend of musical thought can serve, collaterally, an entirely different purpose.

In Opus 30, No. 2, there is an abundance of the C-minor Beethoven for the simplest of reasons: It is in C minor. Thus it is the unique outcropping of the emotional involvement that Beethoven invariably brought to the tonality, or the tonality to Beethoven, between the incidental references in the C-major Piano Concerto (No. 1) and the complete absorption with it in the Third Piano Concerto (in C minor). The sonata has everything of the driving, committed character to be expected, including more than a few suggestions of the thirty-two variations-to-come for piano (1806, also in C minor).

The final dispensation to Tsar Alexander (in return for a valuable ring as well as a suitable fee) is a lighter, definitely playful work in G. Its other than customary interests center on a vivacious finale (a Scherzo is lacking in the three-movement sequence) of a type from which Mendelssohn may very well have derived the impulse for his high-spirited rondos, whether titled capriccioso or otherwise.

6

WHAT IS BEING DEFINED HERE—for the first time known to me—in the references to Schubert and Schumann, Mendelssohn and Chopin, Verdi and Wagner, is the extent to which the musical vocabulary of romanticism, on both sides of the Alps, was evolved, shaped, and codified by Beethoven in these works. As the years in which they were written ushered in a new century, so the works themselves not only proposed new uses for old musical resources, but demonstrated how they could be put to poetic purposes on the highest level.

From the pages of almost any one of these sonatas between Opus 22 and Opus 31 emerge evidences of the strengthening of the enharmonic impulse in Beethoven's writing. This invaluable means of moving music from one key center to another provided, in Beethoven's usage, subtle shifts and deviations from past procedure, unlocked doors into inviting terrain formerly reached only by tedious circumlocution and pointed directions that enabled Schubert, Schumann, and Chopin to reach high ground from which Liszt and Wagner would discern even more remote tonal horizons.

Chromatic connections are another index to the future, whether as ladders leading to the next level of communication—as in the rising, passionate proclamation of the Grave introduction to the "Pathétique" —or merely as a footstool from which to reach for a color from a neighboring key and return it intact in a measure or two. Such an established device as the Neapolitan sixth (or flatted supertonic) was newly evaluated by Beethoven, particularly to provide access to the minor mode for a statement originally made in major.

How such devices were used doubtless stimulated those who were growing up during Beethoven's lifetime and coming to music through his instrumentality. But it was *why* they were used that galvanized the imagination of the emerging generation of musicians in Central Europe. Intellectual energy would command one kind of response; but it was the emotional adrenalin released by Beethoven which fed fancy and fanned fire. Unlike those who created for themselves through means originated by others, Beethoven combined (in rare balance) ingenuity and expressivity, originality and creativity. A composer possessed of either in the measure commanded by Beethoven would have been a figure of history: It was the interaction of the *two* that enabled him to span a vaster territory of musical possibility than any predecessor, indeed to establish a prototype for those infrequent others—Chopin and Wagner, Debussy, and perhaps Stravinsky—whose like dualism has set them apart. Similarly Beethoven could utilize, within the limits of a lifetime, only a portion of the discoveries, innovations, and deviations he poured into his own creations. What remained fertile, exploitable, and rich in suggestion became the elements acted upon by Schubert, Schumann, Wagner, Brahms, and others and which, in retrospect, were characterized by history as "anticipations."

As well as creating a new vocabulary for himself and a thesaurus of devices in which others could find a vocabulary for themselves, Beethoven mapped countless ways in which the language could be shaped to expressive ends. This was, of course, a constant with him throughout his career. But the Opus 22 to Opus 35 bracket includes even more that was exploited by others than any equivalent concentration. A reason could be, of course, that its contents were more immediately accessible, hence more exploitable, to the next generation's men of genius, who were nevertheless not of the *genus* Beethoven.

The life and vitality of the individual movements embodied within the dozen or so sonatas just discussed were such that they gave rise to entities to which others (or their publishers) gave the names of Impromptu, Intermezzo, *Moments musicaux*, or *Songs Without Words*. On a smaller but no less distinctive scale were the Bagatelles (Opus 33) which, in time, would be recognized as the cocoon from which emerged the *Papillons* ("Butterflies") of Schumann and Grieg. Already there is, in this first collection of Bagatelles (others may be found in Opus 119 and Opus 129), one impish fancy which plays lightly, delightfully, with the listener's attention. It exploits the listener-as-participant gambit which Haydn devised in such a movement as the Andante of the G-major (*Surprise*) Symphony and carries it forward a step in the direction of the deceptive cadence of the Scherzo in Symphony No. 7 and sundry humorous aspects of the Eighth.

In the context of such achievements, the two sets of variations that bring this miraculous sequence to a close might be anticipated as no more than a terminal gesture, a tapering off, both in ingenuity and expressivity. The A-flat Sonata (Opus 26) showed what Beethoven's thinking about variations was at this time, leaving little reason to suppose that he would excel it any time soon.

How extraordinarily different the actuality from the anticipation! The two sets of variations, Opus 34 and Opus 35 (written at the same time, in 1802, in reverse order of their publication), are as different from the variations which had preceded them as they are from each other. Those of Opus 34 were inscribed to the same Barbara de Keglevics (Princess Odeschalchi) for whom Beethoven had written the E-flat Sonata of Opus 7 several years before. They are almost certainly designed to serve her technical abilities, without disserving them. But those in

E-flat (Opus 35, and inscribed to Count Moritz Lichnowsky, a sure indication of Beethoven's high opinion of their importance) are creative beyond anything suggested in the bare "Variations par L. van Beethoven" which he scribbled on the title page of the manuscript.[13]

They are, indeed, an indispensable part of the sonorous chain which linked the aspiring provincial of 1795, who had earned the right to compose dance music for a Künstler ball, to the master who would create the epochal finale of the even more epochal *Eroica* Symphony (No. 3, in E-flat) later in 1803. The theme on which the variations are built emerged from Beethoven's familiarity with dance music and his ability to produce it at will. In type, it is a contredanse, derived, despite the linguistic improbability, from the English country dance. It was written, in all probability, for a ball of the winter season 1800–1801, for which the performing resources were so restricted that the "score" may be read almost as easily as a piano part:

(*continued*)

---

[13] Kinsky: *Das Werk Beethovens*, p. 87. In May 1803, Beethoven expressed his desire to the publisher (Breitkopf and Härtel) that the title page bear an attribution of the theme to the ballet *Prometheus*. Though Beethoven offered to pay for such an alteration himself, the publishing process was too far advanced to make the change possible.

A version for piano appeared soon afterward, but its degree of popularity with the public is unknown. With Beethoven, it was indeed popular. He chose to utilize the same contredanse in the concluding section of the *Prometheus* Ballet, where alterations from the preceding usage began to emerge. It was then (see pp. 138–9) that the vibrations in his mind began to form themselves into variants and more variants for piano, and something like the finale of the *Eroica* is encountered. By the time he had codified the material in his mind as Fifteen Variations with Fugue, there emerged both the premise and the promise of the new world of sound which distinguish the variations of the *Eroica* from all others in music's previous history.

As an instance of the smallest alteration effecting the most vital change, nothing could surpass the shift of a single note in the bass line, across the three stages from contredanse to ballet to variations. The tones actually remain the same—E-flat, B-flat, B-flat, E-flat. But what was

in the music for the ballroom, becomes

for the stage. Lest the change be so inconspicuous as to escape instant recognition, attention may be directed to measure two of the quoted examples. In the example from the contredanse, the bass is a simple E-flat, B-flat, B-flat (repeated on the same pitch), E-flat. In the example from *Prometheus*, the first B-flat has been raised an octave *above* its prior position;

the second B-flat, an octave below, remains as it was. From a simple, functional bass line, the sequence has been converted into a potent, meaningful theme. Or perhaps it would be better to say that, to a mind as resourceful and far-seeing as Beethoven's, the second arrangement became a potent, meaningful theme whose possibilities for enlargement were so exceptional that he made it the opening statement for all that followed:

Out of the relationship thus defined would emerge a design that would require the symphony orchestra for ultimate fulfillment.

VIII

Early Maturity

I

A S CAME TO BE increasingly typical of Beethoven's creativity, a long period of concentration on one kind of expression—in this instance, piano music—tended to impel him toward another development in a totally different direction. Though attached numerically to the sequence of piano works which absorbed him so long, the Opus 35 variations are, chronologically, a bridge to Beethoven's generation of creative impulses which could only be fulfilled in the orchestra.

A close examination of the external chronology as well as the internal musical relationships indicates that the bridge was one which was built, in several spans and arches, from the contredanse of 1800–1801 through the *Prometheus* Ballet to the piano variations and their subsequent destination. Each had a function to perform in the forward movement of Beethoven's thought.

In addition to converting the uneventful bass of the contredanse into a strongly marked, well-defined idea-in-opposition to the fluent melody above, Beethoven utilized the opportunity of the ballet's finale to employ bass and treble, for the first time, in a sequence of variations. In sound, it is more than a spin-off from the C-major Symphony (No. 1). Though the orchestra combination is very much the same, the climax of the ballet is much more sonorous than anything in the symphony.

Prometheus—or *The Creatures of Prometheus*, as Beethoven titled it—was performed for the first time on March 28, 1801, in the Hofburgtheater in Vienna. It is thus the direct orchestral predecessor of the Second Symphony. But its time of origin (late 1800) puts it on the other, earlier side of the long sequence of piano works ranging from the opus numbers of the mid-20s to those of the mid-30s. It is not without relevance to that sequence, nevertheless.

Generally lost in the flood of piano music that rolled from Beethoven's mind during 1801 and part of 1802 is a version for keyboard of the *Prometheus* Ballet, on whose title page is the designation "Opus 24." The familiar identity of this opus number with the F-major Piano and Violin Sonata came about in the later publication procedure, of course. What is of much greater interest is Beethoven's involvement with the piano transcription, which was dedicated to one of his favorite titled ladies: "Princess Lichnowsky, born Countess Thun." In the Kinsky catalogue,[1] it is stated: "Nach einer Mitteilung Czernys stammt die Bearbeitung des Auszugs von Beethoven selbst" ("From a statement of Czerny one attributes the choice of excerpts to Beethoven himself"). In addition to the overture and "Tempesta" which follows it, Beethoven designated ten of the sixteen segments of the ballet for inclusion in the piano transcription. Needless to say, the finale was among them.

The bridge from piano to orchestra would undoubtedly have fallen short of its objective had not Beethoven turned his attention to the orchestra again in 1802. Of the nine symphonies, No. 2, in D, is the one least likely to be known to the average music lover (it is challenged for that unhonorable distinction only by No. 4, in B-flat). No. 1, as the progenitor of all, has its unique place in history as a cunning example of the young man taking his first step on a historic path, like a baby learning to walk and unexpectedly bursting into a trot. Nos. 3, 5, 7, and 9 are beyond question individual, as are Nos. 6 and 8 (each is possessed of a plot—"Heroism," "Fate," "Apotheosis of the Dance," and "Brotherhood" in the first instance; "Pastorale" and "Humorous" in the second —which makes it attractive to conductors in search of parts in which to display themselves). But, in the "historical" view, No. 2 is known, if at all, as the work from which Beethoven made his "giant leap" ahead to the *Eroica*.

But history and the "historical" view are not always synonymous. As there could have been no Second without the First, so the Third without a significantly stronger Second is all but unthinkable. This is not so much because Beethoven added to his physical means: the instrumentation of the Second is substantially the same as that which had sufficed for the First (except that the key specified for clarinets is A rather than C, and trumpets and horns are in D rather than C, in order to facilitate performance in the key of D). But the *way* in which the instruments are used is another matter altogether. The range is con-

[1] Kinsky: *Das Werk Beethovens*, p. 102.

siderably wider, the dynamics and alterations of force considerably greater than anything for dedication to Baron von Swieten or to be performed in the presence of Emperor Franz.

By any standard, the Second Symphony is a work of almost limitless physical energy, high comedic invention, undeviating optimism and congeniality, with a proper interlude of repose in the Larghetto to set off the propulsive first movement from the even more propulsive third. As a product of late 1801, when the second despairing letter to Wegeler was dispatched, and middle 1802, which ended with the blackly despondent Heiligenstadt Testament, the Second Symphony is a perpetual reminder that external miseries are not be equated with inner humours. Or, perhaps more to the point, it is evidence that Beethoven had already learned, through the magnificent strides he had made in the relatively brief time that had elapsed since the "Pathétique" Sonata was written, that art and life must go their separate ways.

Still young enough—not yet thirty by his own faulty reckoning— to regard health, if not happiness, as his reasonable due, he could point to the vitality and high spirits of his newest symphony (as of 1802) as proof of what he *could* do, were all things well with him. For what vitality and high spirits abound in these movements charged with élan and the life force! There is hardly another orchestral work of Beethoven's in which there is much of the coltish, the skittish, and the engaging without a downward twist of the lips here, an undertone of the macabre there to suggest some hidden misgivings. In a worldly way, life was indeed good to Beethoven just then. Beyond steady productivity and the rewards therefrom, he was enjoying the generosity of the attentive if irksome Lichnowsky to the extent of 600 florins a year. The purpose of the stipend was to assure Beethoven's livelihood without teaching or other distractions from composition, until he found an appointment to his liking. (There was, of course, never such an appointment, and despite subsequent underwritings by Vienna's nobility, teaching was, for a long time, a part of Beethoven's economy).

It is also symptomatic of the new character and abundance to be found in the Second Symphony that it is, within the frame of this inquiry, very much what might be called "continuable." Unlike the First Symphony, in which the total musical matter at Beethoven's disposal is consumed in the creative heat of the immediate effort, the second is replete with ideas, thoughts, devices, and energies to fuel the fire of others, as well as of himself.

From the outset, the D-major is clearly a work that faces two ways: to the past, in its utilization of a slow introduction, which is, nevertheless, much bolder in its musical posture than the similar section of its predecessor; and to the future, in its broader, fuller, more ample sonorities. No longer the meager twelve measures that had sufficed for the First Symphony, the introduction to the Second is a broad thirty bars in length, permitting Beethoven to visit neighboring tonalities, and some not so nearby, en route to the point of departure. Along the way he has the opportunity to indulge his fondness for the woodwinds, not only as loyal opposition to the majority voice of the strings, but as a solid body of opinion not hitherto heard in a symphonic forum (the introduction to Mozart's E-flat Symphony, also slow, also wood-windy, may have been latent in Beethoven's thinking). Together these inclinations arouse the anticipations that a proper introduction should: of subject matter to come, and the means by which it will be expounded.

The first twelve measures of the Allegro bear out the anticipations. No longer inclined to the kind of tune Mozart could produce with such facility, or a motive such as Haydn devised with a careful sense of purpose, Beethoven is now motivated toward what Réti would call a cell-structure. Its characteristics, in the present instance, are a rhythmic-melodic entity in the low strings answered by a swirling figure in the first violins, both destined for positions of prominence. Before a strongly contrasting idea is introduced, measure 60 provides a pendant to what has preceded, also vigorous, also assertive, and also much used in the parliamentary procedures that follow. With the second subject come strongly marked accents (*sfz*, for sforzando) and syncopations (offbeat emphasis).

It is hardly surprising that, amid such abundance of resource, more than a little has to be set aside for fulfillment at a later time. As an instance, at measure 120, the bass is the voice for this idea:

As well as varying the dynamic pattern that had preceded, it sets in motion a circular, churning figuration which eventually fulfills itself in the subterranean rumblings of the basses in the finale (measure 358) of Symphony No. 7:

In pursuit of the extended orchestral range mentioned above, it should be noted that the bass line has much more mobility, takes a much more active part in the total interplay of sound, and adds considerably to its weight and substance. It is, indeed, in this symphony that the historic point of separation would be reached in which the bass and cello—companions on the lower end of the tonal structure for much of the eighteenth century—would part company, each to go its own way (see p. 145).

As noted elsewhere, the finely formed line of the Larghetto is not only serenely beautiful in itself, but a source of inspiration for future purposes.[2] When associated with the kind of increasingly personalized embellishment that accrued to Beethoven as he grew older, both the serenity and the beauty are elevated to an even higher rank on the scale of expressivity associated with the Ninth Symphony.

Such a turn of thought in the slow movement of the Second Symphony as

---

[2] Irving Kolodin: *The Continuity of Music* (New York: Alfred A. Knopf; 1969), pp. 30–1. The reference is to the evolution of the Larghetto's opening into the Nocturne of Mendelssohn's *Midsummer Night's Dream* music.

is but the initial concept or seed from which would flower the eloquence in the Ninth's Adagio cantabile (measure 100):

One can also sense in the Larghetto (at measure 185)

another stylistic trait which would mature and deepen into the form of fanciful filigree that makes so tenderly confidential a communication in the Ninth's Adagio as

The sense of a work which looks both ways, in time, is heightened by the tempo and character of the third movement. Now the view *is*

straight ahead. Gone is such a temporizing designation as Menuetto to cloak an incipient Scherzo. This is a Scherzo in name as well as in fact, saturated with the juices of Beethoven's own explosive humor to an inflammable mixture. Any spark of interpretative life induces a rocketing lift that reminds us where the symphonic Scherzo had its first flight.

In the finale, Beethoven ranges wider and digresses further forward in symphonic time than in any prior movement. Indeed, it came to establish something of a pattern for symphonic finales to follow and may be related to (a) an impulse to vary the harmonic norms explored in preceding movements; (b) a desire to carry the listener into other harmonic involvements; (c) a mere surfeit with conformity. Among its epoch-making formulations is the *final separation of the double bass from its traditional partnership with the cello and the assignment to it of a function of its own.*

The impulse first shows itself as early as measure 5 of the Allegro molto, in which it occurs to Beethoven to write a countermelody against the main line in the first violins. It is initially in an ideal register for the violas, but they lack the power to be heard by themselves. The cellos are then called upon to supplement their effort. This carries the countermelody out of any comfortable range for the string bass. Faced with the option of abandoning the countermelody or the traditional partnership of basses and cellos, Beethoven hesitates not at all. Musical sense prevails, and the cellos sing out, as the basses are put at the bottom of the tonal structure, there to perform as only they can.

(continued)

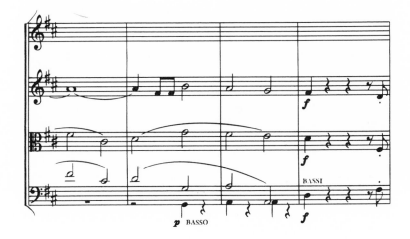

Having thus liberated the cello from decades of bondage to the double bass,[3] Beethoven cultivates its vocal talent wherever his lyric inclination leads him (Second Symphony, Finale, measure 210):

[3] It may be mentioned, for what it is worth, that the score of the *Prometheus* Ballet (published as Opus 43 in 1804) has separate staves for bass and cello, though they are all but identical. The C-minor Symphony was the first in which Beethoven formalized the divided responsibility.

He also encourages it to engage in amorous discourse with the woodwinds. Soon they are not only conversing in a Schubertian way, but in Schubertian terminology:

BEETHOVEN: *Second Symphony, Finale, measure 243*

SCHUBERT: *B-Minor Symphony, second movement, measure* 277

As it gains in force and driving power, the finale soars to an altitude never before attained by such a movement, beyond the melodic tree line to the heights of craggy rhythmic definition where only Beethoven breathed comfortably.

2

THE REPEATED REFERENCE to the Schubert-in-Beethoven has brought us finally to what might be called the Beethoven-in-Schubert. That is to say, the sources are no longer limited to a generalized likeness or inclination acted upon and expanded. They now extend to specific phrases and musical disciplines in Beethoven which reappear at an important point in a masterpiece by Schubert. Why, of all works of Beethoven, it should be the *Second* Symphony to which Schubert reacted strongly invites some attention.

The plain answer is that it is precisely these works of Beethoven's early maturity—the sonatas from Opus 22 to Opus 31, No. 3—which provided spiritual nourishment and intellectual stimulation to a whole generation of composers growing up during Beethoven's lifetime. The ideas they contained were not only provocative but technically accessible, which made them "continuable" in the sense the word has been used in this study.

The instance of Schubert is particularly revealing. He was not only the first great composer to be born (1797) after Beethoven's arrival in Vienna, but the one most closely exposed to his physical being. Schubert's serious musical education began when he was about fifteen, which is to say, in 1812. He was first apprenticed, mentally and spiritually, to Mozart and Haydn, as his earliest symphonies profess. As he developed, the early sonatas and other instrumental works of Beethoven came under his hand and were soon transplanted into his mind.

Lest this be assumed as merely speculative, citation may be made of valuable comment included by Martin Chusid in his edition of Schubert's B-minor (*Unfinished*) Symphony.[4] In his essay entitled "Beethoven and the Unfinished," Chusid quotes from a letter by Anton Holzapfel (a contemporary of Schubert's at the Imperial Seminary between 1808 and 1813, who long outlived the composer). Recalling their days together in the orchestra of the Seminary, Holzapfel wrote: "Year in and year out, at our daily performances, all the [published] symphonies by Josef Haydn and Mozart, the first two symphonies by Beethoven as well as all the Overtures we could tackle at that time, even 'Coriolan' and 'Leonore' (the grand overture to *Fidelio*) were regularly performed. . . ."

From another Seminarian, Schubert's close friend Josef von Spaun, Chusid cites a letter to be found in its entirety in the mammoth documentation by Otto Deutsch: "The adagios from the Haydn symphonies moved him profoundly and of the G minor [K.550] by Mozart he often said to me that it produced a violent emotion without him knowing exactly why. . . . With Beethoven's symphonies in D and B flat his delight reached its climax. Later on he liked the C minor even better."[5] Nor were Schubert's insights into these works limited to what he might

---

[4] Franz Schubert, Symphony in B minor; edited by Martin Chusid (New York: W. W. Norton, Norton's Critical Scores; 1968), p. 100.

[5] Otto Erich Deutsch: *Schubert Memoirs by His Friends* (New York: W. W. Norton; 1958), p. 126. Spaun's letter—written fifty years after the time of the events involved—contains references to the symphonies in "D major and A." Deutsch renders it as "D major and B flat" on the premise that the Fourth (in B-flat) would have been more within the competence of the young players than the Seventh (in A). Some musicologists, Joseph Braunstein among them, dispute this interpretation, contending that, in practical orchestral terms, the Fourth is more difficult.

have heard or observed as a player in the ranks. He was considered bright beyond his subteen years and, in the absence of the instructor, sometimes conducted the orchestra.

Chusid's interest in Schubert's knowledge of the Second Symphony has a specialized involvement. In his essay he advances the premise that it was never Schubert's intention to leave the B-minor Symphony at two movements, nor did he merely put it aside and "forget" to resume work on it. The evidence is contained in the existence, contrary to common belief, of a sketch for a third movement which Schubert had elaborated, in a piano projection, to a total of 128 measures, after which it suddenly breaks off. Here, says Chusid, Schubert encountered a "compositional problem" that prevented him from completing the Scherzo and Trio he had started. This "block" was not dissipated between 1822, when the *Unfinished* was begun, and 1828, when he died.

The answer to this "compositional problem," says Chusid, "may be that while working on the final, orchestral version of the third movement he became consciously aware of the thematic relationship" between his Scherzo and the Trio of Beethoven's Scherzo in the Second Symphony. The relevant musical elements are set forth by Chusid thus:

BEETHOVEN: *Second Symphony, Trio, measures 1–8*

SCHUBERT: *B-Minor Symphony, third movement*
(orchestral version), measures 1–8

SCHUBERT: *B-Minor Symphony, third movement*
(piano sketches), measures 25–32

SCHUBERT: *B-Minor Symphony, third movement*
(piano sketches), Trio, measures 1–8

The immediate question that arises is: Why could not Schubert have rewritten the trio to eliminate the self-incriminating duplication? To the expected question, Chusid has a prepared answer: "Schubert was intentionally seeking to unify the movement of the Unfinished by melodic means. . . . He could not remove the offending themes—those resembling Beethoven's trio—without destroying the completed movements as well as the fragmentary scherzo. The problem was seemingly insoluble and he felt compelled to abandon the composition." It should be borne in mind that, by 1822, all of Beethoven's symphonies but the Ninth were in being, and Schubert's admiration for the C-minor (see p. 148) could well have included the unity of means embodied in the persistence of the ♫♩♩ rhythmic cell.

My interest in Chusid's theory is less with the reasons why Schubert did or did not finish the *Unfinished* than with the evidence his study provides of similarities between Beethoven's Symphony No. 2, in D, and Schubert's No. 8, in B minor (the major–minor kinship of the two works will not escape the reader). Several of his citations are only on the borderline of persuasiveness, but others are close to identities. Only two can be cited here, but the line of thought may be indicated by:

BEETHOVEN: *Second Symphony, Larghetto, measures 12–16*

SCHUBERT: *B-minor Symphony, Andante con moto, measures 68–72*

BEETHOVEN: *Second Symphony, Larghetto, measures 61–62*

SCHUBERT: *B-minor Symphony, Andante con moto, measures* 100–102

The emphasis is, of course, not on plagiarism or purposeful imitation, but on the subtle linkage of design between two inimitable works.

3

EVEN THOUGH VERBAL DOCUMENTATION may be lacking, it is not merely a reasonable assumption but a demonstrable fact that the careers of many other young musicians born in the early years of the nineteenth century partook as strongly of Beethoven's creative conceptions as Schubert's did. The impulse may have differed in kind—Berlioz, born in 1803, did not play the piano and came to Beethoven by another course[6]—but not at all in degree. To Mendelssohn (born in 1809), to Schumann and Chopin (both born in 1810), to Liszt (1811), and to Wagner (1813), the early works of Beethoven sounded the call and proclaimed the faith to which they were responsive in their own beginnings.

The documentation, as I have said, is not quotable in words and sentences. But it is citable in measures and phrases, in musical quotations of the kind that have been instanced from time to time in the preceding pages, and continued to accumulate as their careers and Beethoven's unfolded. His impact on the musical community of Central Europe in the first fifty years of the nineteenth century was somewhat like that of a recurrent earth tremor whose vibrations extend through rolling, deeply subsurface waves to distances remote from the point of origin. How it might be measured on the Richter scale is difficult to compute; on the musical scale, it certainly exceeded 10.1.

In the case of Schumann, for example, the rolling shock waves continued to be a disturbing, if not unsettling, reality throughout his career. The degree of their impact depended on the manner of work he was engaged in at a given time. In one context, they could be heard in so early a piano work as the G-major Toccata (1832) already men-

---

[6] Jacques Barzun: *Berlioz and the Romantic Century*, 2 vols. (Boston: Little, Brown; 1950), I, 99. Ever the prodigious mentality, Berlioz was writing appreciatively of the C-sharp-minor (Opus 131) in 1829, when he was twenty-six and the work, barely three years old, was unknown to most musicians.

tioned; in another, in the symphonies of 1840, whose point of departure was, in more than one way, Beethoven's No. 4 in B-flat; in a third, in the quartets and other chamber music of a few years later. How deeply Schumann was affected by Beethoven's last quartets is readily apparent in his notation of 1830: "Beethoven's B-flat quartet, opus 130, heard for the first time. Ultimate goal!"[7]

Schumann's response was, in a sense, both direct and indirect. The light of Beethoven can be seen reflected, as by a direct beam, in Schumann's own creations. It can also be recognized, refracted into new shapes and shadows, in the music of those who responded most profoundly to the magnetism of Schumann: Brahms and Wagner.[8] The prior citation of Schumann's response to Beethoven's Opus 27, No. 1 (see p. 124), may be expanded to include Opus 54 and, especially, Opus 90. And it pleased Hans von Bülow to isolate four measures in the thirtieth of the *Diabelli* Variations and say of them: "In these four measures we may discover the embryo of all the romanticism of Schumann."[9]

(*continued*)

---

[7] Abraham: *Schumann: A Symposium,* p. 9.

[8] The linkage of two names which became Pope and anti-Pope of warring factions may seem perverse, but both Schumann and Brahms were admirers of early Wagner. As for Wagner, the first act of *Die Walküre* bears indelible testimony to his indebtedness to Schumann, whatever he may have written or said later.

[9] Ludwig van Beethoven, Variations, 2 vols.; Introduction and analytic comment by Hans von Bülow (New York: G. Schirmer; 1898), I, 79.

A devotee of chamber music (such as A. E. F. Dickinson[10]) might point to the slow movement of the A-minor Quartet (Opus 41, No. 1) as a prime instance of how a Beethoven gambit became one for Schumann, by a change of direction:

BEETHOVEN

SCHUMANN

As an instance of the way in which the march of decades altered the frame of reference, one may place the emergence in Wagner's music of what Ernest Newman describes as the "Pathétique-Tristan"[11] spirit side by side with a youthful work of Brahms.

A creation of almost the same time (mid-1850s) as *Tristan*, the C-major Sonata, Opus 1, shows the frame of reference of Brahms (born twenty years after Wagner) to be the much later "Hammerklavier" Sonata (Opus 106) of Beethoven:

[10] Abraham: *Schumann: A Symposium*, see A. E. F. Dickinson's essay, p. 144. The Beethoven measures have been transposed from B-flat into F to facilitate comparison with the Schumann.
[11] Newman: *The Unconscious Beethoven*, p. 79.

On the other hand, what Wagner discerned in the early Opus 13 Sonata led him to a much more revolutionary outcome than anything Brahms arrived at in his total career.

The one, perhaps the only, aspect of romanticism to which Beethoven made little traceable contribution was the part of it represented by the woods and fields of folklore contained in the pastoral poetry of Carl Maria von Weber. His year of birth was 1786, and he was thus well into his teens before the representative music of Beethoven was in general circulation. What was well formed in Weber was nevertheless subject to the impact of *Fidelio* when he came to know it in the final form of 1813. It provided another aspect of human involvement which broadened the scope of Weber's expression in his masterpiece *Der Freischütz*.

Whether or not he perceived any part of himself in Weber's accomplishment, Beethoven was an ardent admirer of *Der Freischütz*, which was introduced to Vienna in November 1821. When they met shortly afterwards in a music shop, Beethoven embraced Weber warmly, and praised him as "a devil of a fellow."

IX

Evolution and Convolution

I

THE PRECEDING REGISTER of persons for whom, by 1802, Beethoven had invented the means for self-discovery may well be incomplete: the company is broad, the terrain wide, the possibilities —within Central Europe alone—verging on the infinite. But for even partial completeness, one more name must be included. That is Beethoven's own.

The path to that conclusion is paved with many blocks, including the comment by Stravinsky, previously quoted (see p. 111), which may be recalled here. It is his reminder that Beethoven, in the piano sonatas, "discovers and sometimes maps out the different territories of several future composers, including himself." Some specific instances have, of course, been noted as they occurred. But the elevation of Stravinsky's observation from the specific to the general prompts even closer attention to the evolution of Beethoven's music from the Second Symphony onward.

No small part of that closer attention has been made possible by Beethoven himself, his growing inclination to record his thoughts— rough and smooth, spontaneous or tortured—in the sketchbooks. The earliest of such memorabilia to appear in print are the so-called Kafka sketchbooks[1] covering works of the 1786–98 period. Valuable as they

---

[1] Beethoven: *Autograph Miscellany* . . .

are, they do not represent any such struggle for clarification and concentration as the famous sketchbooks studied by Nottebohm (or others not known to him which have recently become available).

The suitable conclusion would be that, in the earlier instances, a preponderance of the problems that presented themselves to Beethoven were immediate and manageable. As the ideas began to multiply—in complexity as well as in numbers—and his standards of acceptability grew higher, some means of containing the tide had to be evolved. It is to our everlasting insight and illumination that what evolved was a method not only productive but enduring. There can be little doubt that Beethoven's habit of notating his ideas as they occurred to him and recording, in sequence, the changing configurations from promising to acceptable, preserved, for later use, much that might otherwise have vanished.

Concurrently—perhaps inevitably, as his habit of subjecting new materials to intensive scrutiny became a creative tool—came expressions of dissatisfaction with what he had written previously. The earliest such written comment may be found in the letter of July 1801 (see p. 84) in which he confided the secret of his growing deafness to Karl Amenda. Many months before, he had given his friend a copy of the F-major Quartet (Opus 18, No. 1) with a warm inscription of regard. Now he begs him not to show it to anyone or allow it out of his hands. "I have made some drastic alterations," Beethoven writes, "for only now have I learnt how to write quartets."[2]

It was not much later that Beethoven made a somewhat similar statement to Wenzel Krumpholz, a Viennese musician of Bohemian birth who had attached himself to the young composer in 1795 and remained an enthusiast for many years to come. It was in the aftermath of the completion of the D-major ("Pastoral") Sonata in 1801 that he told Krumpholz: "I am not satisfied with my work up to the present time. From today I mean to take a fresh road."[3]

A well-known, but long unavailable insight into Beethoven's thinking in this crucial period of development came into circulation with the publication in 1962 of the Wielhorsky sketchbook. It derives its name from Michael Jurijevitch Wielhorsky (1788–1856), a Russian musician who acquired the sketchbook in Vienna and took it to Russia. Its contents were known to von Lenz, in the mid-nineteenth century, and

[2] Anderson: *The Letters of Beethoven*, I, 65.
[3] Grove: *Beethoven and His Nine Symphonies*, p. 49.

described by Ludwig Nohl.[4] But it is only within the last decade that publication, in the usual tripartite format,[5] by the Soviet government, has lifted the curtain that fell upon it when it was taken to Moscow.

Of the 173 pages in the rectangular (12" x 9½") sheets, by far the most interesting to me are those beginning on page 12 and running consecutively to page 45. The preceding eleven pages are devoted to sketches for the Piano Sonata, Opus 31, No. 3. It is in E-flat, which may have been a conditioning consideration for the contents of the thirty-three pages that follow. They are the most thoroughgoing evidences imaginable to the processes that produced the Opus 35 Variations and the great *Eroica* Symphony—both, of course, in E-flat. It is hardly likely that this is the first thinking, or writing, Beethoven had done with the *Prometheus* materials since writing the finale of the ballet many months before, or supervising the preparation of the piano transcription published in June 1801. (The creation of the Opus 31, No. 3, Sonata is attributed to spring 1802, meaning that the variations began to take shape at about the same time.)

The presumption that Beethoven had given some prior thought to the material is derived from the first of the sixteen staves on the top of page 12. It begins boldly, and with no indication of rewriting, with the form of the Introduzione col Basso del Tema cited on pages 136–7. That is, the specific addition Beethoven has adduced to the elements already in being, the "given" with which to evolve a new musical equation— theme as bass, bass as treble. It is the opening of the door not only on all the possibilities of the variations to come, but on the finale—and much more—of the *Eroica*.

However, the bold beginning is no guarantee of an all-conquering march to the as yet undefined objective. In the swarming series of variants that gather on the successive pages of sixteen staves (sometimes more than one to a stave), several have a recognizable relationship to forms that pass muster to qualify in the chosen fifteen. Others, promising enough to the lay eye, did not survive the demanding criteria of the expert. It is not until page 23 of the total sequence, or some 175 staves later, that the Basso del Tema emerges as a fugal subject, and the grand design of Opus 35 is firmly established.

Another dozen pages of extensions, elaborations, further formula-

---

[4] Thayer-Forbes (1964), I, 328.
[5] The three volumes comprise: (1) A facsimile of the sketchbook in Beethoven's own hand; (2) A transcription of the entries into modern notation; (3) A critical commentary on the contents.

tions, and more exacting eliminations ensue before Beethoven arrives, on page 33 of the sketchbook, at another extraordinary moment of reckoning. This is the extraction, from all that has preceded, of the ideas that now pass muster for the design that has formed in his mind. It is an index to the fifteen variations he has selected to precede the fugue, which is—two pages further on—written out, in skeleton form, in precise detail. Still to come is the idea of designating three variants that *precede* the theme as Basso del Tema "A due," "A tre," and "A quattro." These are all treatments of the bass which Beethoven decided to separate from the formal fifteen. They have already appeared in the sketches, even with numbers. But when the ground plan is finally fixed, Beethoven tenders them lightly as alternate versions of the Basso del Tema, rather than variations of the theme. No one can quarrel with this logic, for that is, in fact, what they are.

Indeed, as a study in the application of logic to the arrangement and ordering of what had hitherto been a mere collection of random thoughts, these twenty-five or so pages of sketches are of a compulsion beyond compare. They are, however, but a flicker of light compared to the broad, compelling beam Beethoven cast on the littered landscape of forms and shapes that accumulated twenty years later as he exercised his much more mature skills on the theme of Anton Diabelli.

2

IF THE SKETCHBOOK of 1802 is a fascinating index to Beethoven's purposeful procedure in the creation of a scheme embodying fifteen variations and fugue for piano, the spectacle of the master sitting in judgment on himself has an even more absorbing demonstration in the following year. I refer to the finale of the *Eroica*, whose derivation from the variations is invariably mentioned, but never clarified, in the program notes that accompany performances of the work.

For the purposes of a symphonic finale, Beethoven found no cause to label the introductory part "Introduzione col Basso del Tema." Nor was he disposed to identify the succeeding variations by numbers. There was equal logic in the suppression of cadences that would emphasize the separation of its sections. In the interest of greater cohesion, Beethoven invented transitions and connections to enhance symphonic sequence and solidify structural design.

Despite such enlargements and extensions, it will doubtless come as a surprise to most readers that the finale of the *Eroica* is substantially *briefer*, in time span, than the Opus 35 Variations. The normal assumption would be that the finale of the longest symphony written to that time would be more imposing than a mere set of piano variations. It is Beethoven's pleasure to make absolutely clear that a movement could be *both* more imposing and shorter in elapsed time. The principles of "learning how," to which Beethoven referred in his comments to Amenda and Krumpholz, might well have applied to selection and rejection, contraction and elimination. A normal, well-phrased performance of the Opus 35 Variations takes approximately twenty-one minutes; at a suitably similar pace, the finale of the *Eroica* runs to less than twelve minutes.

If there is a categorical reason why the symphony's finale looms larger in the mind than the piano variations—aside from greater resources of the orchestra—it is, unmistakably, Beethoven's ever-sharpening instinct for rejecting the commonplace and retaining the exceptional. Those variants which Beethoven selected with a view to orchestral elaboration are, uniformly, the best that Opus 35 provides. Some others survive as a point of departure. Such a one is No. XV in the piano sequence, labeled "Maggiore." Its glowing mood and leisurely pace (Largo) provide the genesis for the symphony's exalted Poco andante, with its unforgettable oboe solo, which carries the finale to a new height of exaltation before the jubilant conclusion of the movement and the symphony. There is, in the symphonic context, no fugal summation. Rather the duality of the bass-as-treble and the theme-as-bass with which Beethoven had introduced the piano variations is expanded and elaborated in the orchestral treatment, by imitation and other contrapuntal devices. As might be expected, a number of new sections in the finale grow out of the orchestral colorations available to him.

A comparison of those retained with the ones set aside casts some light on Beethoven's criteria, in these specific circumstances. Opus 35 is dotted with variations which exploit the dance derivation of the basic theme. None of that in the symphony! He also indulges in some sportive play with the theme which makes entertaining exposition for the pianist's technique. Again, gone! Anyone who thinks that Beethoven was in the least softminded, or even softhearted, about a musical idea simply because it was his own, need merely consult the cool objectivity, the reasonableness with which he separates what is prime and choice from what is not. Self-indulgence is nonexistent.

What does persist, beyond the context of the symphonic finale, is Beethoven's lingering esteem for a very good idea which doesn't qualify for orchestral elaboration. It is Variation No. VIII in Opus 35, which has, in its musing way, strayed a long distance from the original idea:

(continued)

Not only in mood but in manner it stands apart from any usage of the keyboard common in Beethoven. But a devotee of the composer, alerted to such elements as a running figure in the right hand, with the melody in the left *crossing over* to the treble, would have to award it a measure of familiarity—in the Beethoven to come, if not in the Beethoven that was. Put into a proper context of time, design, and place, it can be recognized as the source of the superb Rondo-Finale of the C-major Sonata for Piano, Opus 53 (universally known as the "Waldstein"), which may be skeletonized thus:

However obvious the connection may be to us today, it was by no means clear to Beethoven in 1803. The sketches of Beethoven's endeavor to put his theme for the finale of the "Waldstein" into a manageable order have been preserved and may be consulted. Among the early forms are:[6]

(continued)

[6] Gustav Nottebohm: *Ein Skizzenbuch von Beethoven aus dem Jahre 1803* (New York and London: Johnson Reprint Corporation; 1970), pp. 63–4. Originally published by Druck und Verlag von Breitkopf und Härtel, Leipzig, 1880.

None of these comes even close to the flowing, serene line of the rondo as it is now revered; however, one element persists from prototype to fulfillment. That is the gravitation to the dominant (with the added seventh) for the "middle" part of the ABA sequence. Not that the "dominant" in such a context is all that unusual; it is perhaps the one, the inevitable, place for it to be. But it is only when Beethoven eventually "recovers" the rondo theme from the mental recesses of the Opus 35 Variations and joins it to a running figuration in the right hand and crosses the left hand into the area of the treble that the new form of the old idea—dominant and all—begins to emerge. As is often the case in such a continuation from a "recovered" original, it is at precisely the same pitch level:

Conscious? Unconscious? Accidental? Volitional? It is impossible to tell. But Nottebohm, in his comment on the sequence of sketches that produced the rondo theme—there is, of course, no reference to any relationship with the section of Opus 35 from which it emerged—brackets Beethoven's thought process with a prior instance he had been discussing by noting that there the composer "also discovered in the middle" of a prior sketch sequence "the kernel of a major theme. . . ."[7]

To a degree this parallels the mental process by which he "recovered" from the finale of the G-major Piano Concerto the outline of the theme which eventually became the chorale of the Ninth Symphony ("Freude, schöner Götter Funken," etc.). In the instance of the variation-as-rondo theme, the second form is not only an intensely creative evolution from the first, but a discriminating as well as imaginative improvement upon it.

Before leaving the "Waldstein" to its established place in the historic sequence, it may be profitable to add the Réti view of its structural formulation. Both the wonder and the curiosity is that this wise observer of Beethoven's mental processes finds that "all its themes are built from the same model with a uniformity not often found in a large musical work."[8] And wonder of all the wonders, Réti finds the "model" embodied in a "stepwise ascent from *tonic to dominant* [italics added] to which a small phrase, a loop, is annexed." And the prime example Réti selects in order to show the model in its simplest form is not a "germ cell" in the first movement, but nothing other than the "main theme of the *Rondo-Finale*," which has been the subject of the preceding discourse. As Réti views it, the particles of the main theme of the Rondo-Finale are:

He adds, "By changing this line to the minor and transposing it a half tone higher, we hear:

which is synonymous with the second theme of the *Allegro*."

As I view it, the whole of the Opus 53 sonata—not merely the

[7] Ibid., p. 64.
[8] Réti: *Thematic Patterns in Sonatas of Beethoven*, p. 166.

Rondo-Finale—emerged from Variation No. VIII of Opus 35. It was there that this form of tonic-dominant relationship, with what Réti calls its "loop," had its inception.

3

If this random instance of a Beethoven thought process working in reverse may be credited to the chance discovery of a connecting link in a sketchbook of 1803, it should not be thought of as either unique or unparalleled. It is the ideological and musical key to unlock the most profound secret in the creation of the *Eroica* Symphony itself; namely, that Beethoven did not, in the common terminology, "utilize" the Opus 35 Variations merely as a basis for the finale of the symphony. Rather, the symphony as a whole owes its origin to the thought processes that produced the Variations, as the "Waldstein" Sonata does to the "model" enunciated in the theme of the Rondo-Finale.

Here, too, there is a connecting link that has only recently become a magical part of the golden chain. I refer to the Wielhorsky sketchbook and the light that its contents shed on the creative processes that produced these variations. "In the swarming series of variants," I have written (see p. 157), "some can be recognized from their later prominence in the 'chosen fifteen,'" but "others, promising enough to the lay eye, did not survive the demanding criteria of the expert."

Of particular interest among them are, on page 16 of the sketchbook, a sequence of measures as follows:

An E-flat Menuetto and a C-minor Todtenmarsch as parts of a

variations-sequence beginning in E-flat? By no means extraordinary—
only if the variations-sequence was preceded by a symphonic sequence
beginning in E-flat, with an E-flat minuet that became a scherzo, and
a C-minor Funeral March that is one of the most famous in the literature.

To be sure, neither has—yet—the conformations of the parallel
movements in the *Eroica*. But it is not too much further along (p. 27
of the sketchbook) that one encounters (again in C minor):

with its very considerable suggestion of what is now the second movement of the *Eroica*. Indeed, combine the upbeat from page 16 of the
sketchbook with an *echt*-Beethoven evolution from the figure of page
27, and the elements of

in the *Eroica* are absolutely evident.

In setting forth the creative processes that produced the variations,

I observed that "these twenty-five or so pages of sketches are of a compulsion beyond compare" (p. 158). Inasmuch as the sketchbook sequence begins on page 12 and ends on page 45, would that not be closer to thirty-five than to twenty-five pages? Yes and no. The total is closer to thirty-five than to twenty-five, *but* after the grand design of the variations has been determined, Beethoven is still fascinated by the processes he has set in motion. Something else is fermenting in his mind, and it is *not* a piano piece.

The clearest indication of the direction in which Beethoven's mind is trending is the insertion of the word fagotto (bassoon) at the following point on page 44 of the sketchbook:

Directly below, the earlier entry of Menuetto has now become Menuetto serioso—which is becoming considerably closer to the scherzo terminology utilized in the *Eroica*—and, on the page following (No. 45 and last that is germane in the Wielhorsky sketchbook), a C-minor figure creeping closer to the Funeral March formulation can be discerned.

Some of this has to be taken on faith, especially by those to whom a bare line of notation may not cue the mind to its more remote, final crystallization. Not only for these, but for any with an interest in the sketchbooks and what they symbolize, I can heartily recommend a series of records in which the English pianist, scholar, and musicologist Denis Matthews brings them to life in an unprecedented way.[9] As expounded in his fascinating blend of the incipient—on the piano—and full-formed (extracts from orchestral recordings, woven into the texture), speculation is replaced by certainty. Indeed, his discussion of the Menuetto serioso and its evolution into the Scherzo of the *Eroica*, and his delineation of just where a series of random chords or a transitional passage fit into the first movement of the symphony, are creative musicology of the first order.

Where, then, one might ask, does the opening E-flat theme of the symphony come to birth? Is it, in fact, the oft-mentioned phrase from Mozart's *Bastien und Bastienne* overture which uses a similar series of notes:

To me, this is not relationship by happenstance. As has been well said by Arnold Schönberg: "Put a hundred chicken eggs under an eagle and even she will not be able to hatch an eagle from these eggs."[10] The *real* source, in my judgment, is the very first variant "A due" of Opus 35, in which the ovum of the eagle that is the *Eroica* is concealed in the counterpoint to the bass figure:

If the theme has not yet made its appearance in the sketchbooks, no matter. At a point late in life when Maurice Ravel was at work on a new score, a friend asked: "How is it going?" "Fine," replied Ravel. "I have everything but the themes." That was his way of saying that form, design, proportion, character were already firmly fixed in mind, and everything else would fall into place. Beethoven had all of this, plus the theme

<hr />

[9] Discourses Ltd., High Street, Tunbridge Wells, Kent, England. The catalogue numbers are ABM 1, 2, and 3.
[10] Arnold Schönberg: *Style and Idea* (New York: Philosophical Library; 1950), p. 201.

for the *Eroica*'s first movement in mind, if not on paper, late in 1802 when the Wielhorsky sketches reveal him occupied with other things. When they were succeeded by the famous sketchbook of 1803 in which Nottebohm presented the emerging materials of the symphony, the preliminary design had been drawn, the marble marked for sculpting.

4

As THE COMPLETION of the *Eroica*, the first performance of the C-minor Concerto, and the beginnings of the "Waldstein" Sonata (Opus 53) have all become identified with 1803, the approach of the Fifth Symphony and the Fourth Concerto might be likened to distant lightning and resultant thunder. Here, too, the Nottebohm researches of a hundred years ago provide an endless fund of information.[11]

Doubtless there were predecessor plans—as there were for the *Eroica*—which have not endured to be appraised. Certainly the steadily greater absorption with the ♩♩♩|♩ pattern precluded a need to have it jotted down in a sketchbook. It was, already, obsessive. As revealed in Nottebohm, the plot of the great C-minor Symphony may also be discerned with the Scherzo roughed out and the shattering first movement definitively determined. Unlike an earlier instance in which he denounced his own use of an idea ("dies ganze Stelle ist gestohlen aus der Mozartschen Sinfonie in C"[12]), he did not find the beginning of the Scherzo (in No. 5) too close to the finale of the G-minor (No. 40) of Mozart for tolerance.

Immediately adjacent to the sketches for the C-minor are (on p. 69) those for the G-major Concerto, No. 4. The mirror likeness of one to the other does not require elaboration. They may be cited as the high and low temperature readings of the rhythmic as well as melodic fever with which Beethoven was to be obsessed for years to come. The emergence of the two sketches to the point where each began to shape a different work brings, full cycle, this inquiry from the point of departure at which it was launched (see p. 5).

The inevitable conclusion has to be that, by the summer of 1803— when the *Eroica* was in full production—Beethoven had set so many musical forces in motion, fertilized and cross-fertilized so many different strains of musical growths, that the harvest would be many years in the

---

[11] Nottebohm: *Ein Skizzenbuch von Beethoven aus dem Jahre 1803*, pp. 70–1.
[12] "Kafka Sketchbook," in Beethoven: *Autograph Miscellany . . .* , II, 228. The work in question was the C-major, *Linz* Symphony (No. 36), which Beethoven had appropriated for a work in G minor.

reaping. The collateral thought must be that the force thus set in motion would, inescapably, assume a volition of its own, inverting the roles of guest and host.

No year is more deserving of such a designation than 1803, in terms, merely, of the ideas projected, the eggs laid, ready for hatching. Not only was it the *annus mirabilis* of the *Eroica* Symphony; it was equally miraculous for the number of involvements clamoring for Beethoven's "immediate" attention, some of them not to be fulfilled for a full five years to come. The premise for this assertion is neither speculative nor intuitive. It is founded on the hard facts and real evidence contained in the sketchbook edited by Nottebohm to which reference has already been made. This invaluable scholar dubbed his cache (a mere seventy-five pages in length but illuminating beyond any imagining) "sketchbook of 1803." However, he honestly acknowledges that the first entry might have been made as early as October 1802, the last as late as April 1804.

No matter. Though it would be of major interest were its contents limited to the beginnings of the C-minor Symphony (No. 5) and the G-major Concerto (No. 4), these are but two among a dozen major works which were coming alive concurrently. Among them—as already discussed—were the C-major Piano Sonata (Opus 53) dedicated to his Bonn patron and continuing friend, Count Waldstein; the opera not yet titled *Fidelio*; the C-major Concerto for Violin, Cello, and Piano with Orchestra, eventually to bear Opus number 56; portions of the oratorio *Christus am Ölberg*, with its nostalgic look at the examples of Haydn (a living presence still, with half a dozen years of life before him); two portions of an F-major composition which emerged, several years later, as the Symphony No. 6, universally known as the *Pastorale*; and extended sections of the *Eroica*. The last named of these include a comment by Nottebohm to the point that its "finale did not take him nearly so long to realize" (the relation to the Opus 35 Variations was still incompletely understood when Nottebohm's volume was published in 1880).[13]

---

[13] Nottebohm: *Ein Skizzenbuch von Beethoven aus dem Jahre 1803*, p. 50. Reference to sketches for 1801–1802, also edited by Nottebohm, enables the reader to establish the circumstances out of which the great Sonata in A, Opus 47, for Piano and Violin (known as the "Kreutzer"), emerged. The earlier volume shows the finale as planned for the Sonata, Opus 30, No. 1, but later deleted because of excessive length. The later one includes a jotting in Beethoven's own hand from which the designation of the work as a whole came into being. "Sonata . . . scritta in un stilo molto concertante quasi come d'un Concerto." Freely translated, this could be construed as "Sonata . . . written in a style very much like a concertante or somewhat the same as a concerto."

5

AMONG THIS DISPLAY of unpolished gems, one stands out to me with the particular identity of a pearl beyond price. I do not refer to the strands of interrelated thoughts contained in the C-minor Symphony and the G-major Concerto, dazzling as they are, but to the much more modest beginnings of the *Pastorale* Symphony. They demonstrate beyond argument the futility of assigning the motivation for so special a work as the *Pastorale* to the year in which it was finally accomplished. They also put into a demonstrable context what has hitherto only been, for me, a speculation.

That was the existence of an inner relationship between the Second and Sixth symphonies which went far beyond their link as "even-numbered" symphonies—Nos. 2, 4, 6, and 8—as opposed to the "odd-numbered"—Nos. 3, 5, 7, and 9. Some Beethoven lore makes the point that "even-numbered" symphonies are, on the whole, of a brighter, more relaxed character than the "odd-numbered" sequence that includes the *Eroica*, the intensely concentrated C-minor, the Bacchanalian Seventh, and the epochal *Chorale*. But there is a touch of the specious, as well as of the accidental, in this reasoning. The announcement for the concert of December 22, 1808, in which the two works were performed for the first time identifies them as: "A Symphony entitled: 'A Recollection of Country Life,' in F major (No. 5) . . . Grand Symphony in C minor (No. 6)."[14] They acquired their established numerical identity when the order of publication brought the assignment of Opus 67 and No. 5 to the C-minor (in April 1809), and Opus 68 and No. 6 to the F-major (in May 1809).

As of the months early in 1802 when Beethoven was at work on the D-major he was, to judge from its sparkling first movement, serene Larghetto, propulsive Scherzo, and laughter-filled finale, a whole man, or as whole as a man harboring the secret he had confided the year before to Wegeler and Amenda could be. At the turn from summer to fall, he encountered for a reason or reasons not wholly known to us, the swift spiritual deflation and emotional downdraft that reduced him to a state of depression unprecedented since the emotional crisis from which emerged the C-minor Sonata of 1798–99 ("Pathétique," Opus 13).

It was during this racking *de profundis* that he imagined himself at the end not merely of his tolerance of life but of his physical ability to

[14] Thayer-Forbes (1964), I, 446.

sustain it. The verbal consequence (the Heiligenstadt Testament) can be quoted to support almost any theses about the Beethoven who persisted, productively. But surely few things are as revealing as the words: "What a humiliation for me when someone standing next to me heard a flute and I *heard nothing* or someone heard a *shepherd singing* and again I heard nothing. . . ."[15] Can a humbler wish be imagined than the final despairing cry: "Oh Providence—grant me at last but one day *of pure joy*—it is so long since real joy echoed in my heart—Oh when—Oh when, Oh Divine One—shall I feel it again in the temple of nature and of mankind—Never?—No—Oh that would be too hard."

As of 1802, Beethoven clearly conceived the Goethean concept of "one day *of pure joy*" as an outward, direct physical experience: the pleasure that comes from spending a day wandering on the land, feeling the sun's warmth, rejoicing in the twittering of bird sounds or of a village band, pausing for rest beside a brook, taking refuge from a sudden storm, and enjoying the spiritual regeneration that accompanies the sun's reappearance. It would be some time before Beethoven would develop the inner resources and the spiritual strength to comprehend that he could still hear the sounds *inwardly* with his mind's ear, re-create, *musically*, every one of the physical sensations just described.

By usual reckoning, it would be at least five years after the Heiligenstadt Testament (Beethoven gives the place name as "Heiglnstadt") before the *Pastorale* began to grow, in 1807–1808.[16] By the unusual reckoning, long buried in the sketchbooks—but not, apparently, pursued previously—it was perhaps only a matter of months. It was certainly no later than the early part of the following summer—when he was again in Heiligenstadt, this time to write the *Eroica*—that he notated the following:[17]

[15] The italics are reproduced as the words were underscored in Beethoven's handwriting. Ferdinand Ries, son of the concert master of the Bonn orchestra, who had come to Vienna at age seventeen, in 1801, to become a pupil and factotum of his father's friend, recounts being present when Beethoven failed to hear a distant flute. Whether the occasion was the same or not cannot be verified. Ferdinand Ries's recollections were published in 1838, eleven years *after* the Heiligenstadt Testament was published in the *Allegemeine Musikalische Zeitung* in the fall of 1827. (See Thayer-Forbes [1964], I, 306–7.)

[16] Kinsky: *Das Werk Beethovens*, p. 161.

[17] Nottebohm: *Ein Skizzenbuch von Beethoven aus dem Jahre 1803*, p. 55.

Peasants at play? Perhaps. As it stands, it is simply a random idea lacking in identity and only later assigned its ordained place in the section of the *Pastorale* titled "Lustiges Zusammensein der Landleute" ("Merrymaking of the Peasants"). The next relevant entry not only outlines a familiar rhythmic pattern and repetitive figuration

but bears the description: "Murmeln der Bäche" ("Murmuring of the Brooks").[18]

Clearly the impulse to convert his response to Nature from a physical sensation within himself to a musical and spiritual form beyond himself was stirring in Beethoven long before the *Pastorale* became its durable embodiment. The unanswered, perhaps unanswerable question is: To what extent was this reversion to a prior thought volitional, to what extent involuntary? Did Beethoven cultivate the sketchbooks as sources for material when the time became ripe for this usage, or did the ideas recur at the prompting of an unconscious creative urge? There are, to my knowledge, no unquestionable answers to such questions, for the simple reason that the existence of the sketchbooks was generally unknown during Beethoven's lifetime. When the books became known, there was no Beethoven to answer the questions they raised.

But there may be, here and there, ways of puzzling out an answer and supporting its validity through circumstantial if not direct evidence. In the instance of the *Pastorale*, the long-buried references by Nottebohm in materials related to the *Eroica* have, within recent years, been augmented by publication of a sketchbook depicting Beethoven's evolution of the symphony itself.[19] The fifty pages of drafts bearing on the creation of each movement sequentially may not provide all the possible answers; but they do, without doubt, promote the asking of more intelligent questions.

For purposes of the queries thus propounded, access to such progressive sketches is of inestimable value. Our long familiarity with the finished work tells us that nothing in it appears exactly as it did in the sketches, either of 1807–1808 or of 1803. The tantalizing, all-embracing

---

[18] Ibid., p. 56.
[19] Ludwig van Beethoven: *Ein Skizzenbuch zur Pastoral Symphonie op. 68*, 2 vols., with an Introduction by Dagmar Weise (Bonn: Beethovenhaus; 1961), II, 27.

consideration is: Can one determine, from the later sketches, whether Beethoven had recourse to the first form of the same ideas, and if so, under what circumstances?

The first nine pages of the sketches—which, incidentally, are superscribed "1808"—show Beethoven absorbed wholly with the problem of getting his thoughts on the first movement in order. He is fairly clear in his mind on the purpose he is pursuing in this "Sinfonia caracteristica oder Erinnerung an das Landleben" ("Characteristic Symphony or Recollection of the Country Life"), as it is described at the bottom of the first sheaf of sixteen staves. It is an ambulatory exposition, suggestive of the walk in the country it would finally depict. Characteristic not only of the then-dubbed "Sinfonia caracteristica" but of all sketches, these personalized jottings conform to the kind of shorthand Beethoven evolved for his own informational purposes. Key signatures are absent; modifications of tonality are derived from the use of accidentals—a natural sign (♮) here, a sharp (♯) there—to remind him of harmonic developments along the way. A repetition of a passage is rarely written out; often it is indicated either by a repeat sign ‖: or ⌒ (meaning more of the same). When reconsideration of the first form of an idea suggests that another direction would be more profitable, the discarded measures are simply struck out

and *Meilleur* ("Better") is written over the preferred form. Given some familiarity with his own form of code, one can follow in fair detail the elaboration and sophistication of the opening matter to the 513 measures it occupies in the finished score.

It is on the fifteenth printed page[20]—with no indication of one movement finished and another begun—that one encounters a recurrence of the first materials related to the sketches of 1803:

This is the form to which the rough draft (shown on page 171) has now evolved. The undercurrent of sound previously labeled "Murmeln der

[20] Ibid., p. 15.

Bäche" has acquired a melodic overtone, but it does not satisfy Beethoven's criteria of the amount of movement such an overtone should have. Another few measures, and it has been altered to

The superscription "2te mal Clar et Fagt" means that Beethoven is reminding himself that, when the opening is repeated, the form it takes the second time is to be given to clarinets and bassoons. Eventually he decided to *begin* the movement this way, with the violins performing the phrase just noted, the woodwinds held in reserve until its repetition.

It is not until many pages farther on in the sketches—in which alternate possibilities for the first two movements and a suggestion of the storm have been dealt with—that another idea of 1803 recurs. As noted previously, it is not there identified with the country, as the sketch inscribed "Murmeln der Bäche" unquestionably is. Now it has been worked into the sequence of what is the third section of the symphony —"Lustiges Zusammensein der Landleute" ("Merrymaking of the Peasants")—as a kind of trio to the dance sequence. It is even preceded by a double bar, demarking it from what had gone before. Relocated in the context of F major, it reads:

Remembered? Recaptured? Retrieved? Reproduced? My inclination is to the last of these possibilities. The rhythmic detail is not only oddly idiosyncratic in itself, but almost identical with both its first (p. 172) and its final form. Its appearance at this place, in so fully perfected a series of details, suggests to me that Beethoven was not working, in 1808, with something unremembered, or only half remembered. Rather it is my belief that he was utilizing a point of departure already in being, fitted into a pattern for which he had finally found its ordained place.

Is this then a token of Beethoven spending hours of his time scrutinizing old sketchbooks, searching for usable—or reusable—materials as a

penny-conscious householder might sift ashes in search of a few uncon-
sumed coals? The probability of such a procedure does not fill me with
assurance. It does not strike me as compatible with other headstrong
attributes of an impatient Beethoven. Nor does the concept of a conscious conning of the past as a guide to future accord with the effort he
expended on shaping the theme for the Rondo-Finale of the "Waldstein" to his exacting standard—though the essential elements were already organically available in Variation VIII of Opus 35.

I would define the two fragments in the sketchbook of 1803 not as
two random, if related, ideas but as the generative elements of a *work*
revolving around a murmuring brook and other pastoral elements. That
is to say, they were not ideas in search of a *métier* in which they would
eventually be utilized, but the building blocks of a scheme he would
eventually find time to realize . . . as, indeed, he did.

There is, after all, no guarantee that the material contained in the
sketchbook for 1808, valuable as it is, collects all the thoughts that went
into the evolution of the *Pastorale* symphony between 1803 and 1807.
Some other links may have been lost, others buried in sketchbooks not yet
processed for general scrutiny. The mention of a passage in the sketches
suggesting a storm (it is marked "Donn," which I interpret as shorthand
for *Donner*, or "Thunder"[21]) recalls that it was only within recent years
that another link in the long chain of Beethoven's musical development
suggested itself to me.

That was the appearance, in recorded as well as printed form, of
Grétry's overture to *Le Jugement de Midas*.[22] His purposefully coloristic
use of the oboe as shepherd's pipe—in measures 59 *ff.*—after a storm,
almost certainly lingered in Beethoven's mind from its performance in
Bonn in 1781 (see p. 44) to become the dimly remembered source of
the similar use of the oboe after his storm in the *Pastorale* Symphony.

It would, in any case, be a mistake to deduce from any specific
example a procedure that pertained to his work in general, or that he
was basically a simple, fathomable personality whose patterns of be-
havior, musical or personal, could be set down in neat, symmetrical rows,
all balanced and congruent. Not only did he have one order of mental
capacity where music was concerned and a totally different one where
other matters—brothers, nephew, friends, patrons, publishers—were

---

[21] Ibid., p. 29.
[22] André Grétry, *Le Jugement de Midas*; original text edited by Antonio de
Almeida (Paris: Heugel & Cie.; 1961). The catalogue number of the recorded
performance by the New Philharmonia Orchestra under the direction of Raymond
Leppard is Philips PHS 900–235.

involved, he also had differing orders of valuations about musical matters in varying situations and circumstances.

One apparent contradiction about his memory was nevertheless wholly firm and fixed. As previously noted, Schindler concluded (p. 19): "His memory of events of the past was always extraordinarily poor."[23] On another occasion, when Beethoven was being pushed hard by an interrogator to explain some feat of aesthetic association, he replied: "My memory is so trustworthy that I am sure it will not forget, even after a period of years, a theme I have once committed to memory."[24]

Between what he couldn't remember of 1796 and what he couldn't forget of 1789 are delicately poised the mysterious functionings of a mind exquisitely balanced to do the one thing for which it will always be remembered: to organize a new world of order from an old miscellany of sound.

[23] Schindler: *Beethoven as I Knew Him*, p. 63.
[24] Robbins Landon: *Beethoven*, p. 298. The answer was noted by the visitor, Louis Schlösser.

Bringing in the Harvest

NOUGH HAS BEEN SAID of the musical events of 1803 (from the concert of the spring in which the Third Concerto was first performed, through the creation of the *Eroica*, and the beginnings of the struggle to subjugate the ♫♪♩ syndrome) to leave little doubt of its preeminent place in Beethoven's musical development. But it also may be characterized as the year in which Beethoven achieved the emotional and psychological breakthrough necessary for the iconoclast, philosopher, and seer he eventually became.

The evidence is both verbal and tonal. If one reads correctly the evidence cited in the *Pastorale* sketch on page 171, nothing is left to speculation or surmise. Decades of acquaintance with the Heiligenstadt Testament and the image it conveys of a man cast into bitter despair by his inability to hear a sound quite audible to a companion have conditioned many—myself included—to the view that it would take years for Beethoven to attain another state of mind. That would be the period between the commitment of the Testament to paper in the fall of 1802 and the sketches that signaled the beginning of work on the *Pastorale* late in 1807.

These, clearly, mark the sublimation of the primitive, physical reaction to a spiritual one "higher on the cultural scale," to borrow the phraseology in Webster's New International Dictionary. It was through such a psychic transformation that the no-longer audible physical pleasures of a day in the country were converted by Beethoven into a "Pastoral-Sinfonie oder Erinnerung an das Landleben" ("Pastoral Symphony or Recollection of the Country Life").[1]

But recent, more thorough acquaintance than was hitherto possible with Nottebohm and the sketchbooks of 1803[2] has drastically reduced that time period from years to months. The key to this revelation is contained not merely in the assignment to 1803 of the earliest sketches connected with a "nature" symphony, but in the nature of that "nature" symphony. It would be one that not merely contained material both good-humored and reflective (peasants at play, and a scene beside a brook). It would also be one in which the creator would mimic in music a sound he might no longer be able to hear, specifically the "Murmeln der Bäche" ("Murmuring of the Brooks"), which became the "Scene am Bach" of the *Pastorale*.

How much Beethoven could enjoy in 1803 of his country surroundings cannot be stated with certainty. Were his condition the same as that which gave rise to the previous year's despair, he would have been able to hear relatively little. Were it, for the while, somewhat better, he might have heard quite a bit more. Schindler records that, in 1823, Beethoven pointed out to him the tree under which he sat as he jotted down the brook theme "while the yellow-hammers were singing above me, and the quails, nightingales and cuckoos [were] calling all around."[3] But Schindler had no way of knowing whether Beethoven was referring to the first impulse of 1803 or the renewal and fulfillment of it in 1807–1808.

In either case, the equanimity of mind, the serenity of spirit required to accept a "Recollection" as a valid substitute for an actuality, defines this period of months as crucial to Beethoven's continued functioning. It settles beyond dispute his awareness that pleasures normal for a whole man were increasingly to be denied to him. It also defines unmistakably his capacity to make the deprivation serve his own special, abnormal needs.

By coincidence or otherwise, it was in this same series of months that Beethoven put into music his pledge to "seize Fate by the throat."[4] Whether or not the ♪♪♪|♩ motif was indeed associated in Beethoven's mind with "Fate knocking at the door," the concept was well within his

---

[1] Kinsky: *Das Werk Beethovens*, p. 163. Beethoven's own designation in a letter of March 20, 1809, to Breitkopf and Härtel, publishers of the score.

[2] Nottebohm: *Beethoveniana* and *Ein Skizzenbuch von Beethoven* and *Ein Skizzenbuch von Beethoven aus dem Jahre 1803*. These long out-of-print, extremely rare volumes were reissued, with an Introduction by Paul Henry Lang, by Johnson Reprint Corporation, New York, 1970.

[3] Grove: *Beethoven and His Nine Symphonies*, p. 211.

[4] In a letter written to Wegeler in 1801.

mental orbit. Remote as it is from the pastoral pleasures of the Sixth Symphony, the Fifth is nevertheless an equally remarkable instance of a negative converted into a positive. Taken together, they suggest that whatever effect his affliction had on other priority objectives—as a virtuoso, as a social being, even as a prospective husband and father— it only tended to intensify Beethoven's single-minded concentration on the life purpose which took precedence over all the rest.

2

IF 1803 WAS INDEED THE YEAR of the psychological breakthrough I have attributed to it, the flood of music thus released continued to flow in almost supernatural abundance for years to come. From a collation of all the available evidence—beginnings as well as endings, bare sketches and fully evolved masterpieces—the conclusion is unavoidable that every- thing Beethoven did between 1803 and 1810 was part of a continuous, cyclical turmoil of creation.

It doubtless served a useful purpose, during the formative state of appreciation, for Wilhelm von Lenz[5] to group Beethoven's work into periods: early, middle, and late. There are few composers of quality to whom such a division might not roughly apply. But the more closely one observes the elements that entered into Beethoven's ever-evolving mental processes, the stronger the conclusion becomes that such a divi- sion fits his output loosely rather than closely. Within the seven-year period from 1803–10, Beethoven created by far the greatest bulk of the music for which he is best known. With the exception of opera, he was dealing with categories of composition he had attempted previously: symphonies, concertos, sonatas, quartets, trios, overtures, etc. But there is, in almost every instance, a vast intensification of content, a broadening of means, a conscious striving for unity and cohesion not to be found either in his earlier treatment of such disciplines or in their treatment by any of his predecessors.

The works that emerged from this interplay of elements can be classified under a series of headings:

CONCERTO SONATA
HEROIC SYMPHONY
SYMPHONIC QUARTET
ORCHESTRAL OPERA

[5] Wilhelm von Lenz: *Beethoven et ses trois styles* (St. Petersburg, Russia; 1852).

The CONCERTO SONATA, beginning with the Opus 47, in A, for piano and violin, is one such heading. It has become well known—more through Tolstoy's novel than the virtuoso to whom it was dedicated—as the "Kreutzer."[6] It might be better identified by the description Beethoven attached to the title page when it was published in 1805: "Sonata per il Pianoforte ed un violino obligato scritta in uno stilo molto concertante quasi come d'un Concerto." An outgrowth of the A-major Sonata of Opus 30, No. 1, it shares with the *Eroica* Symphony and the "Waldstein" Sonata the distinction of having a predestined objective from the start. The famous finale, having been detached from Opus 30, No. 1, because it tended to overshadow what had preceded, called into being three prefatory movements which would be congruent with it. In such wise, a new "stilo molto concertante quasi come d'un Concerto" was born.

Equally unprecedented among the duo sonatas was the A-major, Opus 69, for piano and cello. It is as remote from the limitations and restrictions by which Beethoven was content to abide in his Opus 5 sonatas (dedicated to the King of Prussia) as the Opus 47 is from the likably primitive duos for piano and violin of Opus 12. The expansion relates to, but is by no means defined by, the broadening of the cello's technical resources by his old friend of Bonn orchestra days, Bernhard Romberg. They had met in Vienna during the 1790s, and Beethoven kept in touch with Romberg's later career in Paris, Berlin, and London. The C-major (Triple) Concerto of Opus 56 was created to be performed by a group of which Archduke Rudolph was the pianist and Anton Kraft, another celebrated virtuoso of the day, the cellist. From these two sources Beethoven derived not so much the impulse to create a work difficult to perform as the means to fulfill an expressive pattern of unprecedented eloquence and architectural scope.

Within this same span of time—1803–10—Beethoven compounded all he had learned about the three solo instruments, to create a pair of trios (1808) which remain unique in the literature. Here, again, the concerto-sonata concept is basic. Performers familiar with the broad range of the trio literature extol them as the first in which each of the three instruments has a similar range of opportunity and responsibility. The D-minor (Opus 70, No. 1)—called the "Geister," or "Ghost," Trio because of its obsessively mournful slow movement—demonstrates this equality of involvement in one way. The E-flat (Opus 70, No. 2), whose superb slow movement is founded on a simpler form of the lyric

---

[6] Rodolphe Kreutzer, who never played it.

idea Beethoven invented for the Opus 26 Piano Sonata, exemplifies it in another. As a deliberately colorful accent to the almost chastely diatonic character of theme, Beethoven provides a wayward, downward cascade of chromatics that Chopin might have envied.

Thus, within a span of barely twenty-five opus numbers (47 for the "Kreutzer," 69 for the cello sonata, and 70 for the trio), Beethoven created a totally new concept of the duple and triple sonata.

As much could be said for the solo sonatas (piano) of this period, to which there has already been more than casual mention. Either the "Waldstein" (published in 1805 as Opus 53) or the "Appassionata" (published in 1807 as Opus 57) could have borne the title Schumann invented for his Opus 14: *Concert sans orchestra*. The musical conception in each assuredly has such scope, but Beethoven's talent for verbalizing his musical objectives was not nearly as striking as Schumann's.

In both, Beethoven's rigorous sense of proportion sits in judgment on the creative process as it fulfilled itself. In the "Waldstein" it became his objective opinion that the work would profit by the detachment from it of the slow movement, because it added more to length than to interest. In the "Appassionata," the tidal wave of energy he poured into the opening section overran the conventional sign for a repetition, which prior composers had automatically inserted at the end of an exposition. As Eric Blom[7] observantly notes, it was in such a tempest of creation that Beethoven decided the moment had come to break away from a practice observed by Mozart in dozens of sonatas and symphonies, and Haydn in hundreds. The movement plunges on its way, relieving the performer of any necessity for a judgment on either the need or desirability of a repetition. It is a moment of artistic truth as consequential to all future thinking on a basic musical convention as the definitive separation of cellos and basses into independent elements in the finale of the Second Symphony (see p. 144).

Much has already been said about the emergence of the HEROIC SYMPHONY, whether numbered 3 or 5. No. 3 has one set of specifics to make it a landmark—magnitude, content, unprecedented formal design; No. 5 has another—dramatic impact, dynamic contrast, underlying structural unity. But the Fifth also has its twin in a work for solo instrument and orchestra, which the Third Symphony does not. Due attention has been directed to the thematic link between the G-major Concerto and the C-minor Symphony provided by the ♫♩♩ rhythmic pattern. Even without it, the aesthetic link between them would be of transcendent

---

[7] Blom: *Beethoven's Pianoforte Sonatas Discussed*, p. 165.

importance. For the first time in a work of either category, a composer has gone beyond the hitherto accepted pattern of four self-sufficient, separately segmented movements to a belief in the importance of overall unity *between* the movements as well as *within* them.

The classic instance is the dramatic bridge passage of the symphony in which the throbbing pulsation of the timpani marking the ♩♩♩|♩ rhythm provides an almost human heartbeat of anticipation from the Scherzo to the finale. It is commonly agreed that this was an afterthought, added after almost everything else about the symphony had been determined. But the sequence of completion (1806 for the concerto, 1808 for the symphony) leaves no doubt that the dissolution of the concerto's Andante con moto into an equivocal cadence, marked *segue il rondo* ("the rondo follows"), was its spiritual antecedent. A subtle evolution in boldness of procedure may be remarked: there is no finalizing double bar at the end of the symphony's Scherzo, the instruction now is *attacca,* and the cadence is resolved by the opening C-major chord of the finale.

In the two other solo concertos of this period—the last that Beethoven was motivated to complete[8]—the principle of unity is not merely affirmed but expanded. In the Violin Concerto (Opus 61, in D major, completed in 1806) Beethoven builds on the kind of instrumental writing projected in the Opus 20 Septet and the two Romanzas of Opus 40 and Opus 50 to evolve a structure in which the finale follows the slow movement without interruption. In the E-flat Piano Concerto (Opus 73, completed in 1809), the content of such a work is, for the first time, *wholly* predetermined by the composer. Not only are the slow movement and finale welded inseparably, the cadenzas are Beethoven's own, leaving no option for extraneous matter. Mendelssohn incorporated all these precepts into his E-minor Violin Concerto (completed in 1844) and proved himself more papal than the pope by making a continuous entity of all three movements. Schumann did not quite equal the rigor of this procedure in his A-minor Piano Concerto, completed in the following year, possibly because it accumulated over several years. The first movement, written in 1841, was conceived as a self-contained fantasia. However, all the cadenza passages are Schumann's own, and when he decided to make a three-movement concerto of it, he celebrated the joyous reunion of old and new by linking the intermezzo to the finale with a musical "welcome home" derived from the opening theme of the whole work.

While such unifying concepts were coming to fulfillment in Bee-

---

[8] Late in life, Beethoven began a sixth piano concerto, but set it aside after sketching much of the first movement.

thoven's mind, he abided by prior practice in two other major works. The B-flat Symphony (completed in 1806) was undertaken at a time when the first two movements of the C-minor had been completed. He had received a commission from the Count Franz von Oppersdorf,[9] a noble friend of Prince Lichnowsky, and he intended to fulfill it with the dedication of the C-minor. However, protocol prevailed; the C-minor was inscribed to Beethoven's earlier patron, Lichnowsky, and Oppersdorf received the B-flat Symphony for his 350 florins.

If the B-flat was written as relief from the heavy going of the C-minor, Oppersdorf's name has nevertheless been perpetuated by a creation of singular individuality, musical beauty, and orchestral elegance. As for the Triple Concerto, it was begun in 1803 on behalf of the Archduke Rudolph, an amateur of the piano and a Beethoven pupil. It is thus a work conditioned by certain specific considerations.

3

AMID ALL THE CELEBRATED, world-shaking, epoch-making accomplishments of this incredibly productive period, one appeals to me as peerless in originality, intellectual vitality, and musical fertility. This is the musical content of the trio of quartets grouped in Opus 59, universally known as the "Razumovskys" because they were commissioned by the Count of that name. He was Imperial Russia's long-term Ambassador to Vienna, who had become sufficiently Westernized to marry Elisabeth, daughter of the Count and Countess of Thun. None but a music lover could qualify to be son-in-law to a family which had earned the dedication of Mozart's *Linz* Symphony (No. 36, in C, K.425) and been among his patrons in the 1784 list (see p. 65). Razumovsky had proven his devotion to the art by subscribing to Beethoven's Opus 1 Trios in 1795, along with four members of the Thun family, including his wife (see p. 65).

In addition to entertaining his social and musical peers in one of Vienna's most imposing palaces, Razumovsky indulged himself by maintaining perhaps the best string quartet the world had yet known. Its leader was Beethoven's lifelong friend Ignaz Schuppanzigh, its violist Franz Weiss, and its cellist Joseph Linke. The second violinist at this time (1805–10) was Louis Sina, who had to accept the possibility of being preempted from time to time by his employer, a capable (second) violinist. In addition to a suitable fee for writing the works at Razumovsky's instigation, Beethoven was assured of first-class performances by Schuppanzigh and his fellow professionals. His only obligation was to

[9] Thayer-Forbes (1964), I, 402.

honor his patron by including some examples of Russian folk music. Thus Beethoven set an example for a whole host of Russian composers from Glinka to Stravinsky by demonstrating the richness of this fertile soil. He even preceded Mussorgsky in electing to use—in the Trio (to the Scherzo) of Opus 59, No. 2—the great melody of which so much is made in the Coronation Scene of *Boris*, decades later.[10]

The selection of the Razumovsky Quartets for the place of priority assigned to them among the great symphonies, concerti, and sonatas of this period may impress some as arbitrary or capricious. But the choice is related to specific aesthetic, musical, and historical factors. Among all the instrumental elements by which music has been made over hundreds of years, the string quartet, by the very nature of its organization, is unique. It is an enduring, unchanging but enormously changeable entity whose physical elements serve Elliot Carter's latest conversation piece no less than Haydn's familiarly dainty F-major Quartet (Opus 3, No. 5).[11] Its range of resources has not been enlarged by the accretion of timbres and tone colors which make William Schuman's orchestra totally different from Robert Schumann's. Nor has its mechanical means undergone constant transformation. Today's piano is as different from the one for which Beethoven wrote the "Hammerklavier" Sonata (Opus 106) as that instrument was from the primitive device which served him for the works of Opus 2. The sound of the two violins, viola, and cello has altered hardly at all.

Thus, the ways in which the results achieved by Beethoven or Borodin, Mendelssohn or Stravinsky, Smetana or Debussy differ from those of Mozart and Haydn depend entirely on the sonorous image in the composer's mind and his ability to realize it on paper. What Beethoven accomplished in these three works—whose sound builds on the foundation of the C-major Quintet, Opus 29, as well as the quartets of Opus 18—is nothing less than the creation of the SYMPHONIC QUARTET. In the concerto sonata and the heroic symphony, a bigger, broader sound source than previously existed could be invoked to implement his purpose. In the Razumovsky Quartets, the intellectual input determined wholly the acoustical output.

What, exactly, are the constituent elements of what I characterize as the "symphonic quartet"? It is a form of writing in which *all* the play-

---

[10] The English text of the words to which it is sung by the chorus is rendered by Ernest Newman in his *More Stories of Famous Operas* (New York: Alfred A. Knopf; 1943), p. 567, as "To the sun in all splendour risen be glory, glory."

[11] Its attribution to Haydn is now questioned by some musicologists, but the content remains of its own distinction.

ers bear an equal share of the performance load, and in which the give and take of expression assumes the highest technical proficiency from each of the four. This equality of requirement makes a new, unified *instrument* of what had been an uneven assemblage of players. As employed for the swirl and richness of textures that make up the Razumovskys, the string quartet was an instrument of which Beethoven was the creator as certainly as Adolphe Sax invented the saxophone or Jonas Chickering the full metal plate for the grand piano. The difference is that they devised new mechanical means of achieving a sound image, whereas Beethoven conceived a musical need for which old mechanical means could be broadened and transformed.

The dramatic demonstration can be found in the first measures of the first Razumovsky Quartet, Opus 59, No. 1 (in F). To achieve his objective of a tonal design moving from the depths to the heights of a four-octave span, Beethoven does not hesitate to entrust its crucial first statement to a traditionally weak link in the sonorous chain, the cello. To be sure, this particular Linke (Joseph) was much above the average of his time. But the presumption must be that, by now, Beethoven was following his impulse where it led him, rather than suiting himself to the capacities of a specific performer. It is part of the legend of the birth of these works that Linke, who must have rejoiced at the first opportunity to perform the noble theme with which the F-major Razumovsky Quartet is launched, thought otherwise about the beginning of the scherzando. Its repeated B-flat in the rhythmic pattern ⅜ ♫ ♫| ♫ ♫|♫♫♫♫ |♩ impressed him as some form of joke. It was, indeed, but on a cosmic scale which justified Beethoven's abrupt comment to another non-believer: "They are not for you, but for a later age."[12]

Given the will to work their way through its technical challenges, the performers would find that each of the works asserts an individual character, a musical point of view, an artistic compulsion and sense of purpose rarely found in the best preceding quartets, whether by Haydn, Mozart, or Beethoven himself. Whatever the special character of each work—spaciously dramatic in No. 1, broodingly lyric in No. 2, or classically architectural in No. 3—each achieves a totality of expression as far beyond the scope of any prior quartet as the *Eroica* dwarfs the dimensions of any prior symphony.

Among the details which contribute to a constant sense of new discoveries, fresh devices, and unfamiliar gambits are innovations of construction as well as of expression. One would look in vain for either

---

[12] Thayer-Forbes (1964), I, 409.

a first or a second ending in the opening movement of the F-major, with its grand swinging tune that extends over nineteen measures before it finds a point of rest. There is, in fact, nothing like a repeat sign through the first three movements, which merely means that Beethoven had something new to say each time a theme reappeared.

As in the first movement of the "Appassionata," he bypasses a repetition of any kind. Next comes an Allegretto vivace in which, for the first time in the long history of the menuet and what emerged from it, there is no *Da Capo*, or return to the beginning, after the trio. Rather there is—after the reappearance of the muttering, mysterious opening— a revolving cycle of scherzo and trio elements. Vincent d'Indy doggedly determines this procedure to comprise a variant of sonata form.[13] It is rather more reasonably the two scherzando-two trio sequence which Joseph Kerman plots.[14] In either case, it adds another instance, in this tumultuous time, to Beethoven's precedent-shattering gestures by which composers henceforth, to eternity, were liberated from prior conventions. It also opened the way for even more intricate extensions of scherzo-trio liberties in his own works, such as the B-flat Piano Sonata (Opus 106) and the E-flat Quartet (Opus 127). In the excitement of this innovation —and its subsequent reverberation in the works of Schumann, Brahms, Dvořák, Bruckner, Mahler, etc.—there might be some temptation to overlook others. Mention must be made, at least, of the enharmonic change (at measure 180) of the Menuet by which A-sharp—again, the questing ♪♪♪♪♪ |♩ figure !—becomes B-flat across the barline. This opens a whole new vista of key connections and points a way that Schubert was quick to follow. As a final detail, the slow movement proceeds directly to the Thème Russe finale without interruption.

In the E-minor (Opus 59, No. 2) the prevailing lyric bias gives rise to an inversion of the "classic" dualism of first and second subjects, as exemplified in both the *Eroica* and the C-minor symphonies. In it, the more dramatic impulse follows rather than leads, resulting in a swing from passive to active, rather than active to passive.

As for the sublime slow movement, commentators without number have undertaken to define its character in words, beginning with Bee-thoven himself. It was to his younger friend and disciple Carl Czerny that Beethoven conveyed the experience that had prompted music of such extraordinary serenity and breadth: contemplation of the celestial dome on a particularly starry night. This analogy achieved a new shade

[13] Vincent d'Indy: *Beethoven: A Critical Biography* (Boston: Boston Music Co.; 1912), p. 44.
[14] Kerman: *The Beethoven Quartets*, p. 101.

of meaning to me through a parallel unearthed by Martin Cooper in the research that produced his Beethoven book.[15] From the writings of Johann Michael Sailer, theologian, Bishop of Regensburg, and author of three books found in Beethoven's library, Cooper has culled the observation: "It is one and the same artistic impulse that sees in the night sky Nature's own great cathedral and conceives and produces St. Peter's in Rome, St. Paul's in London, the Stephanskirche in Vienna and the Frauenkirche in Munich." This overlap of identities might have subtly impelled Beethoven to recall the second movement of the second Razumovsky Quartet when it became necessary for him to deal with the musical problem of the Benedictus in the *Missa Solemnis* (see p. 250).

This great central movement of the central work of the Opus 59 quartets tends to overshadow the movements that follow. But, in its own way, and without regard for such an apogee of expression, the C-major (Opus 59, No. 3) is a marvel of sonority, a landmark of sound in its own right. As many as eight voices are heard simultaneously in the first movement, as Beethoven commands double stops from all four instruments (at measure 40). (This device found a later fulfillment in the E-flat, Opus 127, Quartet.) The Andante con moto quasi allegretto reinvents the song without words, in the same key of A minor and with much the same intimation of Mendelssohn's *Italian* Symphony as was noted on page 128 in conjunction with the Opus 28 Piano Sonata. Kerman refers to its "Brahmsian codetta."[16] This would be an inevitable association with a movement which pioneered the formulation of "quasi" frequently employed by Brahms. In order to justify it, the music must have something of a dual character as, for example, in the third movement of Brahms' Second Symphony, then, now, and forever called Allegretto grazioso, quasi andantino.

As for the fugal finale, it could well have been born out of a retrospect to Mozart's employment of fugal techniques in the finales of his G-major (K.387) Quartet and the C-major (*Jupiter*) Symphony, as well as in the *Zauberflöte* overture. Beethoven borrows from them the capacity latent in successive entries and imitations for building momentum and excitement, but adds his own intellectual energy and spiritual animation. Here Beethoven surveys the whole range of contrapuntal writing and selects from it what is of advantage to a movement that is basically homophonic. He is, in effect, carrying forward the impulse that urged him to attach a fugal finale to the E-flat Variations of Opus 35. In the

---

[15] Martin Cooper: *Beethoven: The Last Decade* (London: Oxford University Press; 1970), p. 113 and *n*.
[16] Kerman: *The Beethoven Quartets* p. 148.

future are such great expositions of fugal possibilities as the massive conclusion of the B-flat Piano Sonata (Opus 106, "Hammerklavier") and the Grosse Fuge of the B-flat Quartet (Opus 130).

In all of them, Beethoven bestrides, controls, and directs an onrushing surge of music hardly ever equaled by a predecessor and rarely excelled by a successor. The vitality, aliveness, and compulsion of the impulse they contain are uniquely Beethoven's: as totalities, they resound with references to the past, glorifications of the present, and pre-echoes of the future. They stand as absolutes of achievement, not to be likened to, compared with, or measured against anything that followed. They are landmarks as well as signposts—a badge of distinction that can be awarded to few works by anyone at any time.

4

IF THE RAZUMOVSKY QUARTETS show Beethoven at his most musically compelling, his urge to master the problems of dramatic construction exhibit him at his most humanly endearing. Where the involvement was essentially instrumental, as in the *Coriolanus* or *Egmont* overtures—or even the *Leonores*—he was expanding, enlarging, solidifying prior inclinations and aptitudes (see p. 76). Where the problem took in vocal as well as orchestral elements, the glow of the footlights as well as the heat of a human dilemma, he was venturing into new terrain, challenging uncertain means as well as an unfamiliar path. As tended to be the lifelong case with Beethoven, the overriding consideration remained: achievement of the objective. How long it might take or how much effort might be required was not merely incidental—such consideration was all but non-existent.

The history of *Fidelio* (1804–14) is, of all his involvements, an unequaled example of an insatiable, unappeasable urge to rise superior to any problem. It was inherent in the condition of being born Beethoven that a problem existed in order to be solved—not half solved, or partially solved, or solved "up to a point." It had to be solved to a degree of satisfaction that would have worn out the patience of almost any colleague of whom there is record.

The creation of *Fidelio* is also a prime example of the futility of trying to compartment Beethoven's output into such divisions as early, middle, or late. It has already been demonstrated that Beethoven was writing music of *Fidelio* quality in 1790, when most of the works von Lenz assigned to the category of "early" were yet to be born. Much of the basic work on the enduring content of *Fidelio* was crowded into the years between 1804 and 1806, in the high noon of the "middle" period.

But the final, clinching spurts of creation which gave to the score the interpretative highlights for which audiences sit in expectation today were not joined into place until 1814. These include Florestan's vision of "Ein Engel, Leonoren" in his second-act outburst, the heartrending apostrophe to "Freiheit" as the prisoners are driven back to their cells near the end of Act I,[17] and the noble invocation to "Brüder seine Brüder" in the finale of Act II (p. 611 in the Eulenburg miniature score). If one wonders at the omission of Leonore's denunciation of Pizarro beginning "Abscheulicher!", this is an epic of creation in itself (see p. 193). By the time Beethoven finally got the concluding pages of *Fidelio* to sound the way he wanted them to sound, he was closer to fulfilling his aspiration to set Schiller's "Freude" than to the initial impulse contained in the opera.

The whole tortuous process by which *Fidelio* was eventually accomplished has been traced in closer detail by Winton Dean than by any other writer in English.[18] (Willy Hess's classic *Beethovens Oper Fidelio und ihre drei Fassungen* [Zürich: Atlantis Verlag; 1953] has not yet found an English translator.) For the non-German public with a passion for minutiae, Dean's treatise is unsurpassed. My small quibble would be with with his title: "Beethoven and Opera." In any large sense, *Fidelio* is no more an "opera" than *Don Giovanni*, *Norma*, or *Otello* —none of them described by its composer as an opera. Indeed, *Fidelio* is not particularly a "theatrical" work, but it is an intensely dramatic one. The component values of the text are so special that Beethoven spent the last twenty years of his life seeking a counterpart to compose, and ended up rejecting all of those suggested, from writers as eminent as Collin, Rellstab, and Grillparzer.

It is elementary information about *Fidelio* that Beethoven wrote four overtures to serve the same subject: the three *Leonores* and the final effort to which he grudgingly gave the title *Fidelio*.[19] It is less

---

[17] See chart, pp. 190–1.

[18] Denis Arnold and Nigel Fortune, eds.: *The Beethoven Reader* (New York: W. W. Norton; 1971), pp. 331–86.

[19] It was Beethoven's preference from the first that the work be called *Leonore* in tribute to its heroine. For the Viennese producers this was uncomfortably close not only to the title of the French work by J. N. Bouilly—*Lénore ou L'amour conjugal*—on which Beethoven's was based, but another by Paër called *Leonora*. The composer had his way when the first piano reduction, published in 1810 (and based on the version of 1806), bore the title *Leonore*. By 1814, when the second revival brought on the bright, vivacious curtain raiser in E now known as the "*Fidelio*" Overture and universally preferred for that purpose, Beethoven was reconciled to the inevitable.

THE FORMS OF FIDELIO

ORIGINAL SEQUENCE (1805)	INTERMEDIATE (1806)
Overture *Leonore* No. 2 (No. 1 already discarded*).	Overture *Leonore* No. 3.**

ACT I	ACT I
No. 1 Aria: Marzelline: "O wär' ich schon mit dir Vereint."	No. 1 Aria (as before).
No. 2 Duet: Marzelline and Jacquino: "Jetzt, Schätzchen."	No. 2 Duet (as before).
No. 3 Trio: Marzelline, Jacquino, and Rocco: "Ein Mann ist bald genommen."	Omitted.
No. 4 Quartet: preceding, plus Fidelio: "Mir ist so wunderbar."	No. 3 Quartet (No. 4 in 1805 version).
No. 5 Aria: Rocco: "Hat man nicht auch Gold beineben."	Omitted.
No. 6 Trio: Marzelline, Rocco, and Fidelio: "Gut, Söhnchen, gut."	No. 4 Trio (No. 6 in 1805 version).

ACT II	
No. 7 March.	No. 5 March (No. 7 in 1805 version).
No. 8 Aria: Pizarro: "Ha, welch' ein Augenblick!"	No. 6 Aria (No. 8 in 1805 version).
No. 9 Duet: Pizarro and Rocco: "Jetzt, Alter, jetzt."	No. 7 Duet (No. 9 in 1805 version).

* *Leonore* No. 1 did not include the syncopated figure derived from Sonata, Opus 2, No. 1, nor the trumpet call. The phrase later associated with "Ein Engel, Leonoren" is heard at the end of the Overture but not in the vocal aria.

** *Leonore* No. 2 does include the syncopated figure. The use in No. 3 is much more extended. A trumpet call utilized, but *not* in the form in which it became famous. "Ein Engel, Leonoren," is included.

THE FORMS OF FIDELIO

FINAL (1814)	COMMENT (1814)
Overture *Fidelio.****	Not ready for May 1814; *The Ruins of Athens* used instead.

ACT I

No. 1   Duet: Marzelline and Jacquino: "Jetzt, Schätzchen" (No. 2 in previous versions).

No. 2   Aria: Marzelline: "O wär' ich schon mit dir Vereint" (No. 1 in previous versions).

Omitted.

No. 3   Quartet: Marzelline, Jacquino, Rocco, and Fidelio: "Mir ist so wunderbar" (No. 4 in 1805 version, No. 3 in 1806 version).

No. 4   Aria: Rocco: "Hat man nicht auch Gold beineben" (No. 5 in 1805 version, omitted from 1806 version).

No. 5   Trio: Marzelline, Rocco, and Fidelio: "Gut, Söhnchen, gut" (No. 6 in 1805 version, No. 4 in 1806 version).

No. 6   March (No. 7 in 1805 version, No. 5 in 1806 version).

No. 7   Aria: Pizarro: "Ha, welch' ein Augenblick!" (No. 8 in 1805 version, No. 6 in 1806 version).

No. 8   Duet: Pizarro and Rocco: "Jetzt, Alter, jetzt" (No. 9 in 1805 version, No. 7 in 1806 version).

*** *Fidelio* Overture included in performance of May 26, 1814 (first performance was on May 23).

THE FORMS OF FIDELIO

ORIGINAL SEQUENCE (1805)	INTERMEDIATE (1806)
No. 10 Duet: Marzelline and Fidelio: "Um in der Ehe froh zu leben."	Omitted.
No. 11 Recitative and Aria: Fidelio: "Ach, brich noch nicht, du mattes Herz . . . Komm' Hoffnung."	No. 8 Recitative and Aria (No. 11 in 1805 version).
No. 12 Finale: Chorus: "O welche Lust"; Fidelio and Rocco: "Nun sprecht . . . Wir müssen gleich zu Werke schreiten"; Quartet: preceding plus Marzelline and Pizarro: "Ach! Vater, eilt"; Pizarro and Chorus: "Auf euch nur will ich bauen."	No. 9 Finale (much as No. 12 in 1805 version).

ACT III	ACT II
No. 13 Introduction and Aria: Florestan: "Gott! welch' Dunkel hier! . . . In des Lebens Frühlingstagen."	No. 10 Introduction and Aria (No. 13 in 1805 version).
No. 14 Melodrama and Duet: Fidelio and Rocco: "Nur hurtig fort, nur frisch gegraben."	No. 11 Melodrama and Duet (No. 14 in 1805 version).
No. 15 Trio: preceding, plus Pizarro: "Euch werde Lohn."	No. 12 Trio (No. 15 in 1805 version).
No. 16 Quartet: preceding, plus Florestan: "Er sterbe!"	No. 13 Quartet (No. 16 in 1805 version).
No. 17 Duet: Fidelio and Florestan: "O namenlose Freude."	No. 14 Duet (No. 17 in 1805 version).
No. 18 Finale: Don Fernando, Pizarro, Rocco, Florestan, Fidelio, Marzelline, Jacquino, and Chorus: "Zur Rache! . . . O Gott, o welch' ein Augenblick!"; Chorus: "Wer ein holdes Weib errungen."	No. 15 Finale (expanded from 1805 version).

The Forms of Fidelio

FINAL (1814)	COMMENT (1814)
No. 9 Recitative and Aria: Fidelio: "Abscheulicher!",**** followed by "Komm' Hoffnung."	Not ready for first performances. See below.****
No. 10 Finale.	Much expanded over prior Finales, including return of prisoners from garden, not present in *either* previous version.

**** "Abscheulicher!" was not included in its present form until June 1814. In earlier performances of this revival the words were used, but not in their later form, and "Komm' Hoffnung" was omitted.

ACT II

No. 11 Introduction and Aria: Florestan: "Gott! welch' Dunkel hier! . . . In des Lebens Frühlingstagen" (No. 13 in 1805 version, No. 10 in 1806 version).	Much expanded, including E-flat section and vision of "Ein Engel, Leonoren."
No. 12 Melodrama and Duet: Fidelio and Rocco: "Wie kalt ist es . . . Nur hurtig fort, nur frisch gegraben" (No. 14 in 1805 version, No. 11 in 1806 version).	Expanded version of preceding scenes.
No. 13 Trio: preceding, plus Pizarro: "Euch werde Lohn" (No. 15 in 1805 version, No. 12 in 1806 version).	
No. 14 Quartet: preceding, plus Florestan: "Er sterbe!" (No. 16 in 1805 version, No. 13 in 1806 version).	
No. 15 Duet: Fidelio and Florestan: "O namenlose Freude" (No. 17 in 1805 version, No. 14 in 1806 version).	
No. 16 Finale: Don Fernando, Pizarro, Rocco, Florestan, Fidelio, Marzelline, Jacquino, and Chorus.	Much expanded, to include "Heil sei dem Tag," "Brüder," etc.

generally understood that there were, in actuality, three "operas" to go with the four overtures. Little wonder, then, that the anomaly of a masterpiece being born of two aborted efforts is generally unknown.

The failure of the first version has often been attributed to the circumstances of its introduction in the Theater-an-der-Wien (a structure still in use in Vienna). The date was November 20, 1805, shortly after the city had been occupied by French troops. This is rather more charity than the work deserves. Doubtless the absence from the city of the aristocracy partial to Beethoven deprived him of a sympathetic hearing. The French officers who filled the theater were none too indulgent of the work's shortcomings. But these were indeed of crucial importance. Had the project been abandoned at this point, the judgment of history most likely would have been that what was good in the music had been fatally disserved by Beethoven's lack of dramatic competence.

As the accompanying chart depicts (pp. 190–3), some 60 percent of the music now associated with *Fidelio* remained steadfastly in the score from 1805 to 1814 and thereafter. It can, indeed, be heard when a reconstruction of the 1805 score[20] is occasionally given at a festival. But the enduring music, in a first miscalculation, was spread over three acts, with two intermissions, and the subplot, involving the jailer's daughter and her suitor, Jaquino, occupied overmuch of the listener's attention in both the first and second acts of the original. This tends to give it a prolonged *kleinbürgerlich* character, and to distract attention from the drama of self-sacrifice with which Fidelio-Leonore and her spouse, the political prisoner Florestan, are associated. Pizarro does not appear until Act II, and the finales to both the first and second acts are inconclusive. For that matter, the theatergoer attuned to the agitation in Florestan's "In des Lebens Frühlingstagen" in its full form would hardly recognize it as it was first conceived.

When Beethoven's aristocratic partisans returned to Vienna later in the winter, a concentrated effort was undertaken to bring about the revival of a revised *Fidelio*. Among the efforts expended was a six-hour session in the palace of the Prince Lichnowsky in which his wife, Marie Christine (née Thun), presided at the piano as the work was reviewed in the presence of the composer. The objective of the well-meaning participants was to persuade Beethoven to accept the elimination of three sections of the score and the contraction of the three acts into

---

[20] The score had to be reconstructed for an anniversary publication of 1905 rather than reproduced, because no full manuscript of the first version is extant. It was dismembered to bring about the 1806 version, which was published in 1810.

two. The second concession was easier to accomplish than the first. He finally agreed to the deletion of a terzetto for Rocco, Jaquino, and Marzelline, and her second duet with Jaquino. Both of these, though attractive, were expendable. But Rocco's "Gold" aria, which is more than attractive, was also stricken out, to the detriment of the 1806 version. On his own, Beethoven put himself out to rewrite the *Leonore* Overture No. 2[21] and produced the symphonic colossus known as the *Leonore* No. 3. It was admired when it was introduced on March 29, 1806, but also considered inappropriate to the position it occupied. As a curtain raiser, it almost made the raising of the curtain superfluous.

Fidelio, or *Leonore* II, with its *Leonore* No. 3 Overture, might have remained this way, a magnificently mottled and muddled non-solution of a problem cursed through history by the composer's inability to make the most of his best ideas. But further performances were summarily forbidden by Beethoven himself. This was not by reasoned judgment of its shortcomings, but through the intercession of purely mercenary motives. A suspicion that he was not receiving the earnings to which he was entitled caused Beethoven to demand his property from the producers. He also rejected suggestions for performances elsewhere (Prague and Berlin in particular). The episodes deleted from the original score were published separately in 1807. A piano vocal score of the 1806 version, edited by Beethoven's devoted friend Carl Czerny, was finally published in 1810 (see p. 189, *n.* 19).

Nothing more of *Fidelio* might have been heard in the composer's lifetime had not three artists of the Viennese operatic community petitioned Beethoven to permit them to present the work as a benefit (on their own behalves) in 1814. He agreed, with the proviso that they would give it with the revisions he felt to be necessary. It was only then that Beethoven, his initial (1806) heated objection to changes cooled by passage of time, was able to view the whole project more objectively than before.

More objectivity, however, did not include either detachment or disinterest. Rather, he immersed himself in an unqualified effort to "think out the entire work again"[22] and make the whole worthy of its greatest pages. At times the effort to redo the old score must have seemed greater than the challenge to create a new one. Due in part to the collaboration of Georg Friedrich Treitschke, a poet, playwright, and man-about-theaters in Vienna, the dramatic sequence was greatly

---

[21] No. 1 had been discarded before the 1805 première.
[22] Anderson: *The Letters of Beethoven*, I, 479. No. 479.

strengthened, the emotional involvement of the audience tightened, and the dialogue made more explicit.

By the time of its première on May 23, 1814, in the Kärnthnerthor Theater, much had been done to consolidate the best of old and new. Rocco's "Gold" aria had been restored, the overpowering *Leonore* Overture No. 3 had been deleted in favor of a shorter, lighter work more congruent with the first scenes in the jailer's quarters. However, it was not until several days after the opening that the new overture was completed. At the first performances, the *Ruins of Athens* introduction was probably offered instead. Eventually, which is to say in mid-July, Beethoven finally cast into its frigidly molten, ever-reheatable form, Leonore's denunciation of Pizzaro, together with "Komm' Hoffnung" as it now exists.[23] Thus, with major changes in the finales of both acts—at the end of Act I, the prisoners were led back to their cells under Pizarro's ruthless mandate, and the end of Act II was expanded from a glorification of Leonore and Florestan to a hymn on behalf of all mankind— the full span of the dramatic arch for which *Fidelio* is esteemed today was finally in place. Its realization had cost Beethoven untold anguish over most of a decade.

It is worthy of mention that, unlike some other composers who started with a nuclear element of an opera in hand and worked from it to a totality—Charpentier wrote "Depuis le jour" before he undertook the rest of *Louise*; Wagner worked backward, in *Lohengrin*, from the Bridal Chamber Scene of Act III; and Verdi had the exquisite pleasure of knowing that *Falstaff* was headed for the final fugue on "Tutte nel mondo è burla" *before* he set a note of the beginning—Beethoven earned the fulfillment of "Abscheulicher!" as the reward of ten years' involvement.

5

IN OTHER ASPECTS, *Fidelio* had, of course, engaged him for much longer. Dean, in the essay previously mentioned, honors all possible considerations by describing the inclusion of the excerpt from the *Cantata on the Death of Emperor Joseph II* as "a tribute to the continuity of Beethoven's development."[24] It is also worthy of mention that another of the emotional crests of *Fidelio* was conceived independently of that

---

[23] The text of "Abscheulicher!" was utilized in the early performances of 1814, but with a different musical setting than the now-familiar one, and without "Komm' Hoffnung."

[24] Arnold and Fortune: *The Beethoven Reader*, p. 355.

subject, before the sketches of late 1803 led to the elaborations of 1804 and the premiere of 1805. It is the passionate outburst on the words "O namenlose Freude," in which Florestan and Leonore celebrate their joy at his release from bondage by her selfless action. When it first occurred to Beethoven, it was for an opera titled *Vestas Feuer*. In that form it is cited by Nottebohm[25] as:

Nie_ war_ ich_ so _ frich wie heu - te

As appropriated for the purpose in which it became famous, it was altered to:

O   na - men, na - men - lo - se Freu - de!

Another element of considerable importance can be traced to the sketches for the G-major Concerto (No. 4, Opus 58), on which Beethoven was working in 1804. Among them is this figuration marked Finale:

The first two measures are marked for repetition, with the bassoon joining the second time. The pattern then is led to the subdominant. The substance of the sketch is the basis for the Prisoners' Chorus near the end of Act I in *Fidelio*. Here the bassoon begins the melodic line and the clarinet takes it at the repetition, going on thereafter to the pattern as projected:

[25] Nottebohm: *Ein Skizzenbuch von Beethoven aus dem Jahre* 1803, pp. 86–94.

Much is made in the literature of *Fidelio* (and its eventual emergence as a work of uniquely hypnotic appeal) of the effect on the drama of Stephan von Breuning's participation in the reshaping of 1806, and the even more decisive contribution of Treitschke in 1814. Credit to both may be awarded liberally. But some attention should also be directed to the heightening of Beethoven's own dramatic sense through the involvements that produced the *Coriolanus* Overture (for the play of Heinrich Joseph von Collin), and the even more elaborate overture, incidental music, and *Siegessymphonie* (*Triumphal Symphony*) for Goethe's *Egmont*. Each was a proving ground of his capacity to concentrate, compress, and energize dramatic values within minimum playing time. Both served to make the Beethoven of 1814 far more qualified to improve the unexpected opportunity to work a third time on the problem of *Fidelio* than he had been the second time. The results were purchased at a cost he characterized as equivalent to a "martyr's crown," but the effort eventually came to be reckoned worth his time artistically if not financially.

It was on July 18, 1814, that all the pieces were finally in place for a performance—appropriately enough—for the composer's benefit. It was in this form that it was repeated in the fall, for a total of more than a dozen times. Another series of performances, in 1822, doubtless contributed to the high esteem, almost veneration, the composer enjoyed in Vienna in the last years of his life from a public that knew little of his more recondite instrumental works. But a full score was not published until 1826, in Paris. This version, with a French text more prominently printed than the original German, embodied the revisions of 1814 but perversely divided the drama into three acts, as it had been in 1805![26] This may explain why, for decades to come, *Fidelio* was performed in many world capitals with two intermissions.

Perhaps the first, immediate response to Beethoven's labors of 1814 may be heard in the greatest work of Carl Maria von Weber, who died a little more than ten years later (June 5, 1826). It was in 1813 that Weber, aged twenty-seven, was appointed conductor of German opera in Prague. Here his distinguished repertory included *Fidelio* for the first time on November 27, 1814.[27] In 1817, Weber achieved the eminence of the Royal Opera Theater in Dresden, launching a tradition which fueled the fire of Richard Wagner, and later of Richard Strauss.

As a composer, Weber reached historic eminence with the production of *Der Freischütz* in Berlin in 1821. Whether one was aware of the chronology or not, the sequence of happenings could be read in the dramatic demands that Weber put upon Agathe in *Der Freischütz*, Euryanthe of Savoy in *Euryanthe*, and Rezia in *Oberon*. Or if such a generalized statement is unconvincing, consider the specific demands of the most dramatic scenes for Fidelio-Leonore and for Agathe. Both utilize obbligato horn passages to intensify drama, both find the key of E central to the terminal high note, and the point of departure is clearly a chordal flourish for Weber, as it had been for Beethoven before him.

---

[26] An authentic orchestral score did not appear until the collected edition of Beethoven's works sponsored by Breitkopf and Härtel reached series 20 (Dramatic Works) in 1864.

[27] John Warrack: *Carl Maria von Weber* (New York: Macmillan; 1968), p. 157.

FIDELIO

All' mei - ne Pul - se _ schla - gen, und das Herz _ wallt _ un - ge -
How ev - 'ry pulse is _ fly - ing, And my heart _ beats _ loud _ and _

stüm süss ent - zückt ent -
fast, We shall _____ meet in _____

DER FREISCHÜTZ (*continued*)

ge - - gen ihm, _____
joy _____ at last, _____

DER FREISCHÜTZ

How deeply Weber felt about *Fidelio* may be observed from the effort he expended to make his Dresden production of April 29, 1823, of the highest possible quality. He sought out the young, nineteen-year-old Wilhelmine Schröder, who had succeeded Milder in Beethoven's favor (she sang both Leonore and Agathe in Vienna in 1822) to be the central support of his cast. As Schröder-Devrient she became the legendary Leonore to a generation of music lovers. Among them was Richard Wagner, for whom she was not only a peerless Leonore, but his choice to be the first Adriano in *Rienzi*, the first Senta in *Der fliegende Holländer*, and the first Venus in *Tannhäuser*.[28] The link from Beethoven to Wagner through Weber could hardly be more direct.

In his valuable biography of Weber, Warrack identifies a number of other responses of Weber to the example of Beethoven and *Fidelio*. Of special interest are the similarities he draws between the treatment of Pizarro's vengeful "Ha! welch' ein Augenblick" in Act I of *Fidelio* and its echo in Caspar's "Schweig! Schweig!" in *Der Freischütz*.[29]

The admiration of Schumann and Berlioz for *Fidelio* is perhaps better known from their comments in words rather than their responses in tones, both men, of course, being pioneering critics as well as great composers. Berlioz wrote repeatedly of his great admiration for *Fidelio*, typically in *Evenings with the Orchestra*, in which he has one enthusiast say to another: "That music sets your insides on fire. I feel as if I'd swallowed fifteen glasses of brandy."[30]

[28] *Baker's Biographical Dictionary*, ed. Nicholas Slonimsky (New York: G. Schirmer; 1958), pp. 1,462–3.
[29] Warrack: *Carl Maria von Weber*, p. 220.
[30] Hector Berlioz: *Evenings with the Orchestra*, trans, and ed., with Introduction and notes, by Jacques Barzun (New York: Alfred A. Knopf; 1956), p. 187.

Schumann's most eloquent accolade to *Fidelio* was evolved in the aftermath of hearing all four overtures performed at a Leipzig concert directed by Mendelssohn. After examining each in turn he summarized: "Such is the great Four-Ouverture work. Formed after the manner of Nature, we first find it in the roots from which, in the second, the giant trunk arises, stretching its arms right and left, and finally completed by its leafy crown."[31] Only a composer-critic possessed of Schumann's dual capacities could have so happily related the buoyant beauty of the *Fidelio* overture to its antecedents. Or have reminded us how a "martyr's crown" (see p. 199) could be transmitted into "a leafy crown."

Musically, both Schumann and Berlioz responded to the example of such works for orchestra as the *Coriolanus* and *Egmont* overtures more than to *Fidelio*. Schumann wrote nothing rightfully to be called a music drama, and Berlioz found his precepts more in the French literature than in the German. But Schumann's *Manfred* Overture and Berlioz's *Corsair* both sail under the colors of Beethoven's orchestra, with its capacity for storytelling and the projection of poetic atmosphere as well as the bold concept of dramatizing a play or commemorating a heroic personality in a concert work.

With Wagner, the subject—which is to say Beethoven himself, as well as his creations—was served in every conceivable way: verbally and musically, consciously and unconsciously. It was, indeed, a close connection between several key measures in *Fidelio* and an equally conspicuous passage in *Lohengrin* which set me off on the long pursuit of such relationships that culminated in *The Continuity of Music*.[32] One extension of that relationship has become apparent to me more recently and may be introduced here.

It may be noted in the source cited above that, in his autobiography, Wagner had attributed the impulse for resuming composition in 1840, after a lapse of some months, to "the deep impression the rendering of the Ninth Symphony had made on me when performed in a way I had never dreamed of."[33] This much in the relationship of *Eine Faust-Ouvertüre* to a work of Beethoven was consciously known to Wagner. He did not realize then—or ever, insofar as there is evidence—that

[31] Robert Schumann: *On Music and Musicians*, ed. Konrad Wolff, trans. Paul Rosenfeld (New York: McGraw-Hill paperback; 1964), p. 102. Schumann's comment is not dated, but the concert was attended by the celebrated London critic Henry F. Chorley. His comment on the program in *Modern German Music*, 2 vols. (London: Smith, Elder and Co.; 1854), attributes it to the season of 1839–40.

[32] Kolodin: *The Continuity of Music*, pp. 25–7.

[33] Richard Wagner: *My Life* (New York: Tudor Publishing Co.; 1936), p. 215.

Beethoven was present not only in the spirit but in the letter. The first, brooding theme of the *Faust* Overture is made up of an octave-spanning question, and a troubled response. The question, clearly, is Wagner's own:

But the answer

is no less clearly of the *genus Coriolan*, rephrased from Beethoven's invention depicting the proud, headstrong Roman general

to a proper parallel for the proud, headstrong German philosopher.

Wagner's response to the magnetism, eventually the mystique, of Beethoven generally, and *Fidelio* specifically, persisted for well over a century with such conductor-composers as Richard Strauss and Gustav Mahler. It began earlier and endured longer with Strauss, who, as late as 1932, might have been found conducting *Fidelio* at Salzburg in the company of such kindred spirits as Lotte Lehmann, Franz Völker, Richard Mayr, and Wilhelm Rode. Long before, *Fidelio*'s direct influence—in the construction of *Elektra*—and its indirect influence, through Wagner—in the creation of *Der Rosenkavalier*—were part of Strauss's blood and bone.

With Mahler, the link was largely interpretative. *Fidelio* was part of his re-creative life-pattern long before he became director of the Vienna

Opera in 1897, but it was in connection with a revival of 1904 that his association with the work became sanctified. For this revival, a scenic design was conceived, on a massive scale, by Alfred Roller. It was duplicated in New York for Mahler's revival of March 1908. For both, it became traditional for Mahler to provide time for the conversion of Roller's setting for the dungeon scene into the final tableaux by interpolating a savagely brilliant performance of the *Leonore* Overture No. 3. This has been held, forever after, as Mahler's innovation,[34] though there is quotable evidence to the contrary.

6

WHYFOR THE MAGNETISM, eventually the mystique, of *Fidelio*? What is the secret of its attraction for a host of listeners, or, at least, a host of a certain kind of listener? Is it primarily or even largely related to the noble, self-sacrificing impulse of Leonore on behalf of her imprisoned husband, or, secondarily, to the indoctrinated person's admiration for the long struggle Beethoven waged and, substantially, won? For some, perhaps. But for most others, these are accessories *after* the fact of becoming faithful to *Fidelio*, rather than causative reasons for such a commitment.

The basic compulsion can be observed, reckoned with, and understood by a glance at the audience that is drawn to it at the Metropolitan in New York, Covent Garden in London, or the Colon in Buenos Aires. I cite these locales as outside the German-speaking countries, where annual attendance at *Fidelio* is equivalent to a renewal of marriage vows for a well-mated, musical-minded *Ehepaar*. One will observe a sizable percentage of opera enthusiasts who will go to anything merely because it is sung. But the assemblage is generally filled out, beefed up, intellectually reinforced by a sizable number of others who rarely go to other things *because* they are sung. They respond to *Fidelio* because it is—in proper fulfillment of the sequence that includes the concerto sonata, the heroic symphony, and the symphonic quartet—the first ORCHESTRAL OPERA.

This may strike some as an ignorant, or arrogant, downgrading of Gluck's *Orfeo* and *Alceste*, or the whole canon of Mozart, from *Die Entführung* to *Die Zauberflöte*. In both, the orchestra has not merely an indispensable but also an energizing part in the total result. Does

---

[34] It is identified as a custom begun by Mahler, in Winton Dean's essay, "Beethoven and Opera," in Arnold and Fortune: *The Beethoven Reader*, p. 373, with the addendum "and followed by Toscanini, Klemperer and other conductors." Other "others"—including Anton Seidl—had an equally valid idea previously.

it, however, have a generative part in such a result? Not, to my way of thinking, to the degree that Beethoven's does in *Fidelio*. (The history of the four overtures is sufficient warrant of the importance Beethoven attached to getting right *in the orchestra* what preceded everything else.) To be sure, these are not considerations that can be weighed in the pans of a scale, and measured by a balance of content on one side or the other. They are, rather, considerations that contribute to a state of mind, to a sense of intellectual pressure as well as musical pleasure, to all the extraneous but indispensable values from which emerge the constituents of a conviction.

Just as a successful recipe may be made up of small pinches of this and a tiny infusion of that, as well as of the big basic ingredients which seem the least dispensable, so a work of musical art may be less the sum of its written parts than a whole of what was passing through the composer's mind at the time of its creation. In *Fidelio*, it is of crucial importance that Beethoven's conditioning included an intimate knowledge of Mozart's stage works. It was the "given" of his creative problem, to which he would add the sum of his experience to create a new totality. Though Beethoven professed his dislike for the ethos of *Don Giovanni*, he did not deny himself a flashing saber thrust of strings as a means to a dramatic end, whether or not the saber was originally in the hands of the dissolute Don.

Unlike Mozart, who was conditioned by the audiences for whom he wrote to deal with Counts and Countesses, Dons and Donnas, or mythological kings and queens, Beethoven in *Fidelio* addressed himself to a social stratum barely recognized by Mozart (Zerlina and Masetto in *Don Giovanni*, Susanna and Figaro in *Le Nozze di Figaro*), and hardly extolled by him. Beethoven's characters, perhaps for the first time in a serious work for the musical stage, are ordinary people with ordinary problems—or relatively so.

Let it be granted that the ordinary wife concerned for the well-being of an imprisoned husband would not be likely to risk mortal harm by masquerading as a male. But the wife for whom Beethoven might have reverence certainly would, as did the French wife on whom Bouilly constructed the story largely reproduced in the text of *Fidelio*.[35] That the action responsive to Beethoven's need is set in Spain rather than France was typical of the relocation practiced for political reasons in the stage works of the time (the French version of *Fidelio* published in 1826 places the action in Germany!). Here, in fact, is a primitive *verismo*, long before the tortuous progress through a century of Italian

[35] Arnold and Fortune: *The Beethoven Reader*, see Winton Dean's essay, "Beethoven and Opera," pp. 340 *ff.*

opera brought about a climate of receptivity in which a *Wozzeck* could be acclaimed.

Thus the magnetism and the mystique of *Fidelio* may be centralized, localized, and concentrated at the point of confluence of two powerful streams: a concern for the affairs and involvements besetting persons recognizably real; and a musical enrichment from which no subtlety or resource, including a canon quartet, is excluded. To them is added a precious ingredient, a special kind of seasoning all Beethoven's own, a pinch of flavor which can best be described as the salt of the earth.

The last named is contained in the rough, potent humor of Beethoven himself, his enkindling response to human distress, his abhorrence of injustice, his compelling belief that rank is an accident of birth and superiority a condition of the person who demonstrates it. These may be values superimposed, through decades of familiarity, upon *Fidelio*, as moss and vines become parts of old, stately trees. They add beauty to the whole only to the extent that the understructure can support them.

There are those, of course, to whom all this is extraneous, beside the point, insufficient compensation for spending an evening minus a hummable tune, a ballet divertissement, or eye-filling spectacle. With all his admiration for the musical content of *Fidelio*, Berlioz thought the idea of a stage work that took place entirely in a prison was depressing to begin with. The anti-Fidelians are, for the most part, people rarely seen at symphony concerts unless the program offered an eminent soloist. They could scarcely understand a conversation that J. B. Förster, a friend of Mahler's, recalls after a performance with the great Katherine Klafsky as Leonore (in 1897). " 'You place *Fidelio* ahead of everything, even the works of Wagner?' Mahler asked. 'Yes, ahead of everything,' replied Förster. Mahler embraced him and said, 'We think alike. We'll always remain friends.' "[36]

Fidelio remains a vitalizing infusion of power, realism, and musical satisfaction in the repertory of an art form that can use every drop of such sustenance it can command. It lends dignity and compassion to any occasion of which it is an adornment, as it has given encouragement to the aspirations of any composer whose ideals rise above the trivial. That it offers employment to much the same kind of principals as *Wozzeck* may be purely coincidental. Nobody is compelled to love one because he loves the other, though it is by no means infrequent. But it is a condition transcending time that Beethoven's persistence, as well as his initiative, did to some extent make Berg's breakthrough possible.

[36] Henry-Louis de La Grange: *Mahler*, Vol. I (Garden City, N.Y.: Doubleday; 1973), p. 381.

XI

The Last of the Crop

I

THE DATES 1804–14, which bracket Beethoven's commitment to *Fidelio,* form a parenthesis around the beginning and ending of the harvest from the seeds and shoots that gave rise to the *Eroica* and everything that followed. Chronologically, the years carried Beethoven from hardly more than thirty (he was, in his estimate, thirty-two when the *Eroica* was written) to a riper forty-plus. Emotionally, they ranged from a time in which he still considered himself a possible—indeed, an eager—candidate for matrimony to an awareness that he would, in all probability, never know the union of equals for which he yearned. Physically they began with Beethoven a versatile creator–re-creator, able to assume an occasional if increasingly infrequent part in the public performance of what he wrote. They ended in his all but total withdrawal from the public arena under the pressure of an irreversible handicap.

Musically, the decade was not only the most productive of his life, but one barely challenged by any composer in history. To be sure, in their most productive decades Mozart wrote more piano concertos, more operas and string quartets, and Haydn wrote more symphonies. But neither extended so systematically the perimeters of the art forms to which he addressed himself. Specialists might know which of a half-dozen Mozart piano concertos was first, fourth, or sixth in the sequence of composition or whether Haydn's Symphony No. 88 preceded No. 83, or if the *Miracle* (No. 96, in D) was written in Paris or London. But as the work-by-work discussion has demonstrated, there are values and concepts in the Fifth Symphony which broaden the symphonic concept of the *Eroica*; and no moderately well-versed chamber music enthusiast could possibly confuse the order of growth by which the saplings of Opus 18 evolved into the stand of musical timber exemplified by the three quartets of Opus 59.

But even the most committed Beethovenian could not contend that this progression continued onward and upward, ever and unceasingly. Thayer, one of the most committed of such devotees, points to 1810 as the beginning of a decade which marks "an astonishing decrease in the composer's productiveness."[1] He does, to be sure, qualify this judgment by measuring this decade against the accomplishments of the preceding decade. On the other hand, if one regards Beethoven's compositional career as a totality rather than as a series of time spans, the "Decrease in Productivity," as Chapter XIII of Thayer's matchless work is headed, was accompanied by an interior growth as remarkable as the works which came into being because of it.

Indeed, as Thayer himself marks 1814 as a "marvelous year," to be set apart from the otherwise fallow ones before and after, perhaps there is something in which year one chooses as a point of departure. Certainly a year in which the slag and cinders of *Fidelio* were re-fused in the intellectual furnace to forge a new, highly resilient entity can hardly be included in a cycle of nonproductivity. I would cite *Fidelio* as the key example of the *ending* of a prior period of productivity rather than as an interruption of a stagnant one. It fleshes out, fulfills, brings to a rounded realization a host of ideas that had been set in motion previously. In the nature of things, it is the last of an old cycle rather than in any respect a foreshadowing of a new.

Indeed, *Fidelio* shares with almost all the music realized by Beethoven, up to and including it, the characteristic of being an organic outgrowth of the many cells and entities alluded to, mentioned, or described on pages 108–38. What Beethoven was throwing out as elements incidental to an early sonata, quartet, or symphony were seeds of both the youthful abundance and the mature harvest that followed. It would take another cycle of introspection, germination, and evolution to develop them fully.

It is an interrelated part of this productivity that a full list of the works born, bred, and matured between 1804 and 1814 includes several of historic importance which have not been touched

[1] Thayer-Forbes (1964), I, 483.

upon to this point. They range through the familiar categories of symphony, quartet, trio, and sonata (both solo and duo) of which much has been said in the prior discussion. They tend to "follow on" lines of development previously projected rather than to break new ground of their own. In some instances, they revert to procedures and practices one would have thought the composer had outgrown. But Beethoven did not think so and that is the reality with which we are confronted.

It was among the happenings of this decade, when everything included in Beethoven's first one hundred opus numbers had been published or contracted for publication, that the idea of a "Complete Edition" of his works began to stir. An extraordinary phenomenon to be considered during any composer's lifetime, it can hardly be argued that eight symphonies, sonatas by the dozens, concertos, quartets, and trios in profusion were insufficient for such a project. To one publisher who made such a suggestion, his old friend Simrock of Bonn days, Beethoven wrote: "Regarding the edition of my complete works we believe here that it would be good to add a *new work* to each type of composition; e.g., to the variations a new work of this kind, to the sonatas, each, etc. etc. . . ."[2]

Though never articulated in so many words, Beethoven's procedure during the years in which his productivity was at its height, up to and including 1814, was very much on this pattern. Had such a complete edition been projected somewhat earlier, the Symphony No. 7, the quartets (Opus 74 or Opus 95), the Violin Sonata (Opus 96), and the B-flat Trio (Opus 97) could have been enthusiastically accepted as "a new work" added to "each type of composition" then in being.

It would be foolhardy to downgrade the Seventh Symphony as an "appendage" to Nos. 5 and 6, or the Eighth as an "echo" of anything that had preceded it. But neither masterpiece attains its rank through the innovative impulses that characterize the Fifth and Sixth. The Seventh is one of the nine I relish hearing more often than three or four others; but that is because of the orchestral means it disposes, the sheer impact of the energy it generates, the titanic wave of sound that it sets in motion rather than for such breathless excitement aroused by the sense of a new world being born as accompanies any proper performance of No. 5. The intent and character of the Seventh is defined as early as the first chord, which proclaims a sonorous experience unlike any other to that time. From the low A in the bass to high A in

[2] Ibid., II, 763. August 5, 1820.

the flute, it covers a full five octaves, or something more than any keyboard instrument then at Beethoven's disposal. No wonder he reacted with such joyous delight in his discovery! It sets in motion a weaving together of many ideas and concepts hitherto mentioned: the repeated rhythmic formulation in the first movement, the harmonic pattern of the trio (in the Scherzo) mentioned *vis-à-vis* the Piano Sonata (Opus 2, No. 3), and the grinding ostinato of the finale evolved from the first movement of the Symphony No. 2. On the other hand, the *Pastorale's* idea of unity through connected movements or the C-minor's integration of the whole structure is not pursued in No. 7. Each of its movements is independent of the other.

In his comment on No. 7, Grove observes: "The Seventh Symphony was completed in 1812. . . ." Then, as if in documentation of the idea of Beethoven creating "a new work to each type of composition," he adds: "During the period of which we are speaking . . . a large number of scarcely less important works were composed—The String Quartets in E flat (Op. 74) and F minor (Op. 95) . . . the Choral Fantasia . . . the Solo Sonatas in F sharp minor, and the [Opus 81a] called 'Les Adieux, l'Absence, et le Retour'. . . the Trios in E flat and D (Op. 70) and in B flat (Op. 97); besides the Variations in D (Op. 76), the Fantasia (Op. 77), and the Sonatina (Op. 79)."[3]

Symphony No. 8 was also a product of 1812, if of a much shorter period of creation than No. 7. This is not so much because it is known to some as the "little No. 8"—which is akin to using a diminutive for describing a less than full-grown tiger. It was, rather, as happy in conception as it sounds in execution: a brilliantly playful knocking about of musical materials in a manner to prompt the observation that the Eighth of Beethoven was the last of Haydn. It makes sportive use of such enlarged resources as the separate bass and cello lines which Beethoven had pioneered a decade before in the finale of Symphony No. 2. But it also holds to such conventions of the Haydn orchestra as paired woodwinds and brass rather than multiples of them. For the first time since Symphony No. 1, Beethoven writes a Scherzo in the guise of a Menuet rather than a Menuet striving to become a Scherzo. The playful finale embodies a Haydnesque motive[4] developed in a way which demonstrates why Beethoven was too proud to describe himself as a "Pupil of Haydn."[5]

Of all the products of the period enumerated by Grove, the one

---

[3] Grove: *Beethoven and His Nine Symphonies*, p. 229.

[4] Grove: ibid., p. 299, cites it as "not improbably an expansion of the opening of the final allegro in a symphony of Haydn's in G." In present terminology, that would be No. 88, in G.

[5] Thayer-Forbes (1964), I, 139.

which strikes me as an enlargement rather than an echo of a preceding standard is the Trio, Opus 97. Universally known as the "Archduke," it deserves its designation for reasons other than its dedication to his pupil-patron Archduke Rudolph. As will be expanded upon in a later section (pp. 236–42), Beethoven's feeling for this young son of Leopold II was a curious mixture of reverence and love. Though the prince was eighteen years his junior, he held Rudolph in something like awe, for other reasons than his faithful adherence to the conditions of the tripartite arrangement of 1809 (see pp. 215–16). An excellent pianist as well as a more than competent composer, Rudolph was honored by Beethoven's dedication to him of a host of important works, among them the concertos Nos. 4 and 5 and the "Les Adieux" sonata.

However much he might have relished these dedications, Rudolph could hardly have savored their content as profoundly as he did the Trio in B-flat. It is well known that Beethoven wrote the Triple Concerto (Opus 56, in C) for the Archduke to play, though it is dedicated, for reasons of policy, to Lichnowsky. The trio plays much upon the kind of passage work for the right hand, cascading sixths and thirds and other bright-sounding devices, which give the piano a place of leadership in the concerto. But the later work does much more than favor the Archduke's technical strengths; it rejoices in the absence of the sometimes intrusive orchestra to develop an endless stream of melodic formulation which can hardly be heard too often or played too well. It is, indeed, not only the "Archduke" of the Beethoven trios but the archtype of Schubert trios to come. These were poured out during the last years of Schubert's life (1828) and published almost at once. They were, one suspects, immediately on the Archduke's list of favorites. It would almost have had to have been "immediately," for the Archduke outlived his benefactor, Beethoven, by only five years, and Schubert by only four.

For reasons which relate more to opportunism than to aesthetics, the great cycle of orchestral works which had climbed ever higher since the First Symphony of 1800 slipped to an abysmal, sub-basement of quality in 1813. For Beethoven, as well as others all over Europe, 1814 was a year to be anticipated. Vienna itself was specially favored as the scene for the Congress designed to put back in suitable places the pieces scattered during the long series of Napoleonic forays all over Europe. As his share of the business opportunities created by Napoleon's downfall, Beethoven agreed to compose—for a music machine devised by Johann Nepomuk Mälzel[6]—a *Battle* Symphony celebrating Wellington's victory at Vittoria (Waterloo was still an obscure village in the

---

[6] Inventor of the metronome.

Lowlands). Its profitability disappointed Beethoven considerably, if not as greatly as the arrangement for orchestra (Opus 91) demeaned his name and talent. He even conceived a lasting animosity for England's Prince Regent,[7] to whom he sent a copy of the score, for not replying with a gift. Perhaps the future King George IV was a keener music lover than Beethoven imagined.

2

BEETHOVEN'S INCLINATION to engage in so vacuous a catchpenny scheme as the *Battle* Symphony (as he sometimes called it), on behalf of a mechanical musicmaker, at a time when his fame in Europe was unprecedented, his music was being published (to his profit) in England and France as well as in Germany and Austria, and performances spread his name from Moscow to Madrid may impress the cynical as no more than could be expected. But there are some collateral factors to be considered before final judgment is passed. They need not be regarded as extenuating circumstances, but they may add to understanding of what, without them, could be construed as an excellent instance of what passeth understanding.

The root fact—in my view—is that as Beethoven was coming near to the exhaustion of the musical force, the dynamic impulse, that had driven him for more than a decade, he was also finding eroding under his feet the terrain on which he had grounded his mature career. He had, as has been abundantly documented, an acute awareness of the undependability of public favor in Vienna. Over a long period of time he had marshaled the artistic forces at his disposal to fight the battle of wits required to evolve a secure, substantial life among the high as well as the lowly born with whom he associated.

Thus, publishers would be encouraged to bid against each other for the privilege of marketing his works, the aristocracy would be required to bear their share of the burden by recognizing the value of a Beethoven dedication, some teaching might be entertained (a Ries or a Czerny, if the pupil were of sufficient talent; a Countess Giulietta Guicciardi, Therese Brunsvik, or Marie Erdödy, or an Archduke Rudolph, if the candidate were sufficiently well-connected). Together with an occasional Akadamie (public program of his own works), the components of a suitable annual income could be devised.

So long as Vienna's own affairs were stable, so were Beethoven's.

---

[7] He became George IV in 1820.

Both came to a crisis in 1809, when the French occupied Vienna, and Beethoven was faced with the choice of accepting an invitation to become court composer to the king of Westphalia[8] (in Kassel) or forgoing its handsome stipend in favor of the amenities as well as the uncertainties of life in Vienna.

Unwilling to contemplate the prospect of a Beethovenless Vienna—or, perhaps, the foreseeable wrath of the public for not doing all in their power to prevent it—the Archduke Rudolph and his fellow music-loving nobles, Princes Kinsky and Lobkowitz, executed a legal document guaranteeing Beethoven 4,000 florins a year for life (as long as he remained in Vienna, or until he accepted an appointment conferring a similar income). Together with expectable earnings from other sources —totaling, say, 2,000 florins a year—he could look forward to an annual income of 6,000 florins a year. This would be the equivalent of 600 English pounds—in the prevailing economy, a sum[9] beyond any question goodly.

The year 1809 was hardly out when the French occupation of Vienna and its subsequent constriction of normal business activities altered monetary values sharply. Needless to say, the alterations were not in Beethoven's favor. Moreover, the contract had only been in force three years when the highborn, well-connected Kinsky was thrown from his horse and injured so badly that he died in less than a day (November 3, 1812). The blow was all the heavier because Kinsky was more than an equal partner in the underwriting. His share of 1,800 florins a year was nearly half the total. Without it, Rudolph's 1,500 and Lobkowitz's 700 were painfully little, especially in a depressed economy. By 1813 the illusion of security had become a mere delusion. Lobkowitz's extravagant involvement in artistic ventures of various sorts had brought him to the verge of insolvency. He now became, in Beethoven's eyes, a "princely rascal"[10] who had to be dunned to discharge his part of the obligation. He did exonerate Kinsky as "one of an opposite character," the presumption being that the family was "good for it."

But it was also to be presumed that months, even years, would elapse before a legal claim could be prepared, processed, and satisfied. It was not, in fact, until the spring of 1815 that a three-and-a-half-year lapse in the Kinsky payments and a nearly four-year arrears in the Lobkowitz account were settled. (Lobkowitz died in 1816, aged forty-four). Then the Kinsky commitment was re-negotiated and reduced to

---

[8] Jérôme Bonaparte.
[9] Anderson: *The Letters of Beethoven*, I, xvii.
[10] Ibid., p. 422.

1,200 florins a year from the original 1,800. It was not the last time that a highborn's promise of generosity to Beethoven proved to be infuriatingly undependable. Hence the increasing receptivity to the offers of well-paying hack work tendered by George Thomson of Edinburgh,[11] and, perhaps, the motivation for cooperating in Mälzel's music-machine scheme.

The eventual reckoning showed that, in the aggregate, the princes or their heirs paid Beethoven an annual amount of 3,400 florins a year until his death. The reasons for Beethoven's uncommonly warm feelings for Archduke Rudolph (see pp. 238–39) might relate to his consistently prompt fulfillment of his own pledge, his willingness to revise the amount upward to meet the devaluation of the coin originally stipulated, and his devotion in applying pressure on the Kinsky-Lobkowitz estates to fulfill their obligations.

If 1812 was a famously bad year for Napoleon, it was hardly better for his onetime admirer, then disappointed detractor, Beethoven. It brought to a climax all the emotional involvements, the yearnings for companionship, and the protestations of "need" for one who would share his life—and, incidentally, relieve his dependence on costly, unruly servants for the domesticity he cherished. Beyond the effect on his finances of delayed payments and currency depreciation, he had suffered a personal blow of greater magnitude. This remained a secret known only to himself and the still-unidentified object of his hopeless love until, like the Heiligenstadt Testament, a parcel of documents bearing on the case was discovered after his death.

She was, of course, the one enduringly famous as the "Immortal Beloved."[12] For lack of a covering envelope, or postmark, or a single clear indication in the three-part communication as to the year to which the July dates (6–7–8) applied, there is no sure clue to when the letters were written and dispatched—if they were dispatched. By common consent of the mystery-minded, and a searching analysis of every factual detail in the letters—weather, postal schedules, conditions of the roads mentioned, and the travels, concurrently, of a prince of the Esterházy clan—every year but 1812 has been ruled out. But this has not ruled *in* any of the numerous female possibilities who might qualify.

It is no part of my purpose to venture a lay opinion of the "Immortal Beloved's" identity where experts continue to differ. It is, rather,

[11] Ibid., p. 154. The first response to Thomson is dated November 1, 1806. They became more frequent in 1809, 1810, 1811, etc.

[12] Emily Anderson prefers the designation "Eternally Beloved." Anderson: *The Letters of Beethoven*, I, 376 n. The phrase, in German, is "Unsterbliche Geliebte."

wholly my purpose to relate this unmistakable turning point in Beethoven's life to any results flowing from it that might have a bearing on his later creative course. Some who challenge 1812 as the year of Beethoven's defeat in his confrontation with the "Immortal Beloved," cite his tender of marriage, in 1811, to Therese Malfatti, and his serious pursuit of Amalie Seebald, later in 1812, as disqualifying counter-circumstances. This hardly has the ring of relevance to me. In my reading, the letters describe a one, an absolute, a Leonore come to life whose attainment would solve forever all the problems *vis-à-vis* women that had plagued Beethoven ever since he conceived the male-female relationship in terms of his mother, whom he adored. That was not to say that he wouldn't entertain possible alternatives or settle for lesser, but acceptable, solutions of the overpowering sex drive he could not commit to a casual, "bestial" relationship.[13]

The lack of counterparts, in almost all the enduring correspondence of Beethoven, to the frenetic, intensely agitated tone of the three letters to the "Immortal Beloved" has inclined some to the view that she might not even have existed among the circle of women known to us. It suggests to me, rather, one indeed known to us but of such astral inaccessibility as to be ruled out, except to a Beethoven momentarily inflamed by an urge he had not hitherto dared to voice in words—or at least in written words.

It is of some passing interest, where inaccessibility is concerned, that Beethoven the plebeian, the rebel, the implacable opponent of privilege, rarely—so far as is known—aspired seriously to a continuing relationship with a woman of his own background. Whether the name was Guicciardi, Brunsvik—two charming sisters, of whom Josephine (later Deym) was his favorite—Erdödy, or Malfatti, they were all of noble birth, destined to marry counts or barons. Even Dorothea von Ertmann,[14] a late entry in the I. B. Sweepstakes, an excellent pianist and an interpreter of his works highly respected by Beethoven, was then (1812) married for a dozen years to a Major, later General, Peter von Ertmann. The place in the sequence held by Amalie Seebald (she was twenty-four in 1812), an accomplished singer who eventually married, but not into the nobility, suggests a lively appreciation by Beethoven of her vivacity and charms rather than a prospective marriage partner. That might be said even more emphatically of the last in the long suc-

[13] Thayer-Forbes (1964), II, 670. "Sensual enjoyment without a union of souls is bestial and will always remain bestial."

[14] George Marek: *Biography of a Genius* (New York: Funk and Wagnalls; 1970), pp. 307–8.

cession of "new" females in his mature life. She was Maria Pachler-Koschak, a beautiful native of Graz, who was twenty and married when they met in 1817. Beethoven, then forty-seven, was unquestionably responsive to her, but the relationship had no known outcome.

A new addition to the list, the result of research done at the time of the two-hundredth anniversary of Beethoven's birth, has been put forward by Maynard Solomon. His candidate does, indeed, conform to my concept of "astral inaccessibility." Born Antonie von Birkenstock in 1780, she became the sister-in-law of the celebrated Bettina von Arnim when she married Bettina's half-brother Franz Brentano. She and her husband were friends *en famille* of Beethoven from about 1809 on. It is well known that she was in Karlsbad, generally accepted as the place to which Beethoven addressed the letters, at the crucial time in July 1812. But Solomon was the first to discover that she was also in Prague at the time it is believed that Beethoven had an assignation with the "beloved."[15]

Solomon has added to his painstaking documentation of these dates interpretations of two Beethoven statements that have long eluded clarification. Found in a collection of notes usually described as a *Tagebuch* (or diary), the statements he reproduces include the following: "Regarding T. nothing is left but to trust in God; never to go where weakness might lead to do wrong: to Him to Him alone, the omniscient God, leave all this." And again: "But towards T. . . . as good as possible; her devotion deserves never to be forgotten." This does not fit Brentano as well as the earlier reference, in a preceding Tagebuch, "In this way with A., everything goes to ruin," does her first name, Antonie. But, to her intimates, Antonie *was* known as *Tonie*, and it might just work. Finally, Antonie's daughter, a favorite of Beethoven's, was named Maximiliane, and might be the "M" encountered at another time who caused Beethoven to write a coded reference to an anguished love affair.

Here, however, the dates are incongruent, though there has also been argument that the "M" might be another initial. Also, less than convincing to me is Solomon's contention that a miniature portrait found among Beethoven's possessions after his death was not that of Countess Marie Erdödy, as it has commonly—because of their close friendship—been identified, but rather that of Antonie Brentano. On the other hand, Beethoven did beyond question dedicate the monumental *Diabelli* Variations to Antonie Brentano more than a decade later, a tribute

[15] Maynard Solomon: "New Light on Beethoven's Letter to an Unknown Woman," *The Musical Quarterly* (G. Schirmer, New York and London), Vol. LVIII, No. 4 (October 1972), p. 572.

to an affection that might, indeed, suggest an "astral inaccessibility."

So much for the pros and the cons of all the Immortal Beloveds. One context in which 1812 might, in itself, have been a crucial factor in his *need* for such a love, whoever it might have been, has been generally overlooked. According to his own belief about his birthdate, 1812, would have marked the year in which the composer had just entered on his forties. That would have sharpened his awareness that he had left behind the still youthful thirties and was verging on middle age. By current standards, such lines of demarcation might be regarded as meaningless, or at least of slight significance, though such anxieties are not unknown. Certainly there is abundant evidence in Beethoven's general correspondence of the period to suggest a feeling that time and opportunity were slipping away from him, that the possibilities of achieving emotional fulfillment or creating a physical image to mirror his physical self as his music mirrored his spiritual self, were dwindling. It was not long before those who knew him best began to notice a deterioration in his appearance, a lack of care in dress and grooming that presaged his retirement into a world of his own. This was not so much a change of personality as a reversion to the one he had brought with him from Bonn.

3

THE LAST DESPERATE HOPE that there might be, after all, another kind of happiness for him, began to fill his mind late in 1815. Unlike those other illusions, which had been dispelled by the parents of a prospective partner (such as Malfatti's) or by a realistic rejection of his potential as a lifetime partner, this was to endure as long as he lived. But it is doubtful that he derived even a fractional share of compensation for the agitation, the time-consuming frustration, or the material means he invested in a relationship whose cost to him was, finally, mortal.

Though it was none of his business, Beethoven did not approve of the women chosen in marriage by either of his brothers. Insofar as Johann's Therese was concerned, he had no option but to tolerate her, as both outlived him. But with Carl Casper Anton, the case was different. In the early summer of 1815 it became apparent that he was, at age forty-one-and-a-half, suffering so seriously from consumption that he probably would not live out the year.[16] The consequences of the family conversa-

---

[16] It is an interesting side aspect of Beethoven's misbelief about his own age that the death announcement of November 20, 1815, described Carl as "aged 38." A footnote to this in Thayer-Forbes (1964), II, on p. 625 reminds the reader, "actually he was 41½ years old since he was baptized on April 8, 1774."

tions concerning the guardianship of his son, Karl, are spelled out in a will dated November 14, 1815. The relevant clause is numbered 5, and reads:

> I appoint my brother Ludwig van Beethoven guardian. Inasmuch as this, my deeply beloved brother, has often aided me with true brotherly love in the most magnanimous and noblest manner, I ask, in full confidence and trust in his noble heart, that he shall bestow the love and friendship which he often showed me, upon my son Karl, and do all that is possible to promote the intellectual training and further welfare of my son. I know that he will not deny me this, my request.

An unequivocal statement, it leaves no room for doubt about Carl's apparent intentions. However, the document preserved in the archives of the city of Vienna discloses that the first sentence of this clause was *written*: "Along with my wife I appoint my brother Ludwig van Beethoven co-guardian." The words "Along with my wife" and "co" were written over to render them nonoperative. Beethoven claimed to have come upon the will "by chance" and stricken out the words indicated above[17] because he did not want to be "bound up in this with such a bad woman in a matter of such importance as the education of a child."

Appraised, no doubt, of Beethoven's alteration of the will as written, and very likely under the pressure of his wife—who was, after all, the boy's mother—Carl added a codicil to the will. Remarkably, it bears the date of November 14, though it was not delivered to the court until November 17. It reads:

> Having learned that my brother, Hr. Ludwig van Beethoven, desires after my death to take wholly to himself my son Karl, and wholly to withdraw him from the supervision and training of his mother, and inasmuch as the best of harmony does not exist between my brother and my wife, I have found it necessary to add to my will that I by no means desire that my son be taken away from his mother, but that he shall always and so long as his future career permits remain with his mother, to which end the guardianship of him is to be exercised by her as well as my brother. . . . For the welfare of my child, I recommend *compliance* to my wife and more *moderation* to my brother."[18]

This extraordinary testament is offered in detail because it is central to the interminable sequence of squabbles, contentions, lawsuits,

---

[17] Thayer-Forbes (1964), II, 624–5.
[18] Ibid., p. 625. The italics are in the original text.

depositions, and documents that occupied Beethoven from 1815 until his death, on March 27, 1827. For a dozen years then, Beethoven's attention to the most vital aspects of his life was disturbed, invaded, and preempted by the consequences of his intrusion into an affair that was none of his rightful concern.

That he might, as an attentive uncle, wish to put his resources to the benefit of the only male heir the three Beethoven brothers possessed was eminently in order. That he sought, in return, for domination of the boy's life, usurpation of the place of the mother—his complaint against her was, as a moral man, mortal: she had been unfaithful to her husband—and the presumption to dictate how and where he should be educated, was not merely out of order, it was insufferable. It could only be construed as an obsessive, compulsive, unreasoning outlet for his own emotional needs, as a desperate appeal for the love for which he yearned and which—as a result of his insensate demands on a boy lacking real talent or intellectual distinction—was never forthcoming.

None of this would have a prominent part in a biography of Beethoven's music did it not have a shaping effect upon it. Aside from the irksome, time-consuming paper work which diminished the time he had to devote to his art, the involvements with his nephew added complications of the most mundane and sometimes deceitful kind to his pursuit of a living. At the very least it imposed a financial burden which might have been absorbed, by some self-sacrifice, within his normal pattern of earnings. In defiance of the very *moderation* for which his brother pleaded, it engendered a state of mind in which the uncle undertook to create a legacy to guarantee the boy's welfare after his own death. Whether it was necessary may be questioned. Whether it was desirable may be doubted. Whether it justified all the penury, deprivation, and crafty exploitation of his most exalted works in the years that followed, can only be unequivocally denied.

4

THE LAST OF THE SHAPING FORCES that determined not only the nature of those years but the number of them was, of course, his health. The common conception, among those who have absorbed a great deal of his music and a more than casual amount of information about the man who wrote it, might be stated as follows: Beethoven was, on the whole, a man of robust health and sturdy constitution. He suffered an early attack of smallpox, probably in Bonn, as attested by the pockmarks on his face, for which he was known in his public life. This was followed by a severe illness, probably typhus (see p. 82), sometime after he came to Vienna, which was related to the deficiency in his hearing. This later condition grew progressively worse, developed into debilitating deafness, and became total by the time of the premiere of the Ninth Symphony (1824). In an instance often remarked, the deaf composer could not hear the stormy applause the work aroused, but had to be turned to *see* the audience applauding. Sometime along the way he suffered an illness from which he recovered to write the "Heilige Dankgesang" ("Holy Song of Thanksgiving") of the Opus 132 (A-minor) Quartet. Not long after, he fell ill again, and died after a violent gesture of defiance during a March snow and thunderstorm.[19]

Nothing in the foregoing chronology is invented. But it is a deceptively inadequate rendering of a factor which was a recurrent intrusion on Beethoven's functioning from his late twenties onward—the impairment of his hearing. It was a progressive debility, increasing with each year. But how it increased, with what frequency, and in the specific ways that affected his productivity, has not, to my knowledge, been chronologically tabulated. In the absence of such a graphic, tabular statement of the facts, the appended documentation has been prepared to assist the reader in correlating all factors that entered into Beethoven's "nonproductive" decade and the years that followed (see pp. 326–41).

It may even shift the emphasis from why he produced so little in this final phase of his life to *how* he produced as much as he did. The evidence is all derived from Beethoven's own statements, either in correspondence or in verbal exchanges reported by reputable witnesses. There are those who impute some of Beethoven's claims of "headaches," "chills," "colds," and "digestive complaints" to his desire to avoid unwanted engagements or as convenient excuses for negligence due to other causes. But the steady accretion of longer, traceable periods of confinement, of known reductions in his activity, and documented evidence of his suffering, as well as the recourse to written questions from visitors, which began in 1818, when he could no longer hear spoken words, tell their own story of the curtain that gradually fell between Beethoven and the world around him.

----

[19] Ibid., p. 1,050. The tale of the thunderstorm was perpetuated by Anselm Hüttenbrenner, famous as a friend of Schubert. He was one of those present when Beethoven died. For those who may wonder how the deaf composer could have heard the thunder, it was Hüttenbrenner's version that the room was illuminated by a sudden shaft of lightning which aroused Beethoven's reaction.

XII

Toward a World Apart

I

ETWEEN 1805—when he completed the F-minor Sonata (Opus 57)—and late 1809, Beethoven wrote no piano sonatas. One may associate this neglect with his absorption in other things, or attribute it to the termination of his own career as a performer.[1] In any case, when he was asked by a publisher to break this silence he replied: "I don't like to spend much time composing sonatas for pianoforte solo, but I promise to let you have a few. . . ."[2] One of the few he did write was designed to serve a special purpose of Beethoven's own, and thus escaped his reluctance to spend "much time" on such projects. This was the E-flat Sonata (Opus 81a), known outside German-speaking countries as "Les Adieux," though Beethoven preferred the German title, *Lebewohl,* as more expressive of his sentiments. These were con-

---

[1] Thayer-Forbes (1964), I, 445–7. December 22, 1808, marked his final formal appearance as a performer in a solo "virtuoso" role, in the first performances of his Fourth Piano Concerto (Opus 58) and the Choral Fantasia (Opus 80). Later, extraordinary exceptions were made in the company of others: in a performance (1812) of his Horn Sonata (Opus 17) in the company of Friedrich Starke, a virtuoso whose skill he admired (p. 526); and in 1814, in an introductory rendition of the Opus 97 Trio at a concert for charity in which Schuppanzigh was interested. Ignaz Moscheles, who was twenty, recorded his impression of the event in a diary entry under the date of April 11, 1814: "His playing, apart from the spirit prevailing in it, satisfied me less, for it lacks clearness and precision: still I observed several traces of the grand style of playing which I had long since recognized in his compositions" (Ignaz Moscheles: *Recent Music and Musicians,* edited by his wife and adapted from the original German by A. D. Coleridge [New York: Henry Holt; 1875], p. 8).

[2] Anderson: *The Letters of Beethoven,* I, 244.

ceived as a fond farewell to Archduke Rudolph, who left Vienna on May 4, 1809[3]—in the company of his brother, the Emperor, to avoid the French occupation—an expression of sorrow at his absence, and a joyous tribute to his return nine months later, on January 30, 1810. A derivative in all probability of Bach's "Capriccio on the Departure of a Beloved Brother," it was carefully, lovingly executed by Beethoven. The dates are fixed in the manuscript. Their omission from the printed copy strongly offended the composer.

The other sonatas, of rather more impersonal character and decidedly greater brevity, were the F-sharp-major (Opus 78) dedicated to Therese Brunsvik, which explores a vein of piano writing that might have served Mendelssohn's Rondos; and the Opus 79 in G, which Beethoven asked to have identified as a "Sonata facile or sonatina." Five years elapsed before Beethoven was inclined to venture a solo sonata again, and it was restricted to the two-movement E-minor (Opus 90). It begins with an affectionately contentious dialogue between "Kopf und Hertz" (as Beethoven explained to Count Moritz Lichnowsky, to whom it is dedicated). In the Schumannesque music that ensues, "head and heart" could as well be rendered "Florestan and Eusebius." But the implications are hardly followed through in the second (concluding) movement, a rondo which is Schubertian not merely in mood but in its more than tolerable amount of repetition.

The resumption of a close, intimate involvement with the solo piano in the A-major Sonata (Opus 101) strikes me as indicative of something more than accident or whim. It signals the start of a new cycle of thought and creativity, comparable to the great forward surge that marked the period 1799–1802. It was then (see pp. 109–34) that all the works between Opus 22 and Opus 35 were written, and only one of these—the String Quintet, Opus 29—does not utilize the piano.

A superficial conclusion might be that this renewed interest in the piano was a windfall from a benevolent gesture on behalf of his long-term friend (and sometime detractor) Joseph Linke, the cellist who first regarded the Scherzo of Opus 59, No. 1, as a joke. His place in the quartet maintained by Count Razumovsky disappeared, literally, in smoke when the sumptuous establishment that served as residence, Russian embassy, and concert salon was gutted by fire.[4] Razumovsky did not terminate his musical involvements at once, but rebuilding the palace or continuing his musicales on their prior scale was beyond even

---

his resources. In 1816 Schuppanzigh followed his reputation to Russia, and his fellow quartet members sought out other work to supplement the pensions thoughtfully provided by Razumovsky.[5]

For Linke, this included an attachment to the establishment of the Countess Erdödy, one of Beethoven's oldest, most devoted, and highly musical friends. To salute their artistic union and to send Linke on his way with a priceless addition to the cellist's repertory, Beethoven created in the summer of 1815[6] the two sonatas eventually joined in Opus 102. This would imply a composition date later than the A-major Sonata, Opus 101, which was not finished until the following year. But the origins of Opus 101 (see p. 226) indicate that Beethoven was respecting chronological fidelity as well as exercising a personal preference in ordering the sequence as he did.[7]

The cello sonatas were, nevertheless, the first to bring to full statement a trend of thought that came to be dominant in the works of his last decade. Perhaps the ordained performers, for whom he had high personal as well as professional esteem, had a part in the psychic evolution. In any case, the stranding of the piano's line in and around the string part, the continuous recourse to contrapuntal devices in which the instruments are equal elements, and the eventual direction of the D-major Sonata to a fugal finale marks the two works, if not formally "late" Beethoven, as later than most music lovers might think.

No. 1 begins with a statement by the cello, and the leadership impulse alternates from instrument to instrument; they are rarely heard in the context of solo and accompaniment. Indeed, in continuation of a trend to be observed in the last of the violin sonatas (No. 10, in G, Opus 96, completed in 1812 for the French master Pierre Rode) the notion of the string instrument as an "obbligato" to the piano has been abandoned. No longer is there any suggestion of keyboard preeminence, though the place of priority in the title still goes to the piano (which could, in German as well as English, be a mere matter of alphabetical arrangement—klavier, or piano, preceding violoncello).

In the D-major Sonata, Opus 102, No. 2, suggestions of the old homophonic relationship of solo and accompanying instrument are even more recessive. Beethoven's facility in moving the lines of *both* parts as entities of a single musical formulation prevails in each of the first two movements. It not merely prevails in, but dominates, the finale, an Allegro fugato which grows out of the Adagio without interruption,

[5] Ibid., II, 640.
[6] Ibid., p. 620.
[7] All three works were published in 1817.

a sure indication of Beethoven's impulse-to-unity functioning at its fullest.

By now Beethoven was too old and perhaps too wary to announce to friends that he had "finally" learned how to compose, as he had fifteen or so years before. But one can sense, in the structural layout of the Opus 95 quartet (six tempo designations, grouped—after the first movement—into two uninterrupted sequences) and the Opus 96 sonata, a quest for new disciplines. Or at least, for the means of renewing and regenerating the old ones through devices, procedures, and concepts he had not hitherto exploited, or had long disused.[8] This would mean a combination of contrapuntal formulations with the humanizing drama, contrast, and humors which had characterized the best of his writing for years. They are present in the Opus 102 sonatas in a way not only to gratify their first performers[9] but to exercise an audience-involving spell ever since.

The presence in a sketchbook of 1813 of the germinal sketches for Opus 101 can mean much or little according to their interpretation. They are, to me, decidedly in the "much" category. Among other things, they point to the plain fact that while one part of Beethoven was concocting, with J. N. Mälzel, an opportunistic scheme for taking advantage of a topical happening with a composition for the Panharmonicon, another was engaged in speculative thoughts that would project his influence far into the future.

Unlike many other entries in the sketchbooks, which show Beethoven struggling to subjugate a central thought from which much else would emerge, those for the Opus 101 sonata project a structure partially seen, if not altogether heard. They comprise pieces of a puzzle which appear to differ from most such fragments in lacking an important element to form the picture of which they are a part.

[8] The sixth quartet of Opus 18 ends with a movement combining five separate tempo designations.

[9] Beethoven's friendship with Erdödy was long enough and warm enough to prompt Dana Steichen to prove (in *Beethoven's Beloved* [Garden City, N.Y.: Doubleday; 1957]) that she *must* have been the "Immortal Beloved," though she cannot possibly conform to the fundamental premise that 1812 was the year in which the letters were written. It is a curious footnote to the relationship of Beethoven and Erdödy that he begged off on his promise to dedicate the works to her, adding (in a letter of May 13, 1816) that it need not "alter either you or me." It was Beethoven's intent to inscribe them, instead, to Charles Neate, an English musician who had recently been visiting Vienna, and who might do some good for him in London. Her response is not preserved, but the Kinsky catalogue reveals that the offense to the Countess was resolved by letting the inscription to her stand in the printed edition, and giving Neate a copy of Opus 102, No. 1, inscribed "composée et dédiée à mon ami Mr. Charles Neate" (Kinsky: *Das Werk Beethovens*, p. 283). Though they continued to correspond, Beethoven and Erdödy are not known to have met again. As for the false statements to impress Neate, it is but the first in a long series of deceptions, duplicities, and lies in which Beethoven indulged as he grew older.

As the adjoining examples indicate, the sketches of 1813 describe, in sufficient shorthand detail to serve Beethoven's constructive purposes, the characteristics of two movements of a piano work.[10] He has already assigned the sketches a place in the prospective totality: "2tes Stück [second movement] Allegro Marcia," for the first sketch; "Letzte [Last movement] presto," for the final sketch. Another idea, marked "3tes Stück [third movement] poco Allegretto," has a more mystifying appearance. It did not, as it stands, find a place in the A-major Sonata when it was born three years later, nor do its conformations immediately suggest an alternate usage. A family characteristic that affiliates the sketches for movements two and four with their finished form is worth noting: they are both contrapuntal in design (canonic in the first instance, fugal in the second). The sketch for the second movement has gone far enough into the whole concept to provide a middle section, or trio, for the Marcia. As cited by Nottebohm, the sketches read:

(1)

[10] Gustav Nottebohm: *Zweite Beethoveniana: Nachgelassene Aufsätze* (New York and London: Johnson Reprint Corporation; 1970), pp. 341–3. Originally published by Verlag von C. F. Peters, Leipzig, 1887.

(2)

(3)

(4)

(5)

(6)

No. 1 is an early form of the movement that came to be the Vivace alla marcia of Opus 101. No. 2 is a fuller implementation of its rhythmic design. No. 3 presents the middle section (trio) much as it is today (in reading Beethoven's sketches, one has to imagine flats, sharps, accidentals, etc., which Beethoven sometimes neglected to write, as the notations were meant only for his own purposes). No. 4 is the first form of the last movement. No. 5 is a bit of its next evolution, in which the contrapuntal possibilities are pursued.

In the first stages of familiarity, the location on the staff of sketches Nos. 1 and 2—No. 2, in particular—may be somewhat confusing. They are clearly jottings for a movement in F. One automatically assumes that when Beethoven came to wrestle with the problems of a sonata in A major, he rewrote them in the that key. Wrong! A reference to the sonata shows that the second movement is, indeed, in F—a destination achieved by one of those pivotal modulations to which Beethoven was becoming more and more attached in this phase of his career. That is to say, the A, which is the root tone in the key of A, becomes the third in the key of F. This group of entries might be titled: "How to write a sonata in A from sketches that begin with a movement in F."

This apparent paradox prompts another look at sketch No. 6, the one which has no apparent part in the finished Opus 101. It is, without question, in A minor, as is the third movement of Opus 101. But it is a poco Allegretto in 6/8 time—two specifications wholly at variance with the Adagio ma non troppo in 2/4 which Beethoven wrote to bridge the space between the second and fourth movements of Opus 101.

But if one can imagine him, in an improvisatory mood, taking the basic shape of No. 6 and moving it about the keyboard in various guises and different speeds,[11] it is not impossible for the outcome to become:

And it is only a leap of the mind from an A-minor slow movement to an A-major first movement, for which the late Rudolph Réti might very well have isolated the notes

as the cell from which emerged[12]

---

[11] As in the search for the "Waldstein" finale, noted on pp. 161–2.

For a final insight into the alteration, development, and reshaping of Beethoven's musical objectives over a twenty-year period, reference might be made to a prior A-major sonata in Beethoven's output. It is Opus 2, No. 2, one of those prepared for dedication to Haydn, embodying pre-Vienna elements as well as others evolved in his early years (1792–95) there. The work begins with a figure

not unlike sketch No. 4 (p. 229). But the Beethoven of 1795 can do little with it but exploit its obvious attributes of saucy good humor. For the Beethoven of 1816 it is an idea with immediate opportunities for imitation, duplication, inversion, and elaboration—the idioms and dialectical devices from which so many of the sonatas and quartets that followed Opus 101 were evolved as another way of giving expression to his emotional urges.

What characterizes them as in the mainstream of Beethoven's development is precisely the fact that for all the intellectual connotation of the devices they remain the outlet for emotional urges. The fugue of Opus 101, for example, is a remarkable instance of its kind not for the number and variety of its subjects, or the cleverness of its counterpoint, but because it is, ever and always, expounding a point of view and a state of mind rather than merely manipulating notes.

The terminology required to define the special characteristics of Opus 101—improvisatory, contrapuntal, fugal, canonical—becomes increasingly common in the works to come. Here are the areas of experiment, the first flights of ideas and objectives which are to become of larger consequence and greater dimensions.

A final instance of such objectives may be cited in the link that Beethoven forges between the A-minor slow movement and the A-major finale. It would be perfectly possible for Beethoven to go from one to the other with no connecting link at all—Mozart and Haydn often did it. Possible, yes. But poetic? Not really.

---

[12] See Réti's comment on the "cell" of the same work, p. 163. His text, unfortunately, does not deal with any sonata later than the "Appassionata" (Opus 57).

He converts the prosaic A-minor–A-major interchange into another kind of listener-involving device, by pausing for a momentary reminiscence of the work's opening statement

and arousing the hope that we may hear more of this beautiful formulation. Then he plunges directly into a fugal exposition of the theme he has been holding in reserve all along. An engaging digression in itself, it points the way to the famous "rejection" section of the Ninth Symphony in which all the previous themes pass in review and are found wanting before the chorale theme is put forward and joyously accepted.

2

ANY REFERENCE to a "Hammerklavier" Sonata among Beethoven's thirty-two will, without question, key the reader's mind to the great Opus 106 in B-flat. It is, colloquially, as much the "Hammerklavier" as the C-major, Opus 53, is the "Waldstein," or the E-flat, Opus 81, is "Les Adieux." Though included among the last five to which Beethoven applied the term "Hammerklavier," the A-major, Opus 101, is, clearly, not so responsive to the implications of strength and spaciousness in the word as the B-flat. As it happens, the congruence of the word and the music in the B-flat is something of an accident, in any case. At this time of life, Beethoven was increasingly responsive to the premise that German-speaking composers should use German musical terminology wherever possible. This applied no less to tempo markings (langsam rather than adagio, lebhaft rather than vivace) than it did to instruments themselves. "Hammerklavier" was hardly a translation for pianoforte (which would have been something more like weiche-stärke [soft-loud]); it is more descriptive of an instrument whose strings are struck by a hammer rather than plucked by a quill.

Beethoven was also in constant search of an instrument that would compensate for his ever less responsive hearing. During a stay in Nussdorf, in the summer of 1817, Beethoven wrote to the wife of his old friend, the piano maker Streicher, with an urgent message for her husband: "Ask him for my sake to do me the favor of adjusting one of your pianos for my weakened hearing so that it is as loud as possible. I need it."[13] Even while Beethoven was assuring Frau Streicher that her husband was "the one person who is in the position to send me the kind of piano that I need," another was building the instrument that would serve Beethoven's "need" better than he could imagine. This was the English manufacturer Thomas Broadwood, who had become acquainted with the composer during a visit to the continent and was aware of his hearing difficulties. At the end of 1817 he sent from London (by way of Trieste) a six-octave Broadwood, whose arrival in Vienna Beethoven gratefully acknowledged on February 3, 1818. Streicher, who was charged with uncrating the precious cargo and preparing it for Beethoven's use, agreed that its tone was beautiful, but thought the heavy English action made it all but impossible to play. Beethoven vehemently disagreed and reveled in its fullness of sound and extended range.[14] He had it sent to Mödling where he spent the summers of 1818, 1819, and 1820. It is described as having a compass of six octaves from C, five leger-lines below the bass staff.

This would leave it lacking an octave and a third at the bottom, and an octave at the top, to match the range of the present-day 88-note concert grand.

The regenerative effect of Opus 101 on Beethoven's impulse toward piano writing may be read in the letter he wrote to the Steiner company in January 1817 regarding the sonata's dedication. He recognized that plans for publication were well along, but requested that it be inscribed "Sonata for the Pianoforte or Hammer-Klavier composed and dedicated to the Baroness Dorothea Ertmann. . . ." He offers to pay for the engraving of a new plate if one has already been made. Should it not be possible, he suggests that "this title ["Hammer-klavier"] be reserved for another new sonata which I shall compose." To which he adds, in a tone of gaiety he often employed in addressing the firm's representative, Tobias Haslinger, "*to bring another sonata into the world,*

[13] Thayer-Forbes (1964), II, 690.
[14] Ibid., p. 695.

all that is necessary is that the . . . mines should be opened."[15] From this Haslinger was to infer that Beethoven was happy with the outcome of Opus 101, and would write another sonata upon payment of a suitable fee.

The sketches that have been preserved of what eventually became *the* "Hammerklavier" (Opus 106) are among the most interesting of those bearing on his later works. They are assigned by Nottebohm to fall 1817,[16] suggesting that the fine new instrument sent to him by Broadwood did not have a part in its inception. But it must certainly have had a part in its germination and growth. Much of the work on the first two movements was done at Mödling during the summer months of 1818.

As is now beginning to emerge as a pattern in the works of this late period, the sketches tend to define the *kind* of work that is agitating Beethoven's mind rather than its specific details. One discerns a first, proclamative motive juxtaposed to a conciliatory second, though neither is captured in the sharply defined contours of the finished work. There are graphic hints of imitations, fugatos, passages in descending sixths, etc. As the sketches proceed, they cover longer stretches recognizable as parts of the finished first movement, though, again, not in precisely notated form. The rhythmic thrust of the battle cry with which the composer summons the listener to attention as the work opens has not yet been defined, but one detail of the *final* page has. That is the fanfaring passage beginning eighteen measures before the end of the movement. In its sketch form it reads:

Vi - vat   vi - vat   vi - vat ru - dol - phus

This was, of course, no random Rudolph (or rudolphus) but the one, the only, individual of that name to whom Beethoven might address such a musically fervent blessing, or on whose behalf such a wish for *gesundheit* might be offered. The suggestion is that he intended to convert this fragment of the "Hammerklavier" into a four part chorus to be performed for the Archduke on his name day (April 17). It is a clear, written index to the ever-tightening bonds of interest by which Beethoven and the most devoted of his patrons were being intertwined and then inseparably interconnected.

[15] Anderson: *The Letters of Beethoven*, II, 657.
[16] Nottebohm: *Zweite Beethoveniana*, pp. 123–7.

Nearly two years elapsed before the sonata was ready for the Archduke's attention. As always, this letter of June 1819[17] greets the Archduke as "Your Imperial Highness," thereafter employing "Y.I.H." as an acceptable abbreviation. The communication was prompted by the news then being circulated in Vienna that the Archduke had been elevated to the rank of Archbishop. ". . . an enlarged sphere of activity," rejoices Beethoven, "is going . . . to be opened to you and your fine and noble qualities." Beseeching "your most gracious indulgence," he submits, in elegantly handwritten copies, tokens of esteem he had meant to deliver to Rudolph on his name day in 1818 but had been prevented from doing by ill-health.

Several "distressing circumstances" (a euphemism for difficulties with his nephew) had also intervened. In atonement for the delay, he mentions that in addition "to the two pieces in my handwriting composed for Y.I.H.'s name-day, I have added two more, the second of which is a grand Fugato . . . which will soon be published[18] and which was long ago dedicated entirely *in my heart* to Y.I.H." It was perhaps less modesty than a lack of words to supplement what he had already communicated so eloquently in tone that deterred Beethoven from categorizing the Adagio which complemented the Grand Fugato and completed the even grander design of the B-flat Sonata, Opus 106.

For Igor Stravinsky the Adagio was characterized by a "spaciousness" which is a formidable "hazard for composers-to-come." To him "the movement is the richest harmonically in all of the Sonatas." This "mammoth sonata" as a whole "resembles the later quartet in the same key [Opus 130] . . . in its extraordinary fecundity, huge dimensions and radical substance. Both works challenge our powers of absorption even now, in fact still await full appreciation from a future generation."[19]

As none of the letters from the Archbishop's side of the Beethoven correspondence have survived, or at least have been reproduced to prove that they survive, one can only wonder what powers of comprehension he applied to the magnitude of Beethoven's offering on behalf of his name day.[20] Still to come was the fulfillment of a promise contained in the same letter: "The day on which a High Mass composed by me will be performed during the ceremonies solemnized for Your Imperial

---

[17] Anderson: *The Letters of Beethoven*, II, 813. In a footnote on the same page, Miss Anderson mentions that Rudolph had been created a Cardinal (by Pius VII) on April 24.

[18] September 1819.

[19] *Harper's*, CCXL (No. 1,440), (May 1970), 42.

[20] April 17, 1818, might have had a special significance for Beethoven because it marked the thirtieth "official" birthday of Rudolph, who was born in 1788.

Highness will be the most glorious day of my life; and God will enlighten me so that my poor talents may contribute to the glorification of that solemn day—"[21]

3

Barring the miraculous, there will always continue to be doubts and uncertainties as to the identity of Beethoven's "Immortal Beloved." But there is, to me, neither doubt nor uncertainty as to who was—in the broadest sense of the words—his "Mortal Beloved." He was unquestionably Johann Joseph Archduke Rudolph Rainier, born in Florence in 1788, the youngest son of the Grand Duke of Tuscany, who became Leopold II of Austria in 1790. Rudolph's father was a brother of Beethoven's Elector at Bonn, Maximilian Franz, which, in turn, made Rudolph the Elector's nephew.

From 1790, Rudolph was reared in Vienna, and soon began to demonstrate musical interests of an uncommon sort. Some evidence indicates that he began to study with Beethoven as early as 1803 or 1804.[22] He would then have been in his mid-teens. Along with a predisposition to music, he inherited the Hapsburg's tendency to epilepsy. Heredity or other causes also predisposed him to gout; as a result, Beethoven's letters to him make almost as many references to the Archduke's ill-health as to his own.

The first of these letters, attributed to Baden (1810),[23] suggests the easy _bonhomie_ of the relationship which prevailed between master and pupil. Writes Beethoven:

> I see that Your Imperial Highness wants to have the effects of my music tried on horses as well. All right. But I must see whether the riders will thereby be enabled to make a few skilful somersaults— Well, well, I cannot help laughing at the idea of Your Imperial Highness's thinking of me on this occasion as well. And for that favour I shall remain as long as I live your most willing servant
>
> Ludwig van Beethoven
>
> NB. The music for horses which you have asked for will be brought to Your Imperial Highness at the fastest gallop.[24]

---

[21] Anderson: _The Letters of Beethoven_, II, 814–15.

[22] Ibid., I, 291 _n_.

[23] Ibid., I, 291. The Archduke had a summer palace in Baden, one of Beethoven's favorite retreats from the heat of Vienna. This meant that lessons were on the schedule in summer as well as in winter, especially in the years 1812, 1813, 1816, and 1819, when Rudolph is known to have spent the warm months in Baden. (Nettl: _Beethoven Encyclopaedia_, p. 202.)

[24] Kinsky: _Das Werk Beethovens_, WoO 21, 22, 23, pp. 460–1.

The reference is, in all probability (see below), to military music written by Beethoven for Archduke Anton, Rudolph's older brother by ten years, on behalf of one of the regiments of which he was Hochmeister (Grand Master). In the summer of 1810 Beethoven wrote several pieces of military music for use in Baden. Included was a polonaise that might have been used for mounted troops or in conjunction with some maneuvers in which they were participants.

That Beethoven should give so much consideration to one who had barely reached his majority when he became Beethoven's patron in 1809 suggests one of two possibilities:

1. A strong sense of obligation intensified by the Archduke's rank in the Austrian aristocracy of the time, and the influential place he occupied among Beethoven's benefactors, even if he was not the most generous of them.

2. A genuine fondness for the young man as a person of aesthetic sensitivity and musical gifts uncommon even among the most cultivated amateurs. Beethoven esteemed the Countesses Erdödy and Ertmann as performers who interpreted his music as well as any professionals of the time. But Rudolph also earned his respect as a composer whose talents were steadily profiting from hard work under Beethoven's close supervision.

There is little cause for doubt that reason number 1 was dominant as of 1810, when the first of the recorded letters was probably written.[25] In the years that followed, few if any names are more frequently represented among the recipients of Beethoven's correspondence than Rudolph's. Part of this was due to the ongoing teacher-pupil relationship, whether in Vienna or Baden. More than a few of the ninety-odd letters preserved by Rudolph's librarian are no more than brief notes offering apologies—mostly ill-health—for Beethoven's inability to fulfill a teaching session, or begging approval for an alternate hour on a subsequent day.

But a substantial number of them bear on musical considerations which illuminate the Archduke's deep appreciation of Beethoven as a creative artist, and his vaulting estimate of the place to which he was entitled among the composers of history. Rudolph established and maintained a complete library of Beethoven's works as they were written, often receiving handwritten copies of works to which the composer

[25] Assignment of the year to a letter lacking it may be credited to one of Emily Anderson's typically shrewd deductions. She correlated the reference to music, horses, and riders with the large quantity of WoO (Without Opus Numbers) works in the Kinsky catalogue and found a Baden entry, in 1810, for military music that could have been used for the purpose.

attached especial importance—such as the piano-cello sonatas of Opus 102—before they were published. Reciprocally, Beethoven drew upon the library when need arose to have copied a work of which he had no accessible score.

On at least one occasion (in 1811) Rudolph ordered a major musical festivity in his own surroundings at his own expense. Internal evidence suggests that the works performed were the symphonies Four, Five, and Six, plus a couple of overtures.[26] Needless to say, Beethoven was appreciative of the opportunity to rehear these works and of the effort, as well as the money, the Archduke expended to bring it about. The Archduke was also a participant in the happenings that brought about the creation of a violin sonata (Opus 96, in G) for Pierre Rode. Beethoven's letters bearing on his reasons for writing the work as he did convey clearly his estimate of Rudolph as one with whom he could discuss a professional matter in a professional way.

On the other hand, the draining obligation to be at the Archduke's disposal at certain hours several times a week, summer as well as winter, often found Beethoven irked or unable to comply. The repeated recourse to "ill-health," "a cold," "confined to bed," "doctor's orders," as excuses for his nonappearance tend to become monotonously recurrent, indeed suspiciously repititious when documents spread over several years are read from a book in a matter of minutes. Beethoven himself gives evidence of having created such suspicion in a letter of 1815 which begins: "Your Imperial Highness! You must almost have thought that my illness was feigned. But I assure you it was not."[27]

As time passed, the Archduke's own health began to be more and more a matter for concern. Consequently Beethoven's letters trend more to expressions of commiseration, especially when "gout in the hands"[28] restricted Rudolph from playing the piano. And as he passed thirty and found his own activities circumscribed by such infirmities, Rudolph was more disposed to indulge Beethoven's even larger range of complaints—even when they seemed to fall with regularity in times set aside for lessons or other services on behalf of the royal patron.

For his part, Beethoven became increasingly disposed to invoke the Archduke's non-musical, non-patron powers in instances of need. He took the liberty of bringing Rudolph's influence to bear on "my

---

[26] Anderson: *The Letters of Beethoven*, I, 343. The specifications for the number of instruments required, especially the number of horns in each work, provides Miss Anderson with the basis for her judgment.

[27] Ibid., II, 541.

[28] Ibid., I, 444 *n.*

affair at Prague,"²⁹ a delicate reference to the non-payment by the Kinsky estate of the money owing to him on the tripartite contract (see p. 215). In Beethoven's view, "if Your Imperial Highness would just write a few words or have them written on your behalf, the *affair* would certainly be *speeded up*."³⁰ On another occasion, when the theaters he sought for a concert were unavailable, or not on terms he deemed acceptable, Beethoven invoked the Archduke's assistance in obtaining the use of the University Hall for a program in which the Symphony No. 7 had its first performance.³¹ Later on, when the difficulties pertaining to his nephew were beginning to multiply, he beseeched Rudolph to ask an older brother, Archduke Ludwig, to use his influence in some court over which he had jurisdiction to see that Beethoven's side of the argument was properly heard *vis-à-vis* the boy's mother.³² There is no indication that the Archduke Rudolph was affronted by any of these requests, or failed to act upon them. Indeed, there is documentation in each of the instances noted above that Beethoven's interests were directly advanced to bring about the results he desired.

As they record the march across the years, the letters from Beethoven reveal an upward surge both of identity and dependence. To be sure, both men were growing older, a circumstance predisposing toward closeness. Rudolph's increasingly recurrent illnesses also tended to reduce the gap between the composer and his younger, but no longer youthful, disciple. Moreover, they began to grow closer as man to man rather than as master and pupil, even despite the one's exalted temporal powers and the other's recognizably eternal accomplishments.

Some of this can be read in the formal close of Beethoven's letters, whose term of address was almost invariably "Your Imperial Highness." For the ending, protocol called for nothing less than "Your obedient servant," and for a time this was the form Beethoven employed. But as time went on and urgencies of the moment intruded, one may read "Your Imperial Highness's most obedient servant,"³³ or "Your Imperial Highness's humble servant,"³⁴ or "Your Imperial Highness's faithful and most obedient servant.³⁵ In some instances, "loyal" and "faithful" became interchangeable, as though the composer's "loyalty" might be

---

²⁹ Ibid., pp. 480–1.
³⁰ Ibid. The italics are in the original.
³¹ Ibid., p. 428.
³² Ibid., II, 810.
³³ Ibid., I, 333. 1811.
³⁴ Ibid., p. 366. 1812.
³⁵ Ibid., p. 367. Later in 1812.

in doubt. When he heard that the Archduke was ailing in 1814, Beethoven wrote a note of commiseration in which, after mentioning an illness of his own that had brought him "nearly to death's door" and offering to spend "a few hours, in a musical way" with him, Beethoven signed himself "Y.I.H.'s most obedient and most faithful servant."[36]

Perhaps the most extraordinary demonstrations of devotion contained in the letters of this period are to be found in the ones composed by Beethoven as New Year's greetings to his princely patron. The first to be preserved is dated December 31, 1816. After an opening report on his health—"it will probably be some time before I shall be able to cease worrying about the state of my health"—Beethoven continues:

> The year is coming to an end. My warmest wishes for the welfare of Y.I.H. begin with the New Year. With me, it is true, these wishes neither begin nor end. For every day I cherish those same wishes for Y.I.H. If I may add another wish for myself, then I should like Y.I.H. to allow me to grow and thrive in your grace and favour. The master will constantly strive not to be unworthy of the favour of his illustrious master and pupil—
>
> > *Your Imperial Highness's*
> > *most obedient servant*
> > LUDWIG VAN BEETHOVEN[37]

There are but a few important letters preserved for the year 1817, in part because it was a year of recurrent, severe illness for Beethoven (see pp. 332–3). The Archduke was also in "delicate" health, and spent the summer in Baden, where the composer did not go in this summer (he was in Heiligenstadt and Nussdorf, not too far away). Nevertheless, Beethoven was faithful to his custom at the year's end, this one more subdued in tone than its predecessor, but no less expansive in deference:

> The old year is almost at an end and the new year is approaching. May Y.I.H. too have no sorrows but enjoy the greatest happiness that can be conceived. Those are my wishes for Y.I.H., which can all be comprised in this one wish.—If I may be allowed to talk about myself, well, my health is very shaky and uncertain; and unfortunately I am obliged to live at a great distance from Y.I.H.[38] But this is not going to prevent me from giving myself as soon as possible the pleasure of waiting upon you.—I commend myself to your most gracious thoughts about me, even though I may not

---

[36] Ibid., p. 467.
[37] Ibid., II. 625–6, 631–2.
[38] Beethoven was living at the time in the Landstrasse, then a suburb of Vienna.

seem to deserve them. May Heaven shower special blessings on every day of your life for the good of so many other people.

> *But I shall ever be*
> *Your Imperial Highness's*
> *most obedient servant*
> LUDWIG VAN BEETHOVEN[39]

Unquestionably the most remarkable statements made by Beethoven to his Archduke at this period of their joint adventures are contained in the letters of 1819. They begin with the most effusive, to date, of the New Year greetings. "Welfare, happiness and blessings" are the least of the benefits Beethoven confers on Rudolph. As an explanation for the interruption of their relationship late in 1818, Beethoven cites, without elaboration, "a terrible event . . . in my family circumstances" by which for a time "I was absolutely driven out of my mind."[40] His nephew, who lately had been living under Beethoven's supervision, had run away to his mother.[41] He apologizes for not having reported on his receipt of

> the masterly variations of my highly honoured and illustrious pupil who is a favorite of the Muses. I dare not express my thanks either verbally or in writing for this surprise and for the favour with which I have been honoured. For I am *too lowly placed* and unable, however ardently I may intend or desire to do so, *to repay you in the same coin.* May Heaven be pleased to lend an especially favourable ear to my prayer and to grant my wishes for the health of Y.I.H. In a few days I hope to hear Y.I.H. yourself perform the masterpiece you have sent me; and nothing can delight me more than to assist Y.I.H. to take as soon as possible the seat on Parnassus which has already been prepared for Your Highness.

> *Your Imperial Highness's most obedient*
> *servant in affection and deepest reverence*
> LUDWIG VAN BEETHOVEN

The expressions of "loyalty," "obedience," and "devotion" lavished by Beethoven on Rudolph are understandable, if only in the context of the time. One should also bear in mind the special circumstances of the composer's need, his involvement with Karl, the real or fancied financial stringencies of which he often complained. He may, if only in moments of depression, apprehension, or even aberration, have feared that being

---

[39] Anderson: *The Letters of Beethoven,* II, 724.
[40] Ibid., p. 789. The letter is dated January 1, 1819. The italics are reproduced as written.
[41] Thayer-Forbes (1964), II, 757.

separated from the Archduke—either by the former's death or his own grave "offense"—called for the expressions of concern to which he repeatedly gave voice.

But was it incumbent upon him, the greatest musical mind of his time, to praise so extravagantly a work by a noble, even a noble who was his own pupil and had chosen a theme of his master's—"O Hoffnung"—on which to write forty variations? Or even more, to endorse it as a "masterpiece," a term he would not award to such eminent contemporary professionals as Spohr or to Weber for his *Euryanthe*?

To be sure, the Archduke embellished his effort with a tribute unique among all the royalty with whom Beethoven dealt in his lifetime and to whom he dedicated music he composed. Rudolph reciprocated by dedicating his *own work* to Beethoven.[42] This, together with the use of a Beethoven theme for his variations, may have impelled the master to an expression of commendation meant only for the royal eyes. But however selective the intention, one cannot plead extenuation for the musical judgment of a Beethoven. Either he meant it or he didn't. It would be a sorry commentary on the value the world attaches to the innumerable *other* musical judgments of Beethoven were it to excuse this one—"just once"—as a permissible act of hypocrisy.

Or is it possible, as his own works grew more complicated and his withdrawal from the world more complete, that the eminence of Rudolph, his comprehension (apparent if not real) of what Beethoven was doing as well as his gestures of concern for the cursed complications with Karl, were converted into a kind of affection that came to border on attachment, devotion, even love?

As Napoleon is remembered as the instigator of Beethoven's *Eroica* and, in the end, proved himself unworthy of the composer's esteem, so too is Archduke Rudolph remembered in perpetuity as the instigator of the *Missa Solemnis*. It was on the occasion of the Archduke's next name-day that Beethoven announced the intention quoted on pages 235–6.

Whether Rudolph was, in truth, worthy of the tribute is beside the point. He died in 1832, after only a dozen years as Archbishop. There is no evidence to indicate that Beethoven subsequently passed judgment on his worthiness or unworthiness, no rash act of destroying a dedication because his faith had been misplaced. The Archduke's merit was in the result it engendered, rather than in himself or his qualification for it.

[42] Anderson: *The Letters of Beethoven*, II, 789 n.

XIII

The Sacred Mass,
and the Secular

I

I<small>T IS BY NOW</small> Correct Opinion, following the valuable lead of J. W. N. Sullivan, that, in the music he poured into the last five quartets, Beethoven rose "above the battle."[1] The question inevitably arises: When was the battle joined? On what terrain was it fought? And what was the prize Beethoven earned in order to emerge purified, withdrawn, spiritually superior to those about him?

The battle was not a skirmish fought to a finish in one action. It was a series of encounters drawn out over days and weeks, months and years. It was not a test of physical strength against a tangible opponent, a collision of irresistible force and immovable object. It was an exercise of will, of stamina, and of faith sustained over a longer time than Beethoven had sustained any previous continuous effort. The task was the self-appointed one he assumed to make the *Missa Solemnis* he composed for the enthronement of Archduke Rudolph as Cardinal-Archbishop[2] at Olmütz on March 19, 1820, worthy of a Pope's. In the end,

---

[1] J. W. N. Sullivan: *Beethoven's Spiritual Development* (New York: Alfred A. Knopf; 1927). On the last of its 262 pages, indeed in the very last sentence of his eloquent argument, Sullivan employs the very phrase itself.

[2] Both titles are included in the dedication, whose English version reads: "Dedicated with deepest respect to his Imperial Highness the most Eminent Cardinal Rudolph Archduke of Austria, Prince of Hungary and Bohemia, Archbishop of Ollmütz. (The wording and spelling are reproduced as printed on the title page of the Eulenburg edition, London, edited, with an Introduction by Willy Hess; no date.)

the one glorified was Beethoven himself, for having created what is, on balance, the noblest structure erected to the glory of music to that time.

The rumblings and portents of the encounter to come, its distant tremors and turmoils, may be found in sketches for what became the Ninth Symphony. They preceded by several years anything associated with the *Missa Solemnis*. Among the ideas contained in a sketchbook of 1815 for the second Cello Sonata (Opus 102, in D) is a notation in D minor for a four-measure theme almost identically the motive of the symphony's scherzo. It is marked "Fuge."[3] The next recognizable element of No. 9 intrudes into the sketches for the B-flat Sonata (Opus 106) of 1817. It is greater than a fragment or motive, more like the plot of a whole movement. It shows connecting links and instrumental details clearly related to bridge passages and climaxes of the first Allegro.[4] What it doesn't show is a concept for an opening, let alone the eventual revelation of a musical cosmos as it grows from the nebular to the material to the organic.[5] In a subsequent juxtaposition of the two, the Fuge (or Scherzo) is marked "3te Stück." There is no suggestion, at this point, of an interconnecting link, or how the work will be carrried to its conclusion.

By 1818, there are indications that Beethoven is thinking of two symphonies: one will have vocal elements, one will not. Which will embody the content already sketched cannot be determined. It is, clearly, a work in D minor. How or where the vocal material is utilized might, on the basis of past procedure, be construed as largely a mechanical problem (as for example, the separation of the finale of Opus 30, No. 1, from the rest of that work (see p. 180) and its conversion into the generating force of the A-major, Opus 47 ("Kreutzer"), Sonata. The concept of the scherzo as the *third* movement in a symphonic sequence did not, apparently, lead him where he wants to go. The work on the symphony, or the symphonies, is set aside, not to be resumed in an outward, visible form, for five years.

But within every truly gifted creator there is at work what Mahler termed a "second me,"[6] that "deeper manifestation of the creative will"[7]

---

[3] Nottebohm: *Zweite Beethoveniana*, pp. 157 ff.

[4] Ibid., pp. 159–61.

[5] See definition of "nebular hypothesis" (*Webster's New International Dictionary, Second Edition*, p. 1,634).

[6] La Grange: *Mahler*, Vol. I, p. 580. Mahler's term occurs in a letter describing his surprise and satisfaction at discovering, on resumption of work on the Symphony No. 4 in June 1900, that problems unresolved when he had left off work the previous fall had resolved themselves, mentally, over the winter.

[7] See Foreword.

which intervenes to solve problems when all the marshaled forces of the engaged intellect cannot. For Beethoven it was the outward decision of the engaged intelligence that he apply himself to the act of homage on behalf of his patron, the Archduke Rudolph, by writing a Mass. But the deeper urge may have been prompted by a restless determination to resolve the spiritual dilemma by engaging it on another front.

Some indications exist that Beethoven had begun to think of "a" church work well before the letter of June 1819 in which he announced his intention to Rudolph (see p. 235). The evidence is not to be found, however, in the sketchbooks of 1819–20 which were originally published as the public documentation of the *Missa's* creation.[8] The first begins with sketches for the Credo, justifying Nottebohm's statement of 1887: "Zum Kyrie sind keine Skizzen vorhänden" ("For the Kyrie no sketches exist").[9]

By 1818, however, new sources of information on Beethoven's thoughts and intentions had been added to the sketchbooks. They are the Konversationshefte, or Conversation Books, which Beethoven had devised in the early months of 1818 when his deafness grew so severe he could no longer hear questions addressed to him by visitors. In most instances, he replied verbally, thus his answers do not appear in the text.[10] But often enough the drift of the answer can be deduced from the following question. From time to time, especially when he wanted to be sure his meaning was understood, he wrote it out in his own hand.

Now and then, Beethoven used the rough-textured, crudely bound block of paper as the most accessible medium for preserving some musical thought that had just crossed his mind. In Warren Kirkendale's excellent essay "New Roads to Old Ideas in Beethoven's *Missa Solemnis*"[11] there is a reference to one such entry on page 27, vol. I, of the Conversation Books. Under the handwritten staff may be discerned the syllables "Elee." On the staff are a group of notes in a rising pattern. Above the staff is the abbreviation "dor." Conjecturally, "Elee" could be part of "Kyrie Eleison," with "dor" meaning "Dorian" mode.

A direct association with the *Missa* for Rudolph is compromised by the date assigned to these pages: February–March 1818. This would precede by more than a year the announcement of Rudolph's elevation

---

[8] Ludwig van Beethoven: *Drei Skizzenbücher zur Missa Solemnis*, ed., with an Introduction, by Joseph Schmidt-Görg (Bonn: Beethovenhaus; 1952).

[9] Nottebohm: *Zweite Beethoveniana*, p. 148.

[10] Georg Schünemann, ed.: *Ludwig van Beethovens Konversationshefte* (Berlin: Max Hesse Verlag; 1941), I, II, and III. These texts cover the Conversation Books for a five-year period, 1818–23.

[11] In Lang: *The Creative World of Beethoven*, pp. 163–99.

to Cardinal (in April 1819) or to Archbishop (June 1819). The alternate options are: to assume that the Archduke's ecclesiastical conditioning presupposed such future destinies, and Beethoven had knowledge that it would only be a matter of months, or a year or so; to presume that the notation contained "Auf dem hinteren Deckelblatt" ("On the back cover leaf") might have been made at some time *closer* to the events of 1819; or to conclude that Beethoven had impulses and thoughts relating to church music independent of Archduke Rudolph, whose appointment brought them into focus.

It is, in any case, a certainty that there *were* sketches for the Kyrie of which Nottebohm was unaware. They are contained in the Wittgenstein sketchbook,[12] along with sketches for many of the *Diabelli* Variations (see p. 262). However, Kirkendale is illuminating on the kind of musical thinking that went into the Kyrie, as on numerous other aspects of the *Missa*. He directs attention to the long-standing convention for opening any proper Mass with a *topos*, or "traditional formulation" for this text. The *topos* is a group of sustained, repeated notes, of which Kirkendale cites examples as far back as Biber's *Missa Sancti Henrici* of 1701 and a Cavalli *Missa Concertata* of 1656. He might also have looked into Beethoven's own Mass in C (Opus 86) and discovered, as I did, that this too opens with a Kyrie Eleison on just such repeated tones. The rhythmic values are different, but one is unmistakably the counterpart of the other.

Indeed, the employment of a *topos*, or prescribed opening phrase, could explain the lack of more elaborate sketches for this portion of the Kyrie. The broadening of the rhythmic pattern for the purposes of the "solemn mass" appropriate to Rudolph's high office could have been evolved mentally by Beethoven, the creative effort gone on from there.

12 Ludwig van Beethoven: *Ein Skizzenbuch den Diabelli-Variationen und zur Missa Solemnis*, SV 154, ed., with an Introduction, by Joseph Schmidt-Görg (Bonn: Beethovenhaus; 1972), pp. 18, 19, 20.

This common point of departure toward totally different outcomes invites attention to a supremely beautiful work which is not heard as often as it might be. The C-major Mass (Opus 86) was a product of 1807, when Beethoven would still write a Mass on commission. This one was ordered by Prince Nikolaus Esterházy (II) to commemorate the name day of his wife (née Marie von Liechtenstein). Such a commission was an annual Esterházy custom, which had been fulfilled on six prior occasions by Joseph Haydn. For all its considerable quality, Opus 86 might be described as a Haydn Mass by Beethoven, in which the temperature of the creative effort rarely rises above body heat, and the personal participation is more *pro forma* than *con amore*. Structurally it attains heights beyond Haydn's power, but it often looks backward rather than forward in its choice of musical materials.

As an instance, the mezzo's pronouncement of "Qui tollis peccata mundi" is framed on a musical line more suggestive of Mozart or Gluck than of Beethoven. Nevertheless, and presumably because of an occasional deviation from strict conformity to the expected conventions, the Prince is reputed to have greeted the composer at the work's end by saying: "My dear Beethoven, what have you written there!" Some royalty fanciers attribute this as an attempt at an aristocratic pleasantry,[13] but Beethoven reacted with displeasure. In any case, he took his leave of Eisenstadt on September 13, 1807, the day of the work's performance, and dedicated the score to Prince Ferdinand Kinsky.

Not only was the Beethoven of 1819 a different man physically than he had been a dozen years before. His motivation to write the *Missa Solemnis* was, by the measure of the C-major Mass, as blood is

[13] Mass, Opus 86; see the Eulenburg edition, London, edited, with an Introduction, by Willy Hess (no date), p. vii.

to water, however holy. He not only commissioned *himself* to this act of glorification on behalf of the man to whom he owed so much. He immersed himself in the task with the wholeness of his heart and the fullness of his mind. From the emotional source he derived a depth of involvement in the drama of life and death such as he had rarely expressed since the *Cantata on the Death of the Emperor Joseph* (the then-infant Archduke's uncle). From the intellectual center he invoked a wide survey of much music he had written previously, ordering it to a range of allusions, symbols, and rhetorical gestures greater than are to be found in any prior composition by him.

On the one side, he found his emotional involvement urging him to dimensions of effort he had not contemplated. On the other, the challenge of the timeless text and the musical values it had acquired over centuries put him to an intellectual exertion which projected question upon question and demanded unqualified answers. Clearly the commitment to bring his work to completion by the time the Archduke had become the Archbishop could not be met.[14]

2

As EARLY AS 1818, Beethoven had written a note to himself in a kind of day book he maintained at the time: "In order to write true church music—look for all the plainchants of the monks."[15] This was but the first in a long sequence of other remarks, inquiries, and references bearing on his desire to compose a work that would, in every detail, be worthy of consideration as a true *Missa Solemnis*.

This took in a host of details, for which he sought out sources, plied visitors with questions (the Conversation Books bear on this), and immersed himself in any documentation—philosophical as well as musical—that would contribute to his purpose. As he toured the terrain and digested the points of reference that would guide him to his objective, he also marshaled everything in his own conditioning that would contribute to the fulfillment he sought.

Included were his background as a teen-aged church musician in Bonn, when he became versed in the function of such a section as the Praeludium preceding the Benedictus. Conventionally, it is the organist

---

[14] Thayer-Forbes (1964), II, 743. "Every movement had taken on larger dimensions than had originally been contemplated."

[15] Lang: *The Creative World of Beethoven*, see Warren Kirkendale's essay, "New Roads to Old Ideas in Beethoven's *Missa Solemnis*," p. 174.

who is charged with improvising this bridge passage. Beethoven drew upon his background in Bonn for the creation of an orchestral prelude which glorified this space as it rarely has been before or since. The modal colorations appropriate to other portions of the Mass were part of his indoctrination with Haydn and Albrechtsberger (see p. 59). In such circumstances he might have become acquainted with the latter's setting of the "Gloria in excelsis." It defines the traditional rising pattern which gives to its melodic outline a sense of heavenly ascent

and imparts to Beethoven's version a rough-hewn strength and sense of authenticity

that exceed what he had done along the same lines in Opus 86.[16]

The *tremolando* in music has been associated with trembling, in the physical sense, from the time that the device was first employed by Monteverdi in his *Combattimento di Tancredi e Clorinda* in the early 1600s. Beethoven reached for it, instinctively or with all deliberation, in his slow movement of Opus 18, No. 1. This Adagio has sometimes been associated, through a remark attributed to the composer, with the Tomb Scene of *Romeo and Juliet* (the redoubtable Nottebohm deciphered an inscription over a sketch of it, reading "les derniers soupirs" as "the last sighs").[17] This application of the tremolo may be read into Beethoven's utilization of it in the Crucifixus, in which trembling assuredly has a place. It may also be noted that Beethoven was well-versed in the most famous of all musical responses to the drama of the Crucifixion. In a letter of October 15, 1810, addressed to Breitkopf and Härtel, he requests, among other scores, for the favor of one "in which there is said to be the following Crucifixus with a basso ostinato."[18]

[16] Ibid., p. 166.
[17] Nottebohm: *Zweite Beethoveniana*, p. 485.
[18] Anderson: *The Letters of Beethoven*, I, 299.

(Beethoven's freehand sketch misstates the key [it is E minor, calling for one sharp, rather than E major, with the four sharps he utilizes] but the work he is requesting is, in any case, Bach's B-minor Mass.)

Year by year, Beethoven accumulated means and resources which he would draw upon, knowingly or otherwise, for his life's most formidable achievement. In formulating a setting for Clärchen's death in his incidental music for Goethe's *Egmont*, Beethoven made a note to himself reading, "Death could be expressed by a rest . . ."[19] There are precisely such rests at the appropriate place in the Crucifixus (measure 187) where the orchestra is silent as the tenor voice—what else?—voices the hope of "Et resurrexit." The somber tones of the trombone were plumbed by Beethoven for the "Three Equali" (WoO 30) of 1812 on behalf of a church musician in Linz. They may well have recurred to him when he prefaced the Sanctus with three measures for a brass ensemble.

But one of the most striking uses of instrumental color in the whole of the *Missa Solemnis* comes in the Benedictus. At this moment, in which Beethoven steps back, away from the recitation of sacrifice and suffering, to pronounce the solacing "Blessed is he who cometh in the name of the Lord," he turns to the solo violin for a soaring message of consolation and rejoicing. To some, it is an unchurchly intrusion into what has preceded. To others, it is but Beethoven's way of putting all his musical resources to the service of the purpose to which he has committed himself. To either, it must be recognized as one of the most rarefied, exquisitely beautiful moments in all of Beethoven. It is, indeed, almost but not quite as high a flight of fancy as its prototype in the slow movement of the second Razumovsky Quartet, Opus 59, No. 2. That is the one whose rhapsodic statement, according to Czerny, came to Beethoven's mind as he contemplated the limitless expanse of starry sky on a clear summer's night. It has, too, its relationship (see p. 187) to the philosophy of J. M. Sailer. The palpable echo in the *Missa Solemnis* could be construed as an expression of Thanksgiving to Him who made the firmament of a magnitude to inspire such wonder, fervor and devotion. If there is any disposition to prefer (measures 69 *ff.*)

[19] Lang: *The Creative World of Beethoven*, Kirkendale's essay, p. 179.

in the quartet to

in the *Missa Solemnis,* it would be only because the quartet's first violin has a clear, untrammeled access to the ear. The solo violin in the Mass must share his rapture with the vocal quartet and, eventually, the chorus.

As for the fugal writing which provides the strong spinal column of structure throughout, it is clearly bred in the bone through the strength of hand and mind Beethoven developed in achieving the finales of the Opus 35 Variations, the Opus 59, No. 3, Quartet, and the Opus 106 Sonata (among numerous others). Could Beethoven have written the kind of *Missa Solemnis* he did without the mental exercise that produced the sketches for the first two movements of what eventually became the Ninth Symphony? An unlikely prospect, in my opinion. But it is a *certainty* that he could *not* have achieved the sublime Adagio and the stupendous Choral Finale of the Ninth Symphony without the emotional transformation he underwent in bringing the *Missa* to completion.

3

SUCH CITATIONS OF MATERIALS and means derived from his prior achievements provide a reminder of the richness of the soil in which the *Missa Solemnis* is rooted. It would, in all probability, have grown a superbly beautiful tree in any circumstance. It yielded the sturdy oak it did through the soil's enrichment by Beethoven's ceaseless quest for other, regenerating elements. Some reference has already been made to Beethoven's interest in plainchant, which comes into the Dorian Kyrie, and the antique-sounding "Et incarnatus est" for chorus that precedes its conversion into pure, super-rich Beethoven for the solo soprano voice.

But this was only the beginning of the research that contributed directly to the scope and variety of music in the *Missa Solemnis,* and indirectly to the works he wrote *during and after* its creation. Among the sources he sought out was the *Institutioni armoniche*[20] of Gioseffe Zarlino (1517–90), a Venetian-based maestro di cappella who is better known for theoretical works than for his compositions. During the last months of 1819 and the first months of 1820, entries may be found in the Conversation Books indicating Beethoven's interest in obtaining this material. One visitor confirms, "Wir haben einige alte Italiener—Zarlino,"[21] and in the month that followed, Beethoven confirmed, from an aide of Prince Lobkowitz named Karl Peters, "Wir haben den

[20] *Grove's Dictionary of Music and Musicians,* 5th edn., IX, 400–1.
[21] Schünemann: *Ludwig van Beethovens Konversationshefte,* I, 100.

Zarlino." "Wir" in this instance would refer to the library of his employer, Lobkowitz.[22]

In addition to providing Beethoven with the particular kind of modal information for which he was seeking, the work of Zarlino could also have directed his attention to "the well-known canto fermo" in Book III:[23]

as a basis for his own figure from which evolved "pacem, pacem," one of the most dazzling choral passages in the whole *Missa*:

Indeed, the library of the Archduke Rudolph himself, famous not only for its complete collection of Beethoven's works but for many other musical treasures, was drawn upon for the Mass in his honor as need arose. In a letter of July 29, 1819, following by some weeks the announcement of his intention of writing a Mass (see p. 235), Beethoven wrote to his patron, summering in Baden, to express concern about his health and to mention: "I was in Vienna in order to collect in Y.I.H.'s library what was most useful for me."[24]

Clearly, anything pertaining to the Mass, its traditions and its authentic practices, was of interest to Beethoven's wide-ranging mind, his capacity for absorbing all that pertained to any major project in which he was engaged. One of his recurrent visitors in the period of the

[22] *Ibid.*, p. 193.
[23] *Grove's Dictionary of Music and Musicians*, 5th edn., IX, 401.
[24] Anderson: *The Letters of Beethoven*, II, 822. 1819 was one of the summers Beethoven spent in Mödling.

1820 Conversation Books was a Herr von Janitschek,[25] who reported that the critic August Friedrich Kanne, whose knowledge and credentials Beethoven respected, had "written a History of the Mass. It is now at the Censor's." According to Kirkendale, Kanne's work was never published, but it is his opinion that "even if Beethoven did not read it, he very probably benefited from it through Kanne's advice."[26]

It is well known that the older he grew and the more he came to know his predecessors' music, the greater became Beethoven's esteem for the works of Handel. Direct testimony of this is conveyed in a report compiled by an English visitor, Johann Andreas Stumpff, who visited him at Baden during the summer of 1824. Stumpff came in the company of Tobias Haslinger (see p. 233) and with letters of introduction from other mutual friends. Beethoven was uncommonly cordial to Stumpff and responsive to his questions. The first query (all written out, of course) was "Whom do you consider the greatest composer that ever lived?" "Handel" was Beethoven's instantaneous reply; "to him I bow the knee," and he bent one knee to the floor.[27] It was as a consequence of his visit and the responses it aroused that Stumpff, a German-born musician who had prospered in England as a manufacturer of harps, sent Beethoven the forty-volume complete works of Handel which the composer read with frequently expressed admiration during his last illness.

The indirect expression of Beethoven's high regard for Handel may be read in a variety of earlier works, but nowhere else so conspicuously as in the *Missa Solemnis*. Not only is the choral writing in general affected by Handel's preference for long lines, great sonorities, and ear-filling structures—frequently founded on a fugal theme in the bass— but there are evidences of more specific paternity.

Beethoven's knowledge of Handel at the time of Stumpff's visit was clearly defined when the visitor said: "As you yourself, a peerless artist in the art of music, exalt the merits of Handel so highly above all others, you must certainly own the scores of his principal works." Beethoven's answer was: "I? How should I, a poor devil, have gotten them? Yes, the scores of *Messiah* and *Alexander's Feast* went through my hands."[28] Clearly, *Messiah* went further than through his hands. In addition to the generalized evidence of his study of that score,

[25] Ibid., I, 242. January–March. No Beethoven source known to me contains any further information about Janitschek, even his surname.

[26] Lang: *The Creative World of Beethoven*, p. 199.

[27] Thayer-Forbes (1964), II, 920.

[28] Ibid., I, 290. It was then, says Stumpff, that he decided on his gift to Beethoven.

there are references in the *Missa* to several specific passages in *Messiah*, as Martin Cooper cites in his admirable verbalization of the *Missa* and its antecedents.[29] Kirkendale[30] regards the shape and tone of the Benedictus as an adaptation to Beethoven's purposes of the mood and character of "He shall feed His flock." In his view, the tonal design of the fugal theme underlying "Dona nobis" (p. 350 of the Eulenburg miniature score, at measure 216 of the "Agnus Dei") is based "on a subject from Handel's Hallelujah Chorus." This, clearly, would be "and He shall reign forever and ever."

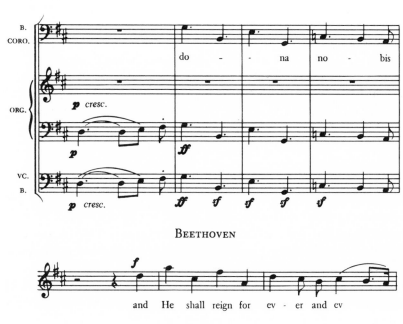

BEETHOVEN

HANDEL

If this was, indeed, an instance of Beethoven borrowing "consciously," it would be the living affirmation of the verbal *devoir*: "To him I bow the knee."

It was by such acts of admiration, cogitation, and investigation that Beethoven created for the *Missa Solemnis* a background of allusion without precedent in his literature. The alphabet of individuals ranged from A for Albrechtsberger to Z for Zarlino, over a time period from Venice in 1565 (when Zarlino became maestro di cappella at St. Mark's)

[29] Martin Cooper: *Beethoven: The Last Decade* (London: Oxford University Press; 1970), pp. 227 and 272.
[30] Lang: *The Creative World of Beethoven*, p. 194.

to Vienna in 1785, when Albrechtsberger wrote the Gloria quoted on page 249. Among others whose attainments and examples entered enduringly into Beethoven's choice of options, alternatives, and examples were J. S. Bach, Luigi Cherubini, the Haydns (Michael as well as Joseph), Handel, Mozart, Kanne, and all the others with whom he consulted and to whose informed opinions he gave the amount of attention they deserved.

It thus becomes understandable why the *Missa Solemnis* should occupy its creator for a time far beyond the period he originally considered probable. The indications are that the Kyrie and Gloria evolved with fair rapidity. They comprise the acts of affirmation, of celebration and praise, for which the musical symbols and their rhetorical equivalents were relatively accessible. According to Nottebohm,[31] the Kyrie was completed (in sketch or outline) in 1818–19, the Gloria by the end of 1819. What then might have delayed Beethoven's conclusion of his task for another *three* years, and what was he doing in the meantime?

4

LEAST OF ALL was he doing nothing. An inordinate amount of his time in these years—1820–23—was preempted by physical illness and the involvement with his nephew, which might be called a form of spiritual illness. But there still was music. In particular, such music as is associated with the last three piano sonatas and the *Variations on a Waltz of Diabelli* (Opus 120). They were all part of the shuttle-and-loom procedure which Beethoven evolved at this time to advance the pattern of the Mass toward completion. It was not uncommon, of course, for Beethoven to be engaged with two or more major works simultaneously. But it was a divinely decreed selectivity—paralleling the direction his mind took in 1802—that impelled him toward music for the piano and nothing but the piano.

Was it psychological or physiological or something of both that made him forget his reluctance (see p. 223) of a decade or so before to "spend much time on solo sonatas"? Anton Schindler, who was at his closest to Beethoven during the period in which the *Missa Solemnis* was being completed (1822), has written: "While composing music for the pianoforte, the master would often go to the instrument and try certain passages, especially those that might present difficulties in performance. At such times he was totally oblivious of anyone present.

---

[31] Nottebohm: *Zweite Beethoveniana*, p. 152.

To this circumstance I owe my acquaintance with the complete sonatas, Opus numbers 106, 109, and 110, and parts of the last sonata, Opus 111. While working on a score, however, he played no instrument, and because it annoyed him to see anyone go through a work that was still incomplete, even those living in the same house heard nothing of a new symphonic work until it was rehearsed."[32]

These being his habits of work, it is at least thinkable that Beethoven may have been drawn toward the piano in order to work manually again with tone and vibration, even if his ability to hear both was minimal. At least while he was in Mödling, during the summers of 1818, 1819, and 1820, he could work with the Broadwood of which he was enamored. The peculiarities of registration which can be noted as a characteristic of the works in A (Opus 101) and B-flat (Opus 106) are even more pronounced in the last three. At a guess, it could be said that more than seventy percent of the writing is concentrated in the top and bottom registers of the instrument, with the middle only occasionally utilized. My conclusion is that these were the parts of the instrument's range from which he could still derive some aural intake; leaving out the middle range clarified his limited perception of the principal lines of what he wrote.

Beethoven may have called these works sonatas out of habit, or simply to preserve a succession in being ("a new example of the same"), but they were, musically, very little like the characteristic sonatas of the past. Beginning with the E-major, they are more like meditations or reveries. This means that they fare best in the versions of those who are less performers than communicators—a Rachmaninoff, Schnabel, Myra Hess, or Wilhelm Backhaus. There are some fine performers—such as Vladimir Horowitz—who consider them works "for the studio" rather than "for the public" precisely because they *are* performers. When asked why, if this were so, Rachmaninoff (whom he idolized) performed the Opus 109 in public, Horowitz responded: "To show it shouldn't be done."

Of the concurrence of the E-major Sonata in Beethoven's mind with thoughts of the Mass there can be no possible doubt. The written notations are to be found in the sketchbook for 1819–20,[33] devoted in large part to the Gloria and Credo of the *Missa Solemnis*. It is indeed eerie, even mysterious, to see the outlines of a delicate bit of tonal filigree among phrases meant to be thundered out by hundreds! The

[32] Schindler: *Beethoven as I Knew Him*, p. 270.
[33] Beethoven: *Drei Skizzenbücher zur Missa Solemnis*, pp. 38–40.

more remarkable then that one was no less representative of his thinking than the other.

My reason for describing these works as meditations or reveries rather than sonatas is contained in the sense of the improvised, the unpremeditated, the spontaneous they convey. The E-major is barely under way with a flowing Vivace line than it pauses for an Adagio that culminates in a series of arpeggios that sweep keyboard-like hands on harp strings for half a dozen elongated measures. Then back to the Vivace, and back once more to the Adagio, and again, in a finalizing way, to the Vivace. It is an outpouring of impulse and musical imagery that takes almost longer to describe than to play. There is more forward movement in the Prestissimo, which serves the function of a Scherzo, but it is hung on the framework of a Rondo, with no pattern of repetitions. Beethoven utilizes repeats only in the third movement, which begins with one of those hymnal tunes (not unlike the slow movement of the Archduke trio) marked Andante molto cantabile ed espressivo. This gives every promise of being a conventionally unconventional slow movement in the tonality of the opening, and perhaps a derivative of its tonal design. He leads it—or is led by it—into a pattern of variations of which Nos. I and IV, he decides, are worthy of being heard again. It evolves into a movement of greater length than either of its predecessors. Eventually he arrives at a sixth variation, which begins as a serene discourse and evolves into a pealing of bells high in the treble, which I would choose to serve as a summarizing finale. Beethoven chooses to end with a reversion to the pure form of the theme with which the movement had begun.

Not unlike Opus 109, the emergence of Opus 110 may be discerned among sketches for the *Missa Solemnis*, in the following year of 1821. The sketches emerge, sequentially, among references to Handel's *Messiah* (see p. 225) and are marked "Neue son." ("new sonata").[34] The first four measures of the sonata apparently came to him much as they were used. They are followed by an outline for the fugue with which the work ends—which is hardly unexpected, as the first four notes of the fugue theme are derived directly from the opening theme of the work as a whole. The space between is occupied by a terse Scherzo, and an even terser Adagio. Brief as it is, those versed in musical terminology as Beethoven conceived it in these years will recognize in this slow movement a preachment, a homily, at once eloquent and consoling.

The feeling that Beethoven has not said all he means to say on the subject is confirmed when he interrupts the fugue to say, again,

[34] Nottebohm: *Zweite Beethoveniana*, p. 465.

what he has said before in the Adagio—this time in even more urgent tones. When the fugue resumes, it is with an inversion of the starting theme, which eventually comes back in its first form. Now it is accompanied by a concluding duet of flutes in the highest register of the keyboard. When one has heard these last three works often enough, they begin to possess interior relationships—such as the A-flat's opening as another variation of the E-major's slow movement—which are literal as well as chronological. For whatever significance it may contain, the date of completion entered into the autograph for Opus 110 is December 25, 1821—Beethoven's Christmas present to himself.

Adjacent to the sketched themes for Opus 110 are ideas for what Beethoven notes as "2te Sonate." The appropriate interpretation of this compositional shorthand would be as a reminder to distinguish it from the A-flat as the foregoing, or "first," sonata of a pair. Some of the jottings are in the key of C minor; others that follow are in B-flat and A-flat. But the one that captures my attention is inscribed "3te Stück presto" and has no key signature at all.[35]

It is, peculiarly, not the eruptive, dramatic opening with which, once heard, Opus 111 is forever identified. Rather than this "crack of doom" chordal formation, it is the jagged, sharp-featured phrase with which the main body of the Allegro con brio is launched, sixteen measures later. Soon enough the outline of the fugal treatment to come is notated, the main lines of the developing movement defined.

Here, again, one encounters one of those striking examples of a thing that *was* recurring in the guise of a thing about to *become*. As identified by Nottebohm,[36] the outline was contained in a book of 1802 devoted in considerable part to sketches for the D-major Symphony (Opus 36, No. 2) and adjacent to a sketch for the Violin and Piano Sonata in A, Opus 30, No. 1.

Somewhat in the manner of the slow movement of Opus 101 (see pp. 228–9), it was a productive *pattern* that etched its way into his mind, not a concept of pace or character. With the first thought, of 1816, Beethoven forged a slow movement out of an Allegro. With the second, of 1802, he shaped a jagged, angry statement out of a brooding, nondemonstrative one:

---

[35] Nottebohm: *Zweite Beethoveniana*, pp. 467–8.
[36] Gustav Nottebohm: *Ein Skizzenbuch von Beethoven* (New York and London: Johnson Reprint Corporation; 1970), p. 19. Originally published by Druck und Verlag Breitkopf und Härtel, Leipzig, 1880. Not to be confused with *Ein Skizzenbuch von Beethoven aus dem Jahre* 1803, published in the same Johnson reprint volume.

But the shape of the musical seedling in both instances is unmistakable.

The question, of course, is: Did Beethoven carry the idea in mind for nearly *twenty* years, secure and hidden during the creation of scores of other works only to finally re-imagine it? Or was there some methodical project by which it was rediscovered? A new light on this perplexing speculation (see p. 7) was beamed recently by an expert on the sketchbooks whose word should carry weight beyond the ordinary. In reviewing the subject of "Beethoven's Early Sketches,"[37] Joseph Kerman writes: "It is sometimes said that the reason he kept them [the sketchbooks] was in order to go back and pick up unused ideas. A number of cases have been pointed out in the literature when he actually did so, but they are really very few. . . ." The likelihood of the theme for Opus 111 being among them is, in my opinion, negligible. The recurrence of 1821 is an act of spontaneous generation in another key, at another speed, and with an altered rhythmic formulation. It strikes me as another example of the retentive resources of Beethoven's mind, its ability to recycle an idea whose possibilities had never been fully explored. In this instance, it was almost certainly the interval (diminished fourth) which retained its power as an irritant until Beethoven liberated it in a productive pattern.

If this tension-loaded Allegro is an instance of an early first thought being utilized in the last of Beethoven's sonatas, the much-quoted, endlessly admired Arietta is quite the opposite—a pioneering instance of the last being first. Who else has dared to make so rarefied a statement the terminal movement of a broadly based sonata structure? Far beyond the stupendously simple melodic design itself is the *enchaînement*—to use a balletic term meaning a sequence of steps or turns—of trills which give it wings, carry it to ever loftier heights until it touches the very top of the keyboard then available to Beethoven.

Was this the reason the sonata was begun in C minor and projected to finish in C major? There could be many less practical explanations. It came to birth at a time[38] when Beethoven was brooding on his treatment of the Agnus Dei and what would follow in the *Missa Solemnis*. It could have been a second form of Benedictus, this one for an indi-

[37] Lang: *The Creative World of Beethoven*, see Joseph Kerman's essay, p. 30 *n.*
[38] Nottebohm: *Zweite Beethoveniana*, pp. 470–1.

vidual's own personal pronouncement at the keyboard—beginning with Beethoven himself.

Each of the last three sonatas, it may be noted, contains the patterns of procedure, the incitements to expression to which Beethoven was compulsively attracted at this time—fugue and variations. They occur at different places, with varying degrees of prominence—but they do, inevitably, occur.

5

AMONG THE EXAMPLE of truths which are stranger than fiction a place of prominence—if not of honor—should be reserved for the publisher who wrote, on receipt of the copy for engraving of Opus 111, to inquire whether perhaps a third movement had not been inadvertently omitted? It is verifiable, if hardly believable, fact that Moritz Schlesinger,[39] who had established a business in Paris, wrote to Beethoven on July 3, 1822, suggesting that perhaps the composer's copyist had been remiss in not sending a finale. The publisher who collaborated with Beethoven on the next, and last, of his works for piano could hardly have had such a complaint. It was the great project on which he had been engaged intermittently since 1819, consisting of thirty-three variations on a waltz by Anton Diabelli. When the composer-publisher heard that Beethoven was taking his theme seriously enough to write several variations on it, he made an extravagant offer—eighty ducats—for the publishing rights. He had to wait years for the results, but they were well worth waiting for.[40]

The earliest group of variations on Diabelli's theme have been identified with early 1819 and "come just before the preliminary sketches for the Kyrie of the *Missa Solemnis*."[41] There are mentions of such variation in correspondence of 1820, and by 1822 Beethoven could advise a prospective publisher "there are many." The composer did not consider his work finished until 1823, which means that it bracketed the whole period of his composition of the *Missa Solemnis*, and much of the time in which he was involved with the Ninth Symphony. The project embodied a massive amount of musical thinking and an exploratory

[39] Thayer-Forbes (1964), II, 786. Adolf Schlesinger was a Berlin publisher with whom Beethoven often did business. His son Moritz began the Paris venture in 1822.

[40] Schindler: *Beethoven as I Knew Him*, p. 252. The amount was eventually set at forty ducats.

[41] Thayer-Forbes (1964), II, 853.

probe of pianistic possibilities which, taken together, comprise a proper valedictory to the keyboard for one of Beethoven's massive achievements. At a total playing time of nearly fifty-five minutes in one standard recording,[42] it is by far the longest among all of Beethoven's solo piano works —in duration the equivalent of the *Eroica* Symphony.

The question of length in a sequence of variations would seem wholly a by-product of the number a composer chose to write. Lacking considerations of organic unity or internal relationship that might govern a sonata or a rondo on an elaborate plan, a sequence of variations could be prolonged indefinitely with relatively little strain. It is, in part, this misconception of Opus 120 which has relegated it to the role of a non-historic Brontosaurus even among people with an appreciation for, say, the Grosse Fuge.

As the Wittgenstein sketchbook demonstrates,[43] the first variations to be written were *not* those numbered 1, 2, 3, etc., in the published sequence. They were, rather, outlines of segments that became Nos. XI, XVIII, XIX, and XXXII (Fuga). Beethoven's utilization of them at scattered, strategic points in the final sequence leaves no doubt that he eventually conceived the variations as possessed of a ground plan. The contents, in consequence, were balanced and organized no less than those of any other extended work. The concept of Opus 120 as a "Variations-Sonata" is supported by the grouping of three extended sections (Nos. 29–31) in slow tempo before the final fugue. Working backward from this finale and slow movement, the earlier episodes can be arranged as introduction, first movement, Scherzo, etc. Indeed, Hans von Bülow[44] urged the performer to avoid fragmentation of the thirty-three into individual entities by grouping them in grand segments of ten, thirteen, five and five. The interpeter is, of course, at liberty to make the groupings according to the logic that satisfies his own criteria.

On behalf of either the prescribed, or a free association of, elements, the following commentary has been devised to describe Beethoven's procedure:

> *Theme:* The theme was derisively described by Beethoven as a *Schusterfleck*, or a witless invention in which repetitions occur sequentially by a stepwise progression up the scale. The outline has the merit of recognizability, meaning that it is hard to disguise.

---

[42] By Stephen Bishop; Philips PHS 900–220. The elapsed time for the two sides is 54'34". By contrast, Vladimir Ashkenazy's version of the "Hammerklavier" Sonata on London CS 6563 totals 42'35".

[43] Beethoven: *Ein Skizzenbuch den Diabelli-Variationen* . . . , pp. 6–19.

[44] Beethoven, Variations, I, 43–91.

I. Alla marcia maestoso: March-like indeed! Beethoven's treatment is good enough to suggest the entrance of the guilds in Wagner's *Die Meistersinger,* the theme with which the overture to that work begins. The effect is heightened by the descending bass line with its jolting passing tone—a Wagnerian touch forty years before Wagner thought of it.

II. Poco allegretto: Broken rhythmic pattern. The repetitions in the theme are respected.

III. L'istesso tempo: The same tempo as before, is the direction. The climbing line in the bass is a form of enrichment whose mastery by Beethoven profited many composers to come.

IV. Un poco piu vivace: This is less a variation of Diabelli's theme than a variant of Beethoven's preceding variation on it. This came to be a procedure by which Brahms and others devised a whole new school of variation writing.

V. Allegro vivace: The trend is to fragmentation, a now familiar device in variation writing—that is, a part of the theme is utilized as a point of departure. The structure of Diabelli's idea is preserved.

VI. Allegro ma non troppo, a serioso: Trills and arpeggios give variety to the further fragmentation of Diabelli's design. "Serioso" applies in greater measure to the second part of the variation, which inverts the pattern and takes on a more dramatic character.

VII. Un poco più allegro: The part of the Diabelli theme that is preserved here, and serves as the connecting link, is the bass line. Over it Beethoven devises a new melodic figure of his own.

VIII. Poco vivace: The paraphrase begins to take on the fanciful latitude of such a dramatic expression as Cyrano's improvisation (descriptive of his nose) in Act I of Rostand's play: " 'Tis a rock—a crag—a cape—A cape? say rather, a peninsula!"[45] As the literary-minded relish Rostand's word play in terms of visual imagery, so the music-minded discern Beethoven's tonal draughtsmanship against a lingering background of Diabelli's pedantic concept.

IX. Allegro pesante e risoluto: Scherzo is the impulse, *stretto* the musical device. (*Stretto* is the Italian term for a contrapuntal formula built on a narrowing time gap in the overlapping of a theme and its answer.)

X. Presto: For the first time, Beethoven disregards the repetitions in Diabelli's theme, and allows his fancy to take him where

---

[45] "C'est un roc! . . . c'est un pic! c'est un cap! . . ." Edmond Rostand: *Cyrano de Bergerac* (Paris: Fasquelle Éditeurs, 1930), p. 44. The English version is Brian Hooker's (New York: Henry Holt; 1923), p. 441.

it will . . . right back into Opus 111, with its deep bass trill and echoes high in the treble.

XI. Allegretto: This is the first to be heard of the "original" variations. It demonstrates how many preliminary alterations could be affected before reaching its kind of flowing contrapuntal interplay.

XII. Un poco più moto: From it emerges something more elaborate in crossing lines and interrelated voices. No formal repetitions.

XIII. Vivace: This typical example of Beethoven's fondness for contrasting *fortes* and *pianos* proceeds directly from No. XII. The rests which separate them caused Beethoven's early commentator, Von Lenz, to describe this variation in terms of its "eloquent pauses . . ." a phrase endorsed as apposite by Hans von Bülow.[46] The pauses become shorter as the pattern evolves.

XIV. Grave e maestoso: From this point forward, Beethoven inclines increasingly to the "transformation" kind of variation which he all but invented. That is, the changes are not in the form of embellishments or fragmentations but are accomplished through extrapolations, deviations, and aggrandizements of the material. Diabelli would, nevertheless, readily recognize the bass line.

XV. Presto scherzando: An instant alteration of mood by means of a lightly fanciful "fanfare" figuration. It is, in effect, a bridge from Scarlatti to Brahms built by Beethoven.

XVI. Allegro: The approximate halfway point in a variation's sequence often produces a reminiscence of the original thematic cell. Beethoven presumes that the listener will not mind a sophisticated, highly chromatic bass line as incidental diversion.

XVII. L'istesso tempo: Not only is the tempo the same as in the foregoing variation; the instruction *attacca subito* indicates that Beethoven thought of it as an outgrowth of No. XVI.

XVIII. Poco moderato: Nos. XVIII and XIX, as previously noted, were among the original four variations, suggesting they were meant as reminders to Diabelli of what he might have done with his theme had he been Beethoven.

XIX. Presto: Here the dialogue becomes a canon at the octave. The progression in measure 12, which begins the upward surge to the cadence, says von Bülow, is "often met with in modern music (Berlioz, Liszt, even as far back as Schubert)."

XX. Andante: Here Beethoven has narrowed the distance to himself to no gap at all. By converting the opening C–G–G into a bass figure, Andante, Beethoven demonstrates that Diabelli's

---

[46] Beethoven, Variations, I, 60.

"Schusterfleck," sequence and all, could become the basis for the much celebrated, greatly extolled "Arietta" of his last piano sonata —which he described as "Adagio molto semplice e cantabile." Is that magical finale, then, Variation XXXIV of the Diabelli set, or should the Variations be better titled "Sonata No. Thirty-Three"? The results inescapably demonstrate that sequence of tones which might be one man's mundane uneventfulness may be—on two famous occasions—another man's divine simplicity.

XXI. *Allegro con brio:* A retake, with a sharper focus, of variation No. VI, this blends the incisiveness of the trill with a restless undercurrent of emotion.

XXII. *Allegro molto:* This is a plunge from the sublime to the risible, an order of pun to which Beethoven was prone, verbally, and which he parallels musically in converting Diabelli into Leporello's "Notte e giorno fatticar" from Mozart's *Don Giovanni*.

XXIII. *Allegro assai:* In Bülow's view this impulsive outburst marks the end of the work's second "grand division."

XXIV. *Andante:* This is the kind of fughetta (as it is titled) that a well-schooled improviser or extemporizer could build on a group of notes picked at random. Beethoven's scheme recalls that he was rated one of the greatest of improvisers when he practiced that art, his notation of it a hardly necessary reminder of his mastery as a composer.

XXV. *Allegro:* A running figure in the bass contests for attention with a skeletonized outline of the theme in the treble.

XXVI. *Allegretto:* A sportive arrangement of elements in a pattern that Schumann would have termed an "Arabesque." Each hand is expected to do its duty as well as the other.

XXVII. *Vivace (L'istesso tempo):* A further expression of the idea expounded in No. XXVI.

XXVIII. *Allegro:* Any resemblance to Diabelli is all but absent in this demonstration of fascinating Beethoven.

{ XXIX. *Adagio ma non troppo:*
{ XXX. *Andante sempre cantabile:*
{ XXXI. *Largo, molto espressivo:* Here Beethoven presumes to expound the ways in which his art, at its purest, digresses most totally from Diabelli's. For the first time, he takes leave of the manners and modes of expression he was practicing in most other works of the time and looks ahead (in No. XXI) to the later quartet impulses, even to the employment of a four-part structure. Frequently the solo line in the "violin" is dominant, but it sometimes flows over into the "cello" register. Bülow isolates the second segment of No. XXX as containing "the embryo of all the romanticism of Schumann." Anyone walking into the room during the

cascading shower of sound in No. XXXI and exclaiming "Chopin!" should be commended, not condemned.

XXXII. Allegro: The listener searching for a direct reference to Diabelli's theme in this grand exhibition of contrapuntal command may be advised, categorically: Don't. Beethoven's transformation evolves into a structure of its own, with intimations of the finale to come in the Ninth Symphony. One advantage for the pianist is that his choraling climaxes will always be heard in tune.

XXXIII. Tempo di Minuetto: The meter (¾) is traditionally that of the minuet, but the patterns evolve into a closing statement on the order of the finales of Opus 110 and 111—disembodied music of an ethereal elevation, for which Diabelli could claim a share of earthly involvement, but very little celestial responsibility.

The *Diabelli* Variations, intruding as they do between the beginning of Beethoven's work on both the Mass and the Ninth Symphony and the accomplishment of those titanic labors, provide a perfect panoramic view of what had been happening to him, philosophically and musically, across those years.

One begins the almost endless quest for the inner essence of this work with a perpetual sense of amazement and admiration for the piling of one skill upon another. But what lures the listener further and further into the labyrinth is the beauty of the vistas, the invitations to reflection, and the bracing air of excitement with which Beethoven embellishes the journey. Eventually one comes to comprehend the motivation for his recourse to the piano and its involvements at this time. He could not only *lose* himself in it; he could also *find* himself again in the challenges and solutions provided by a world devoid of words, symbols, and rhetoric.

6

SUCH WERE THE CONDITIONS and considerations which entered into the extension of his work on the Mass and its eventual completion. Still to be assessed and accomplished when he turned to the writing of Opus numbers 109, 110, 111, and the *Diabelli* Variations (see p. 257) were the Agnus Dei, with its concluding "Donis nobis pacem" and prayer for peace. Unquestionably Beethoven began to write the *Missa Solemnis* to glorify his pupil, friend, and patron, Archduke Rudolph. But, as a necessary precondition, it had to be a work which would previously glorify one other person—Beethoven himself.

For one who stands outside its articles of faith and its promises of salvation, the essence of the Mass is the enormous imagery of its language, its qualities as a work of literature. In the Latin form, it makes a living entity of what is famously known as a dead language. Shaped and smoothed over centuries of usage, the words and their formulation into phrases have the texture of an antique altar of faith polished to a silky evenness by wind-driven sand.

It is noteworthy that through the Kyrie and Gloria, the verbal approach is collective and plural: "Lord have mercy upon us" (Kyrie). "We praise Thee, we bless Thee, we adore Thee" (Gloria). It then becomes personal and singular: "I believe in one God" (Credo); "I expect the resurrection of the dead and the life of the world to come" (end of the Credo). But then, after the Benedictus (which I interpret as a personal statement because it does not mention either plural or singular), the collective is resumed: "O Lamb of God, that takest away the sins of the world, have mercy upon us" (Agnus Dei).

Could the long lapse in the creative process of the *Missa* and the digression to other forms of expression have resulted from Beethoven's inability to resolve his own spiritual conflict? For an extensive and enlightened discussion of Beethoven's response to the Enlightenment, the reader is recommended to Martin Cooper's observations. He makes the good point that Beethoven grew up in Bonn, which was "a stronghold of new ideas under its 'enlightened' Electoral Prince Max Friedrich."[47] (He was succeeded at his death in 1784 by Maximilian Franz, who encouraged Beethoven's musical development.) Beethoven then migrated to Vienna, traditionally a stronghold of Catholic conservatism, where—decades later—Mahler had to accept conversion in order to secure a position he cherished. Arnold Schoenberg only affirmed his Jewishness when he was displaced by the Nazis. That Beethoven acknowledged a Supreme Being is attested by innumerable expressions, from his song "Die Himmel rühmen des Ewigen Ehre" ("The Worship of God in Nature" is a common translation) of 1803, through the Pastoral Symphony and on. But it is Cooper's conclusion, in which I wholly concur, that "For institutional religion he seems to have had little use, or even for any specifically Christian doctrine."[48]

Some might counter-contend that (a) he urged confession on his nephew Karl and (b) himself accepted the last rites of the church on his deathbed. Neither, of itself, can be considered conclusive proof of an attitude. Beethoven could well reason that (a) the church might do his wayward nephew good, where so much else had failed and (b) if

[47] Cooper: *Beethoven*, p. 105.
[48] Ibid., p. 118.

his friends wanted him to have a priest in his dying hours who was he, having tried their patience over weeks and months in the sickroom, to offend them further?

But, in the deepest devotion to his art, he could not wholly reconcile himself to a plea for mercy in which he did not believe. He could not, obviously, change the words and still imagine the results acceptable to a Cardinal-Archbishop. But he could, if he considered it to be his own forum of prayer, order the music to say what he wanted it to say, and thus achieve that inner peace which he required for his own manner of self-satisfaction.

He did, indeed, do it precisely in terms of "inner peace" by inscribing the onset of the "Dona nobis pacem" ("Grant us peace") with his own *addition* to the text of the Mass: "Bitte um innern und äussern Frieden" ("Prayer for inner and outer peace"). That is to say, Beethoven is charging the Deity to whom this plea is addressed with the challenge: If there cannot be "outer peace" in the world—and Beethoven invokes the calls of trumpets and the rolls of drums to sound their deadly alarms as often as the Mass is heard[49]—there can be no inner peace. With the sure sense of the dramatist that he was, the brass and percussion intrude with their menacing military implications after the massed voices have enunciated their cry for "Pacem, pacem" five, six, eight, ten, a *dozen* times in this section of the Mass. It is then that the mezzo voice intrudes, in what is to many the most humane measures of the total work, with an anguished outburst which Beethoven marks *ängstlich* ("fearfully"). As one might have anticipated, it is over tremolando strings, which Beethoven used sparingly and only for highly specific purposes.

It is a cry of fear which, in any proper performance of the Mass, embraces the apprehensions of a world of people, not merely those in the hall. At the end—after the trumpets have sounded fanfares that might raise the dead,[50] and given a brilliant prospect of things to come in the Requiems of Berlioz and Verdi—the cries of "Pacem" are renewed. They strike me not so much as the expressions of prayers or hopes, but as demands, exhortations, *instructions* to those in temporal power rather than a Being on a divine height. For one who had lived all his life with

---

[49] Haydn's use of similar means, on a lesser scale, in his *Mass in Time of War* is well known.

[50] To a musician who visited him in spring 1823, when the *Missa* was completed but not yet performed, Beethoven said: "Even if you do not believe in it, you will be glorified because music is your religion . . . ," and a few sentences further: "You will arise with me from the dead—because you must." *The Beethoven Conversation Books*, III, 160.

war or the threat of war (the Hessians, after all, were being sold for service in the American colonies in the year of Beethoven's birth in Bonn, only a few miles away) spiritual peace without temporal peace was not merely contradictory—it was an anomaly.

Here, finally, the battle has been joined. Beethoven has been to the mountaintop. He has faced his own mortality and recognized that it is, at best, a fragile thing, not least to a man cursed by deafness, afflicted with "a full case of jaundice" (1821), recurrent attacks of gout (1882), and convinced "My life may not be of long duration" (see p. 336). His brooding upon the mysteries of life and death make the *Missa Solemnis,* in its climactic moments, the kind of confrontation that few artists, however farsighted, face in their lifetime. He has expressed, resolutely and with high conviction, his belief in a "Patrem omni-potentem" ("Father Almighty"), his willingness to raise his voice in praise of His holiness because "Heaven and earth are full of Thy glory," and his conviction that blessings shall reward those who come in the name of the Lord (Benedictus).

But does he truly believe that the "Lamb of God" does "take away the sins of the World"? The prayer for inner and outer peace persuades me that the Promised Land Beethoven has discerned is not a divinely ordained, ritualistically ordered, piously attainable Paradise. What he has seen, really, is a vision of a place where *peace* rules without trumpets and drums, a place where men dwell in Brotherhood, where Joy reigns supreme and its magic binds together what custom has driven apart. That is, the place which Schiller has discerned man could make of his world had he but the wit and the will.

It is the measure of Beethoven's enormous spiritual substance that one who began the *Missa* with a full or implied dependence on an outer Being for his hope of peace, attained the higher sense of self-sufficiency to face the facts as his life had taught him to know them, and to accept the reality that "God's work on earth is done by man."

In this, he was also true to his own innermost self. A decade before, he had asked the young Ignaz Moscheles to make the piano score of *Fidelio,* after its final revisions of 1814. The honored young musician applied himself with all energy to the project and finally, after many visits to the master, completed his task. "Under the last number" he wrote in his diary, "I had written 'Fine mit Gottes Hülfe' ['Finished with the help of God']."[51] Beethoven was not home when Moscheles called. When he received the manuscript back with corrections, Moscheles con-

[51] Moscheles: *Recent Music and Musicians,* p. 10.

tinues, Beethoven had added the words "O Mensch, hilf dir selber" ("O man, help thyself").

7

PERHAPS IT IS in such spirit that one should approach the other, the terrestrial, Beethoven. That is, the one—best known perhaps as the author of *Wellington's Victory*—who did not scruple to play one publisher against another in his search for the best terms he could get for what he considered to be his "greatest work," only to promise it to a third and sell it to a fourth. He also solicited subscriptions to the Mass[52] from crowned heads of Europe with the implication that no printed edition would be marketed at any near time. He did, indeed, have to delay the appearance of a published version for nearly a year, for fear of offending his royal customers or, what is worse, providing an excuse for them to demand their money back.

Of all this, the Beethoven literature is explicit in abundance. What has not been sufficiently expounded is the pedestrian pace at which the winged work came to the attention of the music-loving public. Prince Nikolas Boris Galitzin, aged twenty-nine at the time, was a subscriber who also persuaded the Czar of Russia to become Beethoven's patron. Galitzin took pleasure in advising the composer, in April 1824, that a performance had been organized in St. Petersburg on April 6. The information, according to an entry in the Conversation Book of the period, impressed Beethoven deeply—not only because the Russians had been the first to bring about such a performance, but also because his "Oratorium" had been performed in a concert hall rather than a cathedral.

The first hearing Vienna had of any part of the Mass occurred in the Kärnthnerthor Theater on May 7, 1824. It was organized in conjunction with the first performance of the Ninth Symphony. Originally the two works were intended to be given entire, but the length of the symphony restricted the Mass to what was described as "Three Hymns" (Kyrie, Credo, and Agnus Dei).

There was no complete performance in western Europe during Beethoven's lifetime, and there is no sure evidence that the Archduke-Cardinal-Archbishop, on whose behalf Beethoven had labored so hard and so productively, ever heard any part of the work performed. Cer-

---

[52] He even invoked the intercession of the dedicatee, Rudolph, to urge a purchase on the current incumbent of his father's realm, the Grand Duke of Tuscany. Rudolph made the sale. Anderson: *The Letters of Beethoven*, III, 1,055.

tainly he never heard it in its entirety. An elaborately embossed, handwritten copy was delivered to the Archduke "by the composer himself"[53] on March 19, 1823—which is to say, on the eve of the third anniversary of Rudolph's investiture as Archbishop—but his response to that humbling gift is not recorded. (He was in Olmütz at the time of the Vienna concert.)[54]

A curious footnote to the concert and the magnitude of the public response to the music is contained in the Conversation Book for May 1824. One entry reads: "My triumph is now attained; for now I can speak from my heart. Yesterday I still feared secretly that the Mass would be prohibited because I had heard that the Archbishop had protested against it. After all I was right in at first not saying anything to the Police Commissioner. By God, it would have happened."[55] Then, after a pause indicating an unrecorded comment by someone else, it continues: "He surely never has been in the Court Theater. Well, Pax tecum!" The speaker-writer is, presumably, Schindler, and the reference to the Police Commissioner who had withheld permission for the concert, was in deference to disapproval by the resident Archbishop on the performance of a Mass in a theater. Only through the intercession of Prince Lobkowitz, one of the concert's sponsors and guarantors, was the concert permitted to go on. It was repeated on May 23, but with only the Kyrie of the Mass and a miscellany of lighter works to complement the Ninth Symphony.

In the immediate circumstances, the very magnitude of Beethoven's conception worked against it. Full performances, in even the largest cathedral, with the large symphony orchestra, choral ensemble, and vocal quartet stipulated, were unimaginably difficult. The first full performance of which there is reliable record in western Europe occurred in Bonn in 1845 in the fitting circumstances of the dedication of a statue of its native son.[56] The conductor was Ludwig Spohr, though contemporary reports assigned an even larger share of credit to Franz Weber of Cologne, who had done the hard work, over many months, of training a chorus to perform its share of the score. The next occasion did not

---

[53] After the Archduke's death, the treasure became the property of the Gesellschaft der Musikfreunde in Vienna, along with other rarities of the Rudolphinian Collection. Thayer-Forbes (1964), II, 819.

[54] Ibid., p. 908.

[55] Ibid., p. 910.

[56] Schindler: *Beethoven as I Knew Him*, pp. 289–90. A performance in Warndorf, Austria (on the Bohemian border), is assigned to June 29, 1830, and would have been the first since the Vienna concert of May 1824. It is mentioned in Kinsky: *Das Werk Beethovens*, p. 362, but there is no mention of participants or degree of completeness.

come for ten years, when a benefit performance for flood victims of the Lower Rhine was organized by Ferdinand Hiller in Cologne. In May 1856 it was given in Berlin and in November 1856 in Munich. The first known effort to render it as the *Missa Solemnis* Beethoven conceived it to be was organized in the Freiburg Cathedral of Baden in August 1857. The occasion was the hundredth anniversary of the founding of Freiburg University.

This slow pace of dissemination might have been related to the objections that were raised during Beethoven's lifetime—and for some time thereafter—against the very passages which some present-day listeners regard as the work's greatest. The tribute of eventual valuation has long since been paid to the overwhelming effect of the ominous outburst in the Agnus Dei bearing on "inner and outer peace." But to those who encountered it on that first, unforgettable occasion in Vienna nearly a hundred and fifty years ago, the impact was more ominous than overwhelming.

One writer directed attention to the "bizarren Pauken-Schläge"[57] amid so much that was beautiful, and the dubiously perceptive Schindler argued that "the conception of what is appropriate to church music (in our time, at any rate) was not only stretched to its furthest point, it was so completely disregarded that even the artistic wealth of the work could not redeem it."[58] He even took the extraordinary liberty of exercising *his* judgment on the genius of the man, by which his name is remembered, to suggest that "The whole work would be improved if . . . the dramatic section of the Dona that many find justifiably so offensive were omitted." He also had a Beethoven-plus cut to recommend: "One could well skip from the second measures on page 252 of the score to the first measure of page 289. . . ."[59] a mere matter of thirty-seven pages whose creation had cost Beethoven both blood and tears.

In exercising this *post facto* judgment, Schindler was fulfilling Beethoven's evaluation of his "vulgar outlook" and his apprehension that "I have on the whole a certain fear of you, a fear lest some day through your action a great misfortune may befall me." This opinion was expressed in a letter written shortly after the concert of May 7, 1824.[60] It bore on an episode in which Schindler had grossly offended

---

[57] Lang: *The Creative World of Beethoven*, see Warren Kirkendale's essay, "New Roads to Old Ideas in Beethoven's *Missa Solemnis*," p. 163 *n*.

[58] Schindler: *Beethoven as I Knew Him*, p. 285.

[59] Ibid.

[60] Anderson: *The Letters of Beethoven*, III, 1,124.

the composer, and contained Beethoven's suggestion that, in future, he repay Schindler with a gift for "the services you render me," rather than *"have you at my table."*

The high esteem in which Beethoven was held in England was reflected in the many efforts that were made in the last ten years of his life to have him undertake a visit comparable to the well-remembered ones of Haydn, nearly thirty years before. Despite an inordinate amount of correspondence, Beethoven never felt up to it—or, perhaps, secretly shrank from exposing himself to a public not as adjusted to his deafness as the Viennese. But the records of the Philharmonic Society are explicit evidence that London was the first city, after Bonn, to hear the full *Missa Solemnis*, on May 4, 1846.

The program is also unequivocal in stating that, on this occasion, the vocal quartet became an octet—each solo part was performed by *two* voices.[61] Doubtless this was part of a then-prevailing feeling that, because of his deafness or for other physiological reason, Beethoven had miscalculated the ability of the four singers to be heard, especially in the Pleni sunt coeli and the Osanna. This consideration was raised when the Kyrie, Sanctus, and Benedictus were performed at Bonn in 1857 before a gathering of German physicians and scientists. One critic expressed the belief that Beethoven had really intended these sections to be sung by the full chorus, and invited Schindler's clarification. He responded with a lengthy statement. It was, in essence, an affirmation of Beethoven's awareness that he had posed a heavy burden for the soloists. But, after weighing all the objections, the obdurate composer insisted: "Soloists it must be."[62]

Despite its difficulty, the passage was performed at least once as Beethoven specified. That was in the previously mentioned Bonn performance of 1845 under the direction of Spohr, of which a lengthy, detailed, and highly circumstantial account may be found in the writings of that indefatigable eye and ear witness Henry F. Chorley.[63] "At Bonn," he writes, "the solos were toiled through by a quartett of painstaking but ineffective vocalists." Chorley expressed particular compassion for the choristers, saying: "The chorus that is to execute the *allegro con moto*, *Et vitam venturi*, which winds up the 'Credo' with one of the most harassing *codas* ever dreamed of, should be composed of soprani as brilliant as Grisi, of contralti as powerful and rich as Alboni, of tenors

[61] Myles Birkit Foster: *History of the Philharmonic Society of London* (London: John Lane, the Bodley Head; 1912), p. 197.
[62] Schindler: *Beethoven as I Knew Him*, p. 288.
[63] Chorley: *Modern German Music*, II, 276–290.

as vigorous as Duprez and as flexible as Rubini, and of basses as sonorous and mordant as Lablache." Standards of choral execution have, clearly, improved.

For Chorley's admirably catholic taste, the *Missa* was a "stupendous musical work," marred, blemished, and, indeed, disfigured by an excess of aspiration over accomplishment. The difficulties "beyond the bounds of practicable and pleasurable execution" imposed on the chorus, the "too theatrical roll of drum and trumpet, in the *Dona,*" some other instances of the "eccentricities of Beethoven's late compositions" were clearly disturbing to Chorley's conditioning to order, proportion, balance. He had, indeed, a lingering preference for the Mass in C, which was also performed during the Bonn Festival of 1845. But there were vibrations within the *Missa* which went beyond Chorley's mind, directly to his heart, and caused him to raise the question: "Need the clearest admission of these and a few other such specks and disproportions impair our enjoyment of what is glorious and spiritually sublime in this work?" His conclusion came clear: the " 'Missa Solemnis' will always stand as a marvel—as a colossal work, planned on a scale by many a cubit grander than its writer's Mass in C. . . ."

The first American performance was organized in New York by the Church Music Association in 1874, under the direction of James Peck. It was not attempted by even such a progenitor of choral standards as the Cincinnati May Festival during the nineteenth century, nor was it brought into the repertory of a leading American orchestra until 1900. It was then the pleasure of Wilhelm Gericke[64] to organize a special concert for the performance of the "Mass in D" (as it was then described). There were none others by the Boston orchestra for nearly thirty years, the next being offered on March 22 and 27, 1927, under the direction of Serge Koussevitzky.

The last of these dates was, of course, the hundredth anniversary of Beethoven's death. Koussevitzky dignified the event by sponsoring a commemorative address by the *London Times*'s celebrated Ernest Newman. There were other performances elsewhere, not in like manner dignified, by such entities as New York's Friends of Music, of which the conductor was Artur Bodanzky. The New York Philharmonic finally had its landmark performance on March 8, 1934 (repeated on March 9 and 11), with Arturo Toscanini conducting an ensemble that included

[64] Gericke, of Vienna fame, first came to Boston in 1884. His engagement was terminated in 1889 because of illness. Having recovered his health, he was brought back for eight years, beginning in 1898. The date for the single performance of the *Missa Solemnis* was October 15, 1900. M. A. DeWolfe Howe: *The Boston Symphony Orchestra, 1881–1931* (Boston: Houghton Mifflin; 1931), p. 104.

the Schola Cantorum; Elisabeth Rethberg, soprano; Sigrid Onegin, mezzo; Paul Althouse, tenor; and Ezio Pinza, bass. This was followed by three performances more in April of the following year, and a single performance during the Philharmonic's centennial season, on April 22, 1942. For the BBC in London, Toscanini prepared the *Missa* for two performances in May 1939, and he also directed the NBC Symphony in a single performance on December 28, 1940.

Thus Toscanini had rehearsed the work on five separate occasions prior to the NBC broadcast of March 28, 1953 (just a year before his retirement). It resulted in the celebrated RCA recording with the Robert Shaw Chorale; Lois Marshall, soprano; Nan Merriman, mezzo; Eugene Conley, tenor; and Jerome Hines, bass. It was not the first American recording,[65] chronologically, but it was the first to combine the advantages of LP playing time with adequate reproduction of first-class musical elements. It has, in my view, been a paramount, permanent contribution to the understanding and appreciation of Beethoven's accomplishment. More recent recordings directed by Eugene Ormandy, Karl Böhm, Eugen Jochum, and Herbert von Karajan have, without doubt, been responsive to the standard of musicianship embodied in the Toscanini preparation, the supercharged performances of the vocal participants, and the world-wide acclaim with which the reproduction was received. It may be noted, in passing, that Toscanini chose to use the *chorus* to support the solo voices in the passages preceding the Benedictus (see p. 273), and Karajan, in his recording, follows suit.

The consummation of everything Beethoven so devoutly hoped for on behalf of Rudolph finally came early in 1971—a hundred and fifty-one years after the event for which it had been projected—as part of the celebration of the two-hundredth anniversary of the composer's birth (December 16, 1970). On January 14, 1971, the *Missa Solemnis* was performed in St. Peter's, Rome. Wolfgang Sawallisch conducted the orchestra of Radio Italiana, Rome, with the Bavarian Radio Chorus; Ingrid Björner, soprano; Christa Ludwig, mezzo; Placido Domingo, tenor; and Kurt Moll, bass. The TV tape made on that date was shown to American viewers on NBC-TV for the first time on January 24, 1971, and has since been rerun.

The occasion celebrated not only the Beethoven bicentennial but also the fiftieth anniversary of the ordination as priest of Pope Paul,

---

[65] In 1941, RCA Victor issued a two-volume version, on a dozen 78-rpm disks, recorded "live" by the Boston Symphony Orchestra under the direction of Serge Koussevitzky. Richard Burgin's solo violin performance of the Benedictus was interrupted at a mid-point, and other unavoidable intrusions diluted musical pleasure in the results.

who was present. Nothing was omitted, nothing apologized for in this ecumenical acceptance of artistic prerogative and manly emotion.

8

THE CONSUMMATION of Beethoven's most devout other wish—this one on his own behalf—did not have so long to wait. The concert of May 7, 1824, in which the "Three Hymns" of the *Missa Solemnis* were heard for the first time, marked the first performance of the Ninth Symphony before a Viennese audience in the Kärnthnerthor Theater. As he had been preoccupied with the completion of the Mass well into 1822, the accomplishment of the symphony for a performance less than two years later might, by comparison, seem swift. But it should be remembered that parts of a Ninth Symphony had been accumulating even before he began work on the Mass in 1818–19. Its deeper rooted, less specific elements predate all but a few works of Beethoven still regularly heard. Among them, of course, was a plan for setting Schiller's *An der Freude*.

The reasons for Schiller's verses being termed deep-rooted in Beethoven are in no way mysterious: they are rapturous with the kind of imagery, the breadth of imagination, the soaring expansiveness of vision by which the young Beethoven lived and breathed. It would be one thing for someone who knew him when young to recall, in the aftermath of the Ninth Symphony, some such sage words as, "I always expected something perfect, for as long as I knew him he was wholly devoted to the great and sublime." It is another to recall that it was these exact words Bartolomäus Fischenich, a professor at the University of Bonn, employed when he wrote to Charlotte Schiller, in January 1793, about the plan of a young local musician to "compose Schiller's 'Freude' and indeed strophe by strophe. I expect something perfect, for as far as I know he is wholly devoted to the great and the sublime."[66]

How he became acquainted with the Ode in Bonn in the early 1790s, only a few years after it was published in 1785, is not known. Perhaps the more lettered Stephan von Breuning was responsible, or Beethoven may have come upon it during the hours of 1789 he spent at the University.[67] In any case, the disposition existed in Beethoven, and the impulse was sufficiently deep-rooted to endure a gestation period of nearly thirty years.

[66] Thayer-Forbes (1964), I, 121.
[67] Ibid., pp. 93–4. A register of philosophy candidates entered at the University of Bonn in that year includes the names of Anton Reicha, a member of the Elector's orchestra, as well as Beethoven's.

Over the intervening decades, the idea recurred to Beethoven periodically. Once it was on the occasion of a revival of interest in Vienna
in Schiller's plays (during 1809 and 1810).[68] A few years later, without
any known prompting, he wrote a memo to himself to consider the
text as part of an overture. Meanwhile, the fated musical counterpart
was coming to fruition, gradually, mysteriously, but inevitably. To
judge from the written evidence, it all happened so inconspicuously that
Beethoven himself had no awareness of an inherent kinship. Not until
the resumption of work on the D-minor symphony produced the creative
heat to draw the subject and his objective together did a fusion of
elements come about. Hard as it is to imagine such a fusion taking
decades to come about, it is even more difficult to imagine so magnificent a realization by an older, sicker, more worldly composer of a
young man's dream.

The reference to a "D-minor" symphony rather than the "Ninth" is
not merely a matter of paraphrase or semantics. It is not generally known
that, as of 1822, Beethoven was absorbed with plans for *two* major works.
One, in response to a commission from the Philharmonic Society of
London, was, to quote Thayer, "the present Symphony in D minor."[69]
The other, Beethoven identified in his sketches as a "sinfonie allemande"
which was to conclude with a choral finale utilizing a text in German
(hence its mental tag, "allemande"). *Both* were in D minor. The
symphony for London was to conclude with an instrumental finale, which
was so far advanced and enjoyed so high a rating in Beethoven's mind
that it was eventually utilized in another context (see p. 291).

The case for choosing *not* to end the symphony for London with
a setting of a choral text in German was well-reasoned: it would be
inappropriate and might further offend his English friends whom, it
has long been contended, he had ill-served once before.[70] Why it came
about as it did was not reasoned, well or otherwise. It was the product
of a creative drive to complete the Schiller Ode which, once unleashed,

---

[68] Ibid., p. 471.

[69] Ibid., II, 887.

[70] Ibid., pp. 637–8. In sending three already-performed works to the society
rather than the wholly new ones expected for the fee he received. In an article for
The Musical Quarterly (Vol. LIX [July 1973], No. 3, pp. 449–61), David Warren
Hadley documents his contention that the society did *not* expect Beethoven to write
a work specifically for it in 1815, as it did when the commission for the Ninth was
extended in 1824. However, the guarantee by the composer's Viennese agent (in
Beethoven's name) of three works which have been performed "with the greatest
applause" (Anderson, *The Letters of Beethoven*, II, 502–3) was hardly borne out by
the trio dispatched: the overtures titled *The Ruins of Athens*, *König Stephan*, and
Namensfeier. The last-named was performed in London in 1816, the *König Stephan*
not until 1841, and *The Ruins of Athens* not at all by 1912, when a history of the
society's first hundred years (with an index of its repertory) was published.

dictated its own logic. The finale grew out of the music that had *pre-ceded it in the symphony*, a priority which exceeded such considerations as for whom or for where the symphony was being written.

The moment of decision apparently occurred in mid-1823 when, with the first two movements well advanced and the third taking shape, the Schiller text first appears in conjunction with a musical line recognizably familiar. As in a series of sketches extending from late fall 1822, the key is D. Unlike the earlier outlines, the words had finally been joined to a theme similar to that of the Chorale Fantasia (Opus 80, see p. 15), or the finale of the G-major Piano Concerto. Or, to put both in their proper time-perspective, close kin to the second part of a song (to a text by Bürger) dating from 1794-95.[71]

Speculations on the unknown mental processes that brought together, nearly thirty years later, the two impulses of Beethoven in his twenties may be foregone. What is clear and observable are the stresses to which Beethoven subjected his known mental processes to bring the first three movements of the D-minor Symphony and the

[71] "Seufzer eines Ungeliebten und Gegenliebe" is the title of its entry in the Peters edition (1936) of Beethoven's complete songs. "Gegenliebe" begins on p. 166.

choral finale into a congruent partnership. By July 1823[72] the thought of building a musical bridge by some form of recitative was firmly fixed. And it was even projected that themes heard earlier in the work would be introduced. But a verbal reason for their reminiscence was lacking. It was not until Beethoven returned to Vienna in the early fall of 1823 that he announced excitedly to Schindler: "Ich hab's, Ich hab's!"[73] and showed him the sketchbook with the words "Lass uns das Lied des unsterblichen Schiller singen" ("Let us sing the song of the Immortal Schiller"). For Schindler the problem was solved. For Beethoven the problems were just beginning. For, having hit on the idea of a verbal announcement, so to speak, of what was to follow, it was inherent in his nature to mold it, shape it, make and remake it until it came to suit his requirements *exactly*. A prolonged series of sketches are irreplaceably illuminating of the whole procedure. As each earlier theme is presented, the bass voice states, verbally, why it is unacceptable: "Not this—something else [more pleasing?]" (for the first movement). "Nor this either —it is but sport" (for the Scherzo). "And this is too tender" (for the Adagio). "For something else we must seek . . ."[74]

With unimaginable directness, he decides, finally, to let the music speak for itself. After the impatient outburst of the whole wind band has interrupted the dying echos of the slow movement, the cellos and double basses intrude with their recitative. Another discord, and another remonstrance. Then, in turn, the themes of the three movements are offered for consideration. Each is rejected with wordless disdain. Then, in their quiet way, the same low strings tender, lovingly, the perfected form of the chorale theme. They are joined, in an approving vein, by the bassoon—instrumental counterpart of the human baritone—commenting with a variant of its own. All the winds then take up the chorale, reinforced by the timpani. Not until exposed, approved, and elaborated upon by all the instrumental choirs, in rising tiers of tonal brilliance, is a word permitted. Then, after another air-clearing dissonance, the bass proclaims in German (with no mention of Schiller's name) "O friends —not these tones—let us sing something more cheerful and in a spirit of rejoicing," to which the male voices of the chorus reply with cries of "Freude" . . . "Freude." Thus has the prosaic been elevated to the level of the poetic through the composer's faith in the unique power of music to communicate directly and unaided.

It is among the subtleties of Beethoven's attraction to Schiller's Ode

[72] Nottebohm: *Zweite Beethoveniana*, pp. 189–9.
[73] Ibid.
[74] Thayer-Forbes (1964), II, 892–4.

that, in its first form, the Ode was not to *Freude* (Joy) but to *Freiheit* (Freedom)—the same *Freiheit* of which so much is made in *Fidelio*. There is, indeed, one phrase common to both. Schiller wrote: "Wer ein holdes Weib errungen,/Mische seinen Jubel ein." In the libretto, the jubilation of the townspeople at the reunion of Leonore and Florestan is crowned by the words "Wer ein holdes Weib errungen,/Stimm in unsern Jubel ein." In either case, the sentiment is, "He who has a loyal wife discovered,/Let him in our jubilation join" (a version to fit both the sense and the music!). It is the opinion of Dr. Joseph Braunstein that the poet's imagery was probably interpolated into the text of *Fidelio* by one of Beethoven's associates, Joseph Sonnleithner, to whom Schiller's works were well known. (It is Sonnleithner's name which appears as author of the libretto ["freely adapted from the French"] when the 1805 version of *Fidelio* was first performed.) The sentiment embodied in Schiller's phrase was thus deeply imbedded in Beethoven's consciousness long before he settled to the task of setting thirty-two of the ninety-six lines in the Ode.

Aside from its profound philosophic and spiritual content, the extraordinary musical qualities contained in the Ninth Symphony are so numerous and so tightly associated with its total atmosphere that one can hardly be separated from the other. Merely the innovation of associating a sung text with a form of musical expression "always" restricted to instrumental content caused a subsurface tremor which resounded through the musical world for decades to come. From Berlioz's "dramatic symphony" *Roméo et Juliette* through Mahler's Eighth, the option of "the word" has been not merely justified but typified by Beethoven's Ninth. In its dynamism and revolutionary use of *materia musica*, it has outlasted both the *Eroica* and the C-minor Symphonies as repositories of example for generations of composers. Aside from its effect on Berlioz, who got a job in a Parisian printing printing plant as a proofreader of the Ninth when he was still a student, the Ninth caused the *Faust* Overture to erupt in Wagner's mind, kindled the spark for Brahms' First Piano Concerto (in the same key of D minor), and set elusive goals of unity and sequence which Bruckner finally achieved in his Seventh and Eighth Symphonies.[75]

Had there been, as Beethoven planned mentally, a Tenth Symphony, perhaps it would have outranked the Ninth in the number and variety of unfulfilled impulses brought together from earlier works. Whether it is the recitative for the bass voice in the finale, which builds

[75] Kolodin: *The Continuity of Music*, pp. 173–6.

on the recitative of the Piano Sonata Opus 31, No. 2 (also in D minor); or the arabesques of embellishment in the Adagio, which, as noted previously, drive to a higher level of meaning the already beautiful but not so exalted treatment of the Larghetto in the Symphony No. 2; or the contrapuntal elaborations in the *König Stephan* Overture of 1812 (see p. 16), which finalize what had not *yet* become even a shadowy purpose in Beethoven's conscious mind, the new contexts of meaning arouse associations as old as the "Gegenliebe" of 1794 or as new as the recently completed *Missa Solemnis*.

Not illogically, the sound pattern of the Ninth has more affinity with the *Missa* than with any other work in the Beethoven literature. It was, after all, initiated earlier, finished later—hence it partakes both of the conceptual thought and the residue which emerged from the fulfillment of that gigantic project. It is altogether understandable that what Beethoven had come to expect of massed voices in the *Missa* should be carried over into the finale of the Ninth. But the expanded opportunities for acquaintance with the Mass that have accrued from a series of recent recordings leave little doubt that the order of instrumental innovation must be reversed. That is to say, washes of woodwind colorations, accents of percussion, and passages of deep string sound that have, by familiarity, been associated with the symphony are, by reasons of prior usage, more properly related to the Mass. Repeatedly one hears in the Mass—such as the transition in the Credo from major to minor (pp. 168–9 in the Eulenburg scores) or the continuous use of ostinato bass figures—projections of thought which are better known from the symphony than the Mass.

In the vocal domain, the use of the chorus in the finale of *Fidelio* had given some intimation of what Beethoven might expect of the human voice in moments of extreme emotional stress. In the Mass, the capacities of the voice are extended almost to the breaking point; in the Ninth Symphony, the voice is assigned even more impossible tasks. The thought is sometimes advanced that Beethoven, because of his deafness, was indifferent to the strain he imposed upon his singers. It would be a useful revision of attitude were the wholly healthy vocalists to appreciate—as those who have performed the Ninth at festivals in New York, Edinburgh, or Bayreuth appreciate—the invitation to all-out effort, on behalf of incomparable results, that has been extended to them.

The achievement of the desired effect by the solo quartet is predicated more on equality of ability than on singularity of resource. The best conductors—Toscanini, Walter, Furtwängler, Reiner, Szell, Karajan—strive to select voices as much for blend and compatability as for strength or virtuosity. The gathering passion of the four voices in "Alle menschen würden Brüder, wo dein sanfter Flügel weilt" (measures 70–80 in the finale) provides an opportunity for eloquence that should arouse envy, not compassion.

Essentially, the Ninth owes to the *Missa Solemnis* the philosophic framework, the ideological atmosphere, the psychological climate in which it breathes and has its existence. For all his nearly lifelong aspiration to setting Schiller's "An die Freude," it was not until he had addressed himself to the challenge of the super-earthly, and achieved his own "inner and outer peace," that Beethoven could engage in the struggle to improve man's earthly lot.

9

THE WHOLE OF THE NINTH SYMPHONY and the parts of the *Missa Solemnis* that were heard for the first time in the Kärnthnerthor Theater on May 7, 1824, thus made their start on public life concurrently, but they have never been together since. The playing of the sacred music, after agonizing preparation and still more agonizing decisions of how much— or how little—could be included in the already lengthy program, aroused its share of response. But, the pulse-pounding Scherzo of the symphony, with its precedent-shattering *timpani* outbursts, caused the audience to erupt into bedlam. It appeared that a repetition could not be avoided. Beethoven, wielding a baton which the performers had been cautioned to ignore, continued to turn pages oblivious to the turmoil. Either then or at the end of the performance—when the stories were collected fifty years later, they naturally disagreed—Fräulein Unger, the mezzo, pulled Beethoven's sleeve and motioned him to turn around to *see* the applause.[76]

Unlike its formidable co-masterpiece, the fame of the symphony spread even within the few years remaining to Beethoven's life. A second performance (outdoors this time) was given in Vienna before the month was out. The Philharmonic Society of London, which had "merely" commissioned the work, had to swallow its chagrin at being preempted for a Vienna première (and also at having the dedication sold to the King of Prussia). But it could hardly be said to have been unprepared for either possibility.

It had its turn on March 21, 1825, at which time it could proudly

---

[76] Thayer-Forbes (1964), II, 909.

proclaim a "New Grand Characteristic Symphony, composed expressly for this Society."[77]

In Leipzig, a young musician impatient to sample the content of the work in his own way made a piano version of the orchestral score in 1830 because none had been published. He offered it to Schott und Söhne, who rejected the tender with the explanation that "the publishers had not yet decided to issue the Ninth Symphony for piano," but that they would "gladly keep" the laborious effort, offering a score of the *Missa Solemnis* in exchange. "I accepted with great pleasure," wrote Richard Wagner years later of his first dealings, at seventeen, with the firm which would eventually pay him a fortune to publish the *Ring*, *Parsifal*, etc.[78]

In Paris, as already noted (see p. 280), a slightly older musician earned money to fund his studies at the Conservatoire by proofreading the sheets of the Ninth as they went through the press of a Parisian publisher. The work completed his conversion to total adoration of Beethoven, with results familiar to all readers of Hector Berlioz. Together—though unknown to each other—Berlioz and Wagner shared, in 1840, a revealing introduction to the work through the effort of François Antoine Habeneck, founder-conductor of the Orchestre de la Société des Concerts du Conservatoire. The concerts, and the rehearsals that preceded them, Wagner wrote, "exercised a decisive influence in the crisis of my artistic development. . . . I listened repeatedly to Beethoven's Ninth Symphony which, by dint of untiring practise, received such a marvellous interpretation at the hands of this celebrated orchestra, that the picture I had of it in my mind . . . stood before me tangibly in brilliant colors, undimmed, as though it had never been effaced by the Leipzig orchestra who had slaughtered it under Pohlenz's baton."[79]

Berlioz's adoration of the Ninth was converted into action as early as *Harold in Italy* (1834), which contains a section of reminiscences akin

---

[77] Ibid., p. 964. "Characteristic" was a term then in vogue to describe what would today be called "program music." The *Pastorale*, with its delineation of nature, was so described, as was the Ninth by reason of its choral finale.

[78] Wagner: *My Life*, p. 43.

[79] Wagner: *My Life*, p. 214. Reference to the "celebrated orchestra" and omission of the names of vocalists suggest that the performance did not include the finale. The first of Wagner's five separate ventures as conductor of the Ninth Symphony dates from 1846, in Dresden, when he prefaced it with a prose ode of his own creation. Another performance in Dresden followed in 1847, and a third in 1849. He later conducted it in London, in 1855, and, of course, at the dedicatory services for Bayreuth in 1872. The resumption of performances at Bayreuth in 1951 was marked by Wilhelm Furtwängler's direction of the Ninth, the first time in seventy-nine years that music other than Wagner's was heard there. See *My Life*, pp. 397, 412, 465, and 623.

to the rejection section, as *Roméo et Juliette* contains vocal elements though a "dramatic symphony." Both for its philosophic and aesthetic connotations, the Ninth Symphony held, for the remainder of the nineteenth century, a position of singularity attained only in later times by Wagner's *Tristan und Isolde* and Stravinsky's *Le Sacre du printemps*. No fourth has joined the list in the sixty years since *Le Sacre* was first performed in 1913, and its wide-ranging, earth-shaking impact vibrated through the musical world.

On the far side of the Atlantic, the ambition of the Philharmonic Orchestra of New York reached its zenith when, only five years after its founding in 1841, it ventured the American introduction of the Ninth Symphony on May 20, 1846, in Castle Garden (the structure in Battery Park later renowned as the Aquarium).

In the decades since, performances and recordings of the Ninth have proliferated to the extent that scarcely a European city or an American town which cherishes serious consideration for musical distinction has failed to add its name to the list of places where the work has been performed. Despite such proliferation, each new performance remains an event, an occasion, an embellishment of life.

Prior to the spread of recorded versions, outdoor performances in the Hollywood Bowl or New York's Lewisohn Stadium held promise of capacity attendance. Even today the Ninth Symphony possesses a cachet, an aura, an identity not commanded by any other work in the orchestral literature. It stands taller, strides longer, reaches higher toward the Infinite than any work even remotely like it. Unlike the *Missa Solemnis*, it is a celebration of life not of death, of man's earthly possibilities rather than his heavenly speculations.

XIV

Late Beethoven,
and Last

I

ANY IMPRESSION that Beethoven, having realized his two greatest compositional efforts, was devoid either of impulse or resource is dispelled by documents to the contrary. These are not merely the impressions, in letters to his publishers and statements to visitors, that his mind was awash with plans for another Mass, a Tenth Symphony, perhaps even a second opera. They are supported by his responses to the requests for new scores and their spontaneous generation from places as remote from Vienna as Boston, Massachusetts.[1]

The offer which engaged his most enthusiastic response had reached him even before the Mass was wholly finished, and the Ninth Symphony still in process. It was contained in a letter from St. Petersburg dated November 9, 1822, in which Prince Galitzin[2] proposed that Beethoven write two or three string quartets, again leaving the price to the com-

---

[1] Charles C. Perkins: *History of the Handel and Haydn Society of Boston* (Boston: A. Mudge and Son, Printers; 1883), p. 87. The commission was extended through a Viennese banker. Volume III of the *Beethoven Conversation Books*, p. 149, contains a query, "Das Oratorium nach Boston?" Beethoven's elliptical answer was that he would prefer to write only what he wanted to write, but his need for money, as of that time—April 1823—was pressing. At the same time, he insisted, he would *not* write only for money. Nothing came of the offer, for which Beethoven was instructed to "ask any price."

[2] See p. 270.

poser. In his response dated January 25, 1823, Beethoven accepted the offer, stipulating a fee of 50 ducats per quartet. This was the equivalent, in the current money market, of 25 English pounds per work.[3]

Doubtless Beethoven made inquiries to establish the credit of this Galitzin (already known to him, through a reference in the Conversation Books for 1820) before designating "the banker Henikstein in Vienna" as the intermediary for their transaction. Nor is there the least doubt that Beethoven regarded Galitzin as a possible successor to Count Razumovsky as a generator of musical patronage both profitable and productive. The first result of the new Russian involvement was the E-flat Quartet, Opus 127.

Automatically included among the "last five" Beethoven quartets because of the opus number it bears, the E-flat strikes me as the last of Beethoven's late works, rather than the first of his last. Indeed, a plan for such a quartet had been in the making months before the request from Galitzin was received. Undoubtedly the receipt of Galitzin's down payment on a quartet accelerated Beethoven's attention to its execution. But the onset of his absorption with the Ninth Symphony and the performance problems it presented deferred intensive work on the new quartet until after May 1824. It was finished in February 1825, and first performed during the next month at a concert in which Schuppanzigh led the string ensemble.[4]

A powerful, resplendent, and musically satisfying work, the E-flat Quartet is outstanding, in this time of Beethoven's life, for vigor, rhythmic energy, and a host of other attributes that affiliate it, in my mind, with the past—or at least with characteristics that soon became past. Among these was physical health itself. Still to come (later in 1825) was the worst illness of his life to that time.

The reasonable question of whether the E-flat Quartet actually utilizes materials Beethoven had in mind for a work he promised to Peters (in 1822) is considered by Kerman in his commentary, but not resolved. No sketches prior to 1824 are known to exist. Kerman concludes that it makes "very good sense" in terms of other music Beethoven was occupied with at the time (the last of the piano sonatas, or the proofs of Opus 109 and Opus 110). He adds, "it is these works, more than the intervening *Missa Solemnis* and the Ninth Symphony, which develop

---

[3] Thayer-Forbes (1964), II, 815.
[4] Kinsky: *Das Werk Beethovens*, pp. 383–4. Schuppanzigh's seven years abroad (mostly in Russia) had ended in 1823, following which he resumed his place in Vienna's musical life, and in Beethoven's.

the lyric impulse that comes to fruition in the first of the last quartets."[5]

Indeed, if one chooses to make a bold projection *backward* rather than forward, Opus 127 could be termed "the fourth Razumovsky." The obvious link would be through Galitzin and his identification with the country and the musical circles from which Beethoven's prior patron had emerged. But there is a substratum of stylistic character, musical impulse, and renewed, fiery vigor which supports the image—even if Galitzin restricted *his* instructions to a reminder that his instrument was the cello.

Beyond the proclamative Allegro, which arrives at a curious reminiscence of Mozart's C-major Quartet (K.465) at one point:

BEETHOVEN

[5] Kerman: *The Beethoven Quartets,* p. 229.

Mozart

the E-flat earns its high place of distinction as one of Beethoven's best five or six quartets by the richness of the Adagio, ma non troppo, e molto cantabile. It has something in common with the ethereally lofty Molto adagio of Opus 59, No. 2. It is born of a sketch traced to 1824[6] which is subjected to a typical series of alterations before it attains the form for which it is famous. Beethoven then proceeds to a series of variations, in which the interests of his cello-playing patron are not forgotten. There are no concessions to technical limitations, but the melodic flow, prominence of register, and extent of involvement for the bass instrument of the quartet could hardly fail to please Galitzin. It is perhaps among the least remarkable of the slow movements Beethoven would find it in his heart to write in these months, but that still qualifies it as a work whose depth and richness only Beethoven himself could equal or excel.

[6] Nottebohm: *Zweite Beethoveniana*, pp. 210–11.

In the Scherzando vivace, the cello has a leading part in the jagged rhythmic pattern, and the resources evolved in the Scherzo of the Ninth Symphony are utilized in the Scherzo-Trio sequence. Such formal divisions are present, but they are not manipulated in the older way. As in Opus 59, No. 1, all the segments of the post-trio section are written out anew and amended to present an unfamiliar aspect. There is even a hint of a reprise of the "trio" before Beethoven breaks off with one of those abrupt "not now" gestures, and brings the movement to a close. The finale, in my view, is the best quartet conclusion Beethoven wrote since Opus 59, No. 2—limitless in its energy but more varied in its content than that of Opus 59, No. 3.

2

IT WOULD BE an understandable temptation to believe that the work which followed the E-flat Quartet was the B-flat. It is, after all, known as No. 13, is dedicated to Prince Nikolas von Galitzin, and bears Opus number 130. But this is just another of the contradictions that beset late and last Beethoven, such as the attribution of the Rondo, Opus 129, to the same exclusive category because of the number it bears. (It was composed *before* 1800, by the irrefutable evidence of sketches to be found among those for the C-major Piano Concerto, first performed in 1798.)

In the sequence of composition as well of mental climate and spiritual disposition, the A-minor, Opus 132, precedes both the B-flat and the C-sharp-minor. This could, if necessary, be proven by internal evidence. But there is no need for such an exercise in deduction. Ample evidence exists, in letters and Conversation Books, to define 1825 as the year of its creation, and September as the month in which it was first performed. But much else points the unmistakable fact that it was in the A-minor Quartet that Beethoven articulated the musical advances he had made in the *Missa Solemnis* and the Ninth Symphony, and moved ahead to the terrain on which the chamber music to follow would be based.

A particular identity of the A-minor is established by the presence within it of a slow movement which has a special character of its own, even a name by which it is known. That is the Molto adagio inscribed "Heiliger Dankgesang eines Genesenen an die Gottheit, in der lydischen Tonart" ("Holy Song of Thanksgiving from a Convalescent to the Divinity, in the Lydian Mode"). Thousands of persons who know little else about the chamber music of Beethoven came to know about this work from the part it plays in Aldous Huxley's *Point Counterpoint*, and the author's eloquent description of its appeal for his character, Maurice Spandrell.

Why a modal slow movement, and why the Lydian mode in particular? Unquestionably the thoughts of using a modal coloration[7] for a song of thanksgiving derived from Beethoven's long involvement with plainchant and modal resources for the Kyrie of the *Missa Solemnis* (see p. 248). It was midway in the planning of the A-minor Quartet that he was afflicted with an illness of unprecedented seriousness (see Appendix, p. 338). It clung to him for weeks, and not merely distracted him from writing music but from writing of almost every sort between April 9 and May 7, 1825. This provided the motivation, when he began to feel well enough, to write the second song of thanksgiving in his literature. It is an instance of the artistic ground he had traversed since 1807–1808 that the simple terms of praise he had then thought appropriate to the needs of the *Pastorale* were no longer even remotely suitable for his emotional purposes. Unquestionably the choice of the Lydian mode (associated, poetically, with Milton's reference to it in *L'Allegro*: "And ever, against eating cares, Lap me in soft Lydian airs") became identified in Beethoven's mind with Zarlino's comment: ". . . the Lydian mode is a remedy for fatigue of the soul, and similarly, for that of the body."[8]

Out of this distinctive coloration, Beethoven evolved a strain of a solemnity and sobriety rare among all his slow movements (which must number hundreds). The range of allusion is enhanced by tiered, gradually accumulating, layers of sonority which have canonic cross-connections. Finally, after a unison A, the violin picks up the pace, the other strings join the beat, and a gradual resurgence of strength gives pulse to the music. This is in pursuance of Beethoven's marking "Neue Kraft fühlend" ("Feeling of new strength"). A musical poet, such as Beethoven had always been, could hardly resist a reprise of the opening prayer of thanksgiving as proof of the depth of his obligation. But a musical philosopher, such as Beethoven had become, reckons there is nothing like a *real* return of strength to justify prayer. He launches on a new exposition of his renewed state of health to prove that it is indeed present and at his command. This time the measure of gratitude is "Mit innigster Empfindung," a German assertion of "innermost emo-

---

[7] Pundits without number have challenged Beethoven's use of the Lydian mode as being non-authentic and fraught with liberties. He obviously utilized enough of its Lydian character to suit his creative purposes.

[8] Lang: *The Creative World of Beethoven*, see Warren Kirkendale's essay, "New Roads to Old Ideas in Beethoven's *Missa Solemnis*," p. 175.

tion" for which the subjoined Italian expression "Con intimissimo sentimento" sounds like pillow talk. The blend of notes at the very end, with a discordant clash to underscore conviction, is definitely German, not Italian.

Similarly, the Alla marcia that follows confirms health, not infirmity. The pace is "assai vivace" not "vivacissimo," but the measured tread intensifies the sense of power and confidence in the music. And what are the *tremolandos* that intrude between the brief, scherzo-ish Alla marcia and the last movement but a reversion to the rhetoric of the Mass and Ninth: the *tremolandos* in the "trembling" context of the Mass, the recitativo in the violin another abjuration "Nicht diese töne?"

Inevitably, indeed almost chillingly so, the response to the plea for some other kind of music is the finale Beethoven *originally* planned for Symphony No. 9 and set aside in favor of the chorale finale. Having been familiar with it long before that bit of esoteric information came my way, I must say I cannot see it in any other usage but the one for which it became famous, or hear it with any other accents than a strong-handed, soft-hearted first violinist would impart to it. A symphonic finale, with violins by the dozens and other impersonal elements to match? Never. But it rises, in this sublime transformation, to a pitch of onrushing eloquence which no composer prior to Beethoven had ever attained. Remarkably, it has not left him breathless or bereft of spiritual oxygen for still higher flights.

So much of what has been said, if not how it has been said, are clearly recognizable increments of the mental and physical exertions to which Beethoven had subjected himself over the many months preceding 1825. The clues are abundant, the evidences of interrelation unmistakable. But one that has come clear to me recently from the first movement deserves a moment's attention.

It begins ambiguously enough, which is to say with no identity or character other than the sense of something "new." As it gathers momentum and purpose, it surges forward to a predestined point of repose where it engages a fresh lyric idea bearing a tantalizing reminiscence of something else, a form of musical *déjà vu*, or, more precisely, *déjà entendu* ("previously heard"). For those to whom it has always said "A-minor Quartet," a greater familiarity with the *Missa Solemnis* might cause it also to say "Pacem, pacem," and eventually, even "Pacem dona nobis."

In the vocal form (*Missa* pages 328–9) it is first heard from the soprano and tenor in the solo quartet as:

In the instrumental transformation it becomes:[9]

[9] The underlinings indicate the parallel tones in the two melodic lines.

Not all the notes are retained—Beethoven tends to simplify as he re-considers—but the source is beyond question. I do not see a reference to any of this material in the sketches for the Opus 132 quartet repro-duced by Nottebohm[10]—which may have a bearing on the letter from the composer to his nephew Karl quoted below. Certainly one can see, in the discourse of the Song of Thanksgiving, an onset of the person-alized communication that makes the B-flat and C-sharp-minor quartets the extraordinary documents they are. And its pivotal position between the two Allegros that precede and the two Allegros that follow provides a new concept of balance and proportion. The five-segment sequence of the A-minor is a model for further experimentation in the works to come.

The agitation, not to say exaltation, which accompanied Beetho-ven's transports of musical generation has been remarked by several contemporaries who happened to be on the scene when it happened.

[10] Nottebohm: *Zweite Beethoveniana*, pp. 180 and 547.

One was Ries, who encountered Beethoven when the finale of the "Appassionata" was being born; another was Schindler, whose description of the moment when Beethoven conceived the link between the third and fourth movements of the Ninth Symphony has been quoted. But none expressed that degree of excitement as well as Beethoven himself as the time approached for the first performance of the A-minor Quartet. He was in Baden and had given the materials to his friend Holz —a kind of second Schindler whom Beethoven actually liked better—to have copied. Impatient at the delay, he sent an urgent message to his nephew Karl in Vienna:

Baden on Aug. 11 [1825]

Dear Son!

I am worried to death about the quartet, namely the 3, 4, 5 and 6th movements.[11] Holz has taken them along. The first measures of the 3rd movement have been left here, that is to say, 13 in number[12]—*I hear nothing from Holz*—I wrote him yesterday. Usually he writes. What a terrible misfortune if he should have lost it. *Just between us, he is a hard drinker.* Give me reassurance as quickly as possible—you can find out Linke's address at Haslinger's. Haslinger was here yesterday, was very friendly, brought out the periodicals and other things and begged for the new quartets. Don't engage in idle talk, it leads to vulgarities— But for God's sake give me some peace of mind concerning the quartet; what a terrible loss. The main ideas have been written on nothing but small scraps of paper, and I shall never be able to write out the whole thing again in the same way.

Your true father

Even the most gifted novelist could not invent so striking an image of a disoriented creator, the birth behind him, but the pains of labor still in his mind. Clearly the product of an overwrought, distraught, hypersensitized mind, the letter nevertheless depicts graphically—perhaps all too graphically—the flashes of feeling and the flights of fancy that went into the realization of a work on the order of Opus 132. It was, like so much else of Beethoven, a once in a lifetime occurrence which he would "never be able to write" again "in the same way."

---

[11] Thayer-Forbes (1964), II, 957. How Beethoven reduced the six movements to five may be judged from the comment on the B-flat Quartet (see p. 297). Linke was the cellist to whom Holz was to deliver the copy of the manuscript. The italics are reproduced as written.

[12] The "first thirteen bars" of movement three "happen" to be the first complete period of the Heiliger Dankgesang—that they existed separate from the rest of the manuscript suggests they had been rewritten at the last moment.

3

IN ONE OF HIS LESS-KNOWN ESSAYS, Ernest Newman, whose views of Beethoven are famously penetrating, addressed himself to the question of "Beethoven: The Last Phase."[13] Basing his position on certain verbal statements attributed to the composer, as well as to the evidence of his life's work, he notes the presence of not only the "dionysiac frenzy" but also the "dionysiac silence, when the spirit of the worshipper," in the Greek concept, "luxuriated in a new illumination, that of ecstatic quietude." It is in this "inner field of the dionysiac silence that the works of Beethoven's latest phase live and have their being."

Allowing for refinements and adjustments, one can have little doubt of the appropriateness of these views to the B-flat, Opus 130, Quartet. Among the several "farewell" musical addresses of Beethoven's late literature, the B-flat Quartet embodies the most consistently intimate, tender, and affecting music Beethoven ever wrote. Once, sitting at a piano and amusing himself with some passages of a favorite intermezzo, Sir Thomas Beecham extolled Robert Schumann for possession of one quality in greater measure than any other composer. "Intimacy of emotion," stressed Beecham, "intimacy." Through the B-flat Quartet, Beethoven confided to the teen-aged Schumann, as well as to others, that there was such a possibility for music. It makes its meaning clear and unquestionable, while leaving the cause for the tears he shed in the creation of the Cavatina (as he titled the Adagio molto espressivo) his own manly secret. And then, with a mighty shuffling off of restraint, he addressed himself to the frightful orgiastic exuberance of the Grosse Fuge, in which he challenged his own musical capacities to prove that four strings could do the work of forty. The success of his effort is still in doubt, but it will remain a challenge as long as there are players to whom the lure of doing the undoable takes precedence over more comfortable forms of virtuosity.

The temptation to seek a link with earlier works is ever alive in these summarizing quartets—often enough for the good reason that such links can be isolated and demonstrated in the A-minor and C-sharp-minor quartets. The question is: Where to look and how far to carry the search? In circumstances when a quest for subtleties yields no tangible results, it might be that—as in the case of Poe's "Purloined Letter" —the evidence is so apparent it was being overlooked.

---

[13] Ernest Newman: *Testament of Music*, ed. Herbert Van Thal (New York: Alfred A. Knopf; 1963), p. 240.

A clue recalled was Kerman's: "Beethoven had a way of realizing his unfulfilled conceptions." (See p. 7.) "The B-flat quartet," he continues, "helped to clarify what, in 1812, had been dimly and much less beautifully present in his mind." The line of connection thus set out was not in terms of *materials* that recurred to Beethoven from previous usage, in which their full potential had not been realized. Rather, it could be a recapitulation of moods of approach, counterpoises of emphasis which, he felt, as Kerman suggests, able to clarify and more fully realize.

From that point of view the opening movement, with its brooding adagio and forceful allegro in repeated alternations, could be a resumption of the confrontation of passive and active first joined in the slow movement of the Fourth Piano Concerto. The deliberations are much more prolonged, the supplication of the softer, imploring passive more intense, the rejection of the impatient active more brusque and uncompromising. Rather than unisons, the dialogue is fragmented four ways, with the non-consenting viola opposing the determined first and second violins, or exercising its prerogative of joining the importunate cello. At the end, and after some clear references to the recitative arguments first pleaded in the Ninth Symphony, there is no clear-cut victor. The soft sweet voice of persuasion does not triumph over adamant opposition as it did in the work of Beethoven's thirty-third or thirty-fourth year. Now there is, rather, a sense of accommodation, of conciliation, of make-do, in which coexistence is, for a composer in his mid-fifties, a rational solution to human differences.

The Presto, like many Scherzos that have preceded in Beethoven's literature, is terse, insistent, devoid of almost every technical challenge to the performer save rhythmic precision. This is akin to saying that all an actor requires to be a superior Hamlet is to articulate English better than almost anyone ever does. The burden is put not on the first violinist alone, but spread around through the consistently shifting, unison backgrounding of the second violin, viola, and cello.

The following Andante con moto ma non troppo is also marked poco scherzoso. This might leave some doubt in the performers' minds whether it was meant to be a reasonably animated slow movement or something of a slow fast movement. After listening to it a suitable number of times, and bearing in mind Kerman's reference (see above) to it in terms of Beethoven's Eighth Symphony, the sense of a meaning began dimly to dawn. The symphonic movement, it may be recalled, was an Allegretto scherzando. This movement is an Andante, poco scherzoso. Same thing, really, if different in phraseology. In short, what was left "in doubt" in the description was precisely what Beethoven meant to leave in doubt—whether the emphasis was more on scherzo than on andante. If, as Kerman says, the "quartet [of 1825] helped clarify what, in 1812, had been dimly and much less beautifully present in his mind," the result is to make the *motivation* unmistakable, even if the outcome isn't.

Though written documentation is lacking, it is almost a certainty that the Alla danza tedesca was conceived as part of the A-minor Quartet (Opus 132). It would, in other words, have been the sixth movement to which Beethoven referred in his letter of August 11, 1825 (see p. 294), with its frantic plea for Karl to seek out the fate of the manuscript entrusted to Holz. Whatever that association, there is little doubt that Beethoven's title is as often misundersood as it is comprehended—perhaps more often. Some are inclined to read it—as I have myself, in the past—as "Danza alla tedesca," which is to say, "Dance in the German manner." Not so. It says, rather, Alla danza tedesca—"Like a dance in the German manner," which is to say, played in the swaying, undulating manner of an incipient waltz, or a barely sophisticated ländler. In any case, it is profitable to compare it mentally with such a stylized form of rusticity as may be found in the finale of the B-flat (*Archduke*) Trio. In the first instance, all that is necessary for comprehension is present, evident on the surface, asking only for appropriate execution. In the second, what is on the surface is only a clue, or guide, to what is below. It helps if the performers are all of equal ability, capable of providing the minuscule differences of tonal coloration and harmonic insinuation that determine light and shade in such a work.

It is the fashion among some writers to say that Beethoven was not much of a melodist in his early days, markedly inferior to Mozart, Schubert, and Haydn, also to Schumann and Mendelssohn. They are the ones who discover an "unsuspected" wealth of melody in his later, and last, works. Without agreeing at all that his early works are somehow deficient in that precious commodity, I would readily agree that the most melting, the least resistible, and wholly overwhelming melodies are those he wrote late in life—as in the Cavatina of this quartet.

My contribution to the great-greater-greatest ranking of melodists would be the reminder that, as of this time, Beethoven had more to say of life's impacts and urgencies than almost any composer in history, and he somehow found within himself the means with which to say it. There was, at a subsurface point where most composers can probe no deeper, a depth of melodic resource which flooded to the surface in a clear, compelling spurt. Everyone has his or her favorites among Beethoven slow movements, but almost all listeners recognize in the Cavatina an order of communication which even the greatest of composers can achieve only once.

In some circles there purports to be, still, some uncertainty about the proper finale for the B-flat Quartet. Should it be the Grosse Fuge, which he wrote for the purpose and which was performed when the quartet was introduced in Vienna in March 1826, or should it be the much briefer non-fugal Allegro that he substituted at a later date? The reconsideration was urged upon Beethoven by well-meaning friends using the argument—familiar from the Opus 53 ("Waldstein") Sonata—that the movement first proposed was too long for the good of the work.

It may be noted that whether Beethoven agreed with the point of view that was being urged upon him, the publisher regarded the Grosse Fuge as so formidable an obstacle for the average performer that sales in the existing market for home quartet players would be seriously compromised. It was after Beethoven was assured that the Grosse Fuge could be published separately, not only in its original string form but in arrangements for piano duo—for which he would be additionally compensated—that he agreed to write a briefer, less demanding finale. Thus, Beethoven had the best of both worlds as they were offered to him at the time: The work existed to be played as he had imagined it, an alternate finale could be utilized for those to whom it appealed, and he had a new property for piano (four hands) which he could dedicate to his favorite Archbishop (Rudolph).[14]

My own conviction is of relatively recent date and based on two considerations:

1. Is the Grosse Fuge too long? In the aggregate of the five movements which precede it, totaling nearly half an hour in playing time, the Grosse Fuge, taking fifteen minutes to perform, is a finale far better suited to a balanced outcome.

2. Is the Grosse Fuge performable, and if it is, does the effort of performing it confer some gain in substance for the work as a whole?

I have, also in relatively recent years, arrived at the belief that it is well within the capacity of the super-quartets of our time, composed as they are of four highly specialized string players rather than those of former years who "turned to" such a way of life after discouraging

[14] Thayer-Forbes (1964), II, 975.

experiences in other pursuits. Such groups as the Juilliard Quartet and the more recent, perhaps even more proficient, Guarnieri Quartet, have brought to the problem a virtuoso flair and a degree of musical insight which leave no doubt with me that Beethoven knew exactly what he was about in this work.

Together with the *Diabelli* Variations and some aspects of the *Missa Solemnis*, the Grosse Fuge remains the last outpost of unabsorbed Beethoven, the furthest reach of his musical imagination and constructive power. What with the addition to the repertory of the Bartók quartets, which, by agreement, make the most use to date of Beethoven's late example in string writing, and the inclusion of Schoenberg's quartets within the playable literature, few technical problems remain in the Grosse Fuge for either the willing, able performer or the suitably receptive listener.

What Beethoven aspired to was the accomplishment of more than a finalizing, reaffirmation of the place, in quartet writing, for a grand movement on a contrapuntal plan that would make the finale of the C-major Opus 59, No. 3, the equivalent of a talented beginner's exercise. More particularly, it was his own commentary on the Cavatina which had preceded, and to which it was attached by an umbilical cord or chord. Shed all the tears you wish, he is saying, but never forget that life is a hard, uncompromising taskmaster, with the odds heavily weighted against the individual arriving at late middle, or early old age, happy, healthy, and spiritually intact.

The Grosse Fuge is, in a way, his own response to the *Art of the Fugue* which the all but blind Bach undertook at the end of his life and—characteristic of the frustrations that may beset those too optimistic that everything is for the best in the best of all possible worlds—did not live to complete. At an early point in his life, as is well known (see p. 84), Beethoven voiced his resolution to "seize Fate by the throat," and, in the common conception, did just that in the C-minor Symphony. Twenty years later, whether the flesh was able or not, the spirit was still willing to engage in mortal combat, assert its defiance of hardship, and insist upon its immortal durability. Taken all together, the Grosse Fuge is so integral a development of Beethoven's musical life force that a performance of the B-flat Quartet without it lacks fulfillment, or a proper climax.

Then, one may ask, why did he consent to provide the volatile, brief, untaxing finale which he wrote a year later—ironically enough (see p. 312)—as the last act of his musical life? Because there was a publisher crying out that he could not sell Opus 130 with the Grosse Fuge as a finale because his friends did not understand Beethoven's motivations (which he was, doubtless, too proud to explain), and that this was, merely, another instance of the shortcomings of an all-too-imperfect world. After all, the work did exist as he wrote it; and it was there, for those who would someday understand him better than he was understood in Vienna, 1826, to take the full force of his spirit as he distilled it.

4

THE C-SHARP-MINOR QUARTET, Opus 131, is at once the nadir and the zenith of Beethoven. It touches the lowest of emotional states in his troubled life, and it gives voice to them with the highest resources of artistry, technique, and craftsmanship. It is the distinction of this work that, as its contents are beyond praise, so its values are beyond paraphrase. Wagner tried and did very well in his famous interpretative essay, but the music touches nerves and evokes sensations that words are powerless to reach.

It began casually enough with a jotting in a Conversation Book that bridged the years from 1825 to 1826. "It" was the mournful opening phrase of the first section which, to judge from the sketches, emerged with the first six notes—including the crucial intervals B-sharp, C-sharp, A—in both their first and final formulation. The initial notation trails off into a bland continuation of what precedes, but the initial vision of what is to come has been, in the biological term, fixed.

The reference, above, to a "first section" rather than a first movement is by no means accidental. It is an unquestionable contribution to the high esteem which the work enjoys that it achieves once, finally, and insuperably, the ideal of integration for which Beethoven had been striving all his life. It is readily separable into seven main tempo divisions, each flowing into the other without a break, *physical* or *psychological*. The importance of the italics cannot be overemphasized. It is no insurmountable challenge for an able composer to bind one division of a work to another, if that is his desire. It is infinitely more difficult, indeed impossible for one lacking expressive power comparable to Beethoven's, to make each section an inevitable consequence of what has preceded. As an instance: as the Grosse Fuge had provided such later composers as Schoenberg and Bartók with a vista of what four performers could do, technically, so the C-sharp minor gave enduring evidence of the lessons of integration and organic unity Beethoven had learned in his lifetime, and which they were free to emulate in their individual ways (as Schoenberg did in the *Kammersymphonie*, Opus 9, and Bartók in his *Music for Strings, Percussion and Celesta*).

Embodied in Beethoven's accomplishment are psychological as well as musicological capacities of the first order. The work begins, as befits its name, in C-sharp minor and ends forty (score) pages later in C-sharp major. Along the way it visits literally innumerable keys, with never a sense of uncertainty on Beethoven's part of its eventual, secure, destination. The sections occur as they will, in whatever keys have been reached at a point when Beethoven decides another mood is in order. Section two, for example, is in D major, normally a position on the circle of keys as distant from C-sharp minor as one could attain in a hundred or so measures.

But the ear accepts it confidently, because the context has been established by the manner in which this way point has been arrived at. Cadences—or what the English call the "full close"—have been bypassed, delayed, or elided because they are the interruptive antithesis of any ongoing experience. Beethoven's mammoth achievement in giving the whole work the quality of an improvisation is high among the reasons why it has attained a place unique among all the works of his literature.

For an understanding of how it came about, one is indebted to Nottebohm for an insight into one such "improvisatory" detail.[15] It amounts, in the aggregate, to four measures of the score. It is written and rewritten no less than *twelve* times, each time with some variation of detail in the inner voices. It is like a writer searching for *le mot juste* to provide the precise shade of inflection, modification, or coloration the desired adjective will give to a substantive statement. Musically, it can be further subtilized by the interrelated effect of three voices supporting, offsetting, countering, or lessening the effect of the main statement in the first violin.

In the end, the simpler formulation of the first form prevails, but with six different kinds of minuscule differences, ranging from inner embellishments to *pizzicati* in the three supporting instruments that provide a magical degree of impact to the sound as it is finally heard. And to what purpose has Beethoven applied this prodigious labor? Just to such a connecting point from one section to another mentioned above,

[15] Nottebohm: *Beethoveniana*, pp. 54–7.

relative to a cadence procedure. (Preceding the Presto, marked No. 5.)

If there are, here and there, elements of the C-sharp-minor Quartet which arouse recollections of things past, it is not without reason. It is in this work, as an addendum to the Andante, ma non troppo, marked No. 4, that one comes abreast, finally, of the fragment (see pp. 17–19) cited by Nottebohm as the genesis for the slow movement of the C-minor Symphony. Here it recurs in almost the identical form it possessed more than twenty years before, to serve another, no less noble purpose *on its own*. If some mystical reason can be assigned to this recurrence, it could be that, as experience demonstrates, composers may duplicate ideas of others, even *ideas of their own*, in the context of a tonal *register*, a position on the *frequency range*, or at a pressure point of a formal discipline (transitional passage, bridge from first to second motives, coda). In this instance, it is the tonal register that mediates the recurrence: the top line of the bass clef, in A major rather than A-flat major. The rhythmic resemblance proceeds therefrom.

So much is visible to the naked eye, once alerted to the coincidence. But I owe to the cultivated ear of Joseph Braunstein the insight that this may be mere coincidence, not conscious or unconscious reminiscence, least of all cause and effect. He projects this passage in the C-sharp-minor Quartet not as derivation from a cell of twenty years before, but as an offshoot of a much more recent work: the *Missa Solemnis*. His source point is measure 23 of the Benedictus:

(*continued*)

ve - nit, qui ve - nit in no - mi- ne Do-mi-ni,

di - ctus qui_ ve - nit, qui ve - nit- in no -

This adds, to the mere matter of intervallic outline at a certain point on the tonal scale, the truly distinguishing fact of the affecting passage in the C-sharp-minor Quartet: canonic imitation, melodic overlap, extension of the melody at the most critical point:

Note, particularly, at A that the line in the cello extends the original phrase almost exactly as it is extended in the third measure of the passage in the Benedictus (which, in its slow pace and 12/8 meter, compresses the material of two measures into one). I am deeply obliged to Dr. Braunstein for this revealing citation of a further outcome of the *Missa Solemnis* in the late and last quartets. I also see the total pattern as one more instance of Beethoven's pre-Proustian *Remem-*

brance of Things Past as the alchemical source for things present and future.

The gruff rhythmic phrase which initiates the Allegro designated No. 7 also has its prehistory, especially in the not so gruff, nearly march-like form it eventually assumes. Both qualities are inherent in the finale of the E-minor Quartet (Opus 59, No. 2). To a degree it is the endemic form of a Beethoven finale, a way of developing force, thrust, momentum.

There is much, much more to be said of internal structural details, of key relationships, of rhythmic continuity, and other details dear to the heart of Sir Donald Francis Tovey and a legion of his admirers, myself included. But it is almost akin to giving the measurement for the oversized right hand of Michelangelo's *David*, thereby to suggest that a sculptor could model an equivalent masterpiece by incorporating a similar structural subtlety in one detail. One would have to be Michelangelo and exercise his total finesse over marble to make such a single, if vital, detail meaningful, just as one would have to be Beethoven and exercise his total finesse over tone to make "rhythmic continuity" meaningful rather than monotonous.

My particular point of summation would be to borrow from Wagner's famous prose appreciation of the C-sharp-minor, and its celebrated borrowing from Goethe's *Faust*: "The long introductory Adagio . . . I would designate as the awakening on the morning of a day that throughout its tardy course shall not fulfill a single desire: not one."[16] It was in his own Heiligenstadt Testament that Beethoven cried out, "Oh Providence—grant me at last but one day of *pure joy*."[17] It was his power or penalty as the "most *unfortunate fortunate* man"[18] to fulfill, musically, the two most polar of possibilities: his own quest for "one day of *pure joy*" in the Pastoral Symphony, and Faust's day of total disappointment in the C-sharp-minor Quartet—another, inverted, instance of zenith and nadir.

In his discussion of Tovey's commentary on the C-sharp-minor Quartet, Kerman questions the deliberate hyperbole of the eminent Scotsman in characterizing it as "his most unique work." "Can one

---

[16] *Faust*, Scene iv: *Upon the verge of bitter weeping*
  To see the day of disappointment break
  To not one hope of mine—not one—its
  Promise keeping.
Johann von Goethe: *Faust*, trans. Bayard Taylor (New York: Modern Library; 1930), p. 53.
[17] See p. 171.
[18] Thayer-Forbes (1964), II, 798. Beethoven used the phrase in a letter to his brother Johann, dated July 26, 1822.

really uphold the C-sharp-minor quartet," queries Kerman, "as 'more unique' than the B-flat?"[19] Of course, much depends on who the "one" is. But I would blunder into the belief that if Tovey could do it his way, I can do it my way.

My way of implementing Tovey's statement would be to say that the B-flat Quartet, for all its beauty, distinction, and heart-melting beauty, is very much a family affair. It is known to the devotees of the *sixteen* Beethoven quartets, and, of course, to many chamber music enthusiasts who might know only seven or eight, among many compositions by others. But the C-sharp-minor has a separate identity, a special place in history, for reasons dissassociated from any of the other fifteen quartets of Beethoven.

It is, for example, a fact that at its first performance in Paris by the Baillot Quartet in September 1829, not much more than two years after Beethoven's death, a young critic with an aspiration to be a composer took it all in and "fell under the spell of the composer's genius. Here is music, then, which repels almost all those who hear it and which, among a few, produces sensations wholly out of the ordinary. Whence this extraordinary discrepancy?" In addition to answering the question to his own satisfaction—"the envious oppose what is new"[20] —Berlioz absorbed the innovations of the C-sharp-minor Quartet as only the young and gifted can absorb innovations. In addition to many general precepts of string writing useful to the atmosphere for which he was striving in *Roméo et Juliette*, one striking device devised by Beethoven for emphasis, in section 4:

was turned to his own purposes by Berlioz in the *Nuit sereine*:

[19] Kerman: *The Beethoven Quartets*, p. 325.
[20] Barzun: *Berlioz and His Century*, I, 100.

to provide a dramatically incisive accent.

Curiously, it was from another Parisian quartet (the Morin-Chevillard) that Richard Wagner had his first revealing contact with the C-sharp-minor Quartet twenty-five years later. "The inner melody of Beethoven's C-sharp-minor Quartet was revealed to me for the first time [1853]," he wrote.[21] So profound was its impact upon Wagner that, upon his return to Zurich, where he was then living, he gathered four players of the orchestra together, rehearsed them in the quartet, and coached them to a point of proficiency to risk a public performance. It was for this performance (1854) that he wrote the commentary previously quoted. The experience, and the involvement it produced, was

[21] Newman: *The Life of Richard Wagner*, II, 447.

clearly a formative force in the *Tristan* vocabulary just coming to birth at that time (1855).

These two instances, far-reaching in consequence as they might have been, still do not determine whether the C-sharp-minor Quartet was unique in a way that the B-flat was not. Chromatics, after all, are chromatics, and need not appeal to composers of varied backgrounds in similar measure. But the C-sharp-minor is not made up wholly of chromatics. Brahms was not as strongly disposed to chromatics as some others have been. He was still responsive to the hushed appeal of the Adagio ma non troppo, whose throbbing formulation

becomes, in Brahms's second quartet of Opus 51, in A minor,

Finally, if Berlioz and Wagner are too much of a period, and Brahms was decidedly German and even more decidedly disposed to his great fellow-émigré to Vienna, there is still Tchaikovsky. Not the sort of man one would imagine as a partisan of late Beethoven, he has, nevertheless, some of the warmest words of all to say about them. Among them are: "All that is good but superfluous we call padding. Can we find this padding in Beethoven's works? I think we most decidedly do not. On the contrary, it is astonishing how equal, how significant and forceful, this giant among musicians always remains, and how well he understands the art of curbing his vast inspiration, and never loses sight of balanced and traditional forms. In his last quartets, which were long regarded as the productions of an insane and deaf man, there seems to have been some padding until we have studied them thoroughly. But ask someone who is well acquainted with these works, a member of a quartet who plays them frequently, if there is anything superfluous in the C sharp minor quartet. Unless he is an old-fashioned musician, brought up upon Haydn, he would be horrified at the idea of abbreviating or cutting any part of it."[22]

The allusion to the great Russian recalls that the C-sharp-minor followed the three for which Prince Galitzin had contracted, and to whose dedication he was thus not entitled. It bears, instead, an inscription "À Son Excellence Monsieur Le Baron de Stutterheim, Lieutenant." The Lieutenant's credentials among patrons of music for receiving this golden gift of immortal remembrance are unknown. He was, however, as the dedication went on to describe him, "Maréchal de Camp Impérial et Royal d'Autriche, Conseiller aulique actuel de Guerre, Commandant de l'ordre de Léopold d'Autriche, Chevalier de l'ordre militaire de Marie Thérèse et de l'ordre Impérial de Wladimir de Russie et la 3me Classe, Grand-Croix de l'ordre Royal de Sardaigne de Maurice et Lazare, et de l'ordre Royal militaire de St. Georges de la Réunion de Sicile, deuxième propriétaire de 8me Régiment d'Infanterie de ligne Impérial et Royal."[23]

Thus linked were perhaps the greatest of Beethoven's quartets and the most aggravating source of the anguish with which it resounds. It was in summer 1826 that Karl gave Beethoven the worst of their times together by attempting suicide, on July 30. The cause, if not explicit, was certainly related to the frustrations of a young man torn between a mother to whom he could not relate and an uncle who wanted to be more than a relation. It was the young man's choice to pursue a military career, an outcome to which Beethoven would become reluc-

---

[22] Modeste Tchaikovsky: *The Life and Letters of Peter Ilich Tchaikovsky*, ed. from the Russian, with an Introduction, by Rosa Newmarch (London: John Lane, The Bodley Head; no date), pp. 567–8. Letter to the Grand Duke Constantin, October 3, 1888.
[23] Kinsky: *Das Werk Beethovens*, p. 399.

tantly resigned. But the attempted suicide—an offense both criminal and moral in Vienna, with its strong Catholic controls—was an impossible obstacle to overcome without a special dispensation, military, if not moral.

Through the intervention of his old Bonn friend, Stephan von Breuning, with whom Beethoven had finally been reconciled, an approach was made to Stutterheim for Karl to be accommodated in his regiment. The princely gift, for which such a prince as Galitzin might have paid 100 ducats in gold, had its effect. Beethoven parted with one of the personal and treasured of his possessions, and Stutterheim made it possible for Karl to begin soldiering. This occurred shortly after January 1, 1827, when his uncle was mortally ill with the affliction from which he would not recover.

5

MANY MUSICIANS and some musicologists have not yet forgiven Beethoven for following the C-sharp-minor Quartet with a work less qualified to be his "last." If he had to write another, why should it not have been more of a testament, less an example of a will of another sort? Posthumously, Beethoven might enter the explanation that he had no way of knowing that the F-major would be his last as well as his sixteenth quartet. But I doubt that, even so, he would have apologized for leaving the world a reminder of his unquenchable humor after having been for so long absorbed in character revelations of quite a different sort.

If anything categorical may be invoked, it would be a reminder that he did not hesitate to write an Eighth Symphony—also an essay in good humor—after his Seventh. That, too, could have been his "last." Certainly the prospect of a new work in F appealed to his publisher even if he was aware that it was not on the epic scale of its predecessors.

No comment on the F-major Quartet would be even partially complete without some reference to the query "Muss es sein?" and the response "Es muss sein," which precede the finale, and which prompted Beethoven to append the subtitle "Der schwer gefasste Entschluss" ("The very difficult decision") to the title page. It is well known that the question and answer began with a catch-phrase familiar to Beethoven and his friends, and which was the subject of one of the innumerable canons he wrote to amuse himself and his circle. Its appearance in the finale of what became, by an accident of fate, his last quartet has prompted a search for deeper, more subtle associations. I cannot hear the justification for them in the music and see no reason for imputing esoteric reasons to a typical example of Beethoven's jokes.

By any standard light in characters, the quartet is by no means lightweight. It is, intrinsically, an example of relaxation after labor, the mighty mind in pursuit of some fey mental images that presented themselves in the aftermath of the struggle with the C-sharp-minor Quartet. The images were gratefully received, artfully examined, and—in the sense that Beethoven was wholly capable of such a combination of characteristics—bandied about with utmost seriousness. One senses the composer's complete awareness that the listener is expecting serious music from him, and provides it—up to a point. There are unmistakable overtones of a "put-on," of an elaborate pretense at seriousness (the introduction contains a hint of the "riddle" to come) despite the clear suggestions of humor. But every so often (as in measures 85–100) we are reminded that, even at his most playful, Beethoven is Beethoven, with a lion's capacity for rough play. "Play" to be sure, but potentially bruising, in the way that the Scherzo of the Ninth Symphony is bruising. There is even suggestion of an awareness that he is the composer who made a motto of ♫♩|♩ (here ♬|♪).

The Vivace recalls all those sonata movements with syncopated off-beats that Beethoven was writing in his twenties and early thirties. But it builds to a whirling storm of repeated accents (over a fifty-measure course) that all but sucks the listener into the eye of a hurricane. Formal innovations are out of place in a work of this concision, rules Beethoven. Both Scherzo and Trio have their repetitions, with first and second endings.

If formal innovations are ruled out by concision, one hundred of the most beautiful measures Beethoven ever composed are not. He chose to designate the slow movement's pace not only Lento assai, but also cantate e tranquillo—a combination of words not known to me in any prior usage by Beethoven. It is barely seven minutes in length, but once heard it is unforgettable. A simple line in the first violin moving in contrary motion against the cello, or second violin, or the viola (with one or another of the possible permutations) sets up a gravely beautiful chordal pattern. It evolves into one of Beethoven's most affecting melodic designs. For a few measures in the middle episode it becomes a composite of Adagio cantabile (Ninth Symphony), Cavatina (of the B-flat Quartet) and, even, "Heiliger Dankesang" (A-minor Quartet). It comes to a musical crux in an enharmonic transformation in which the written key of D-flat becomes C-sharp (same pitch, entirely different tonal connotations). At the recurrence of the opening chordal melody, the contrary motion possibilities are not merely exploited but subjected to marvellously enhancing elaborations in the first violin.

Perhaps it was the memory of a particularly affecting performance by a quartet during his period in Hamburg (1891–97) that inculcated the Lento assai so deeply in Gustav Mahler's mind that it came out as his own in the slow movement of his Third Symphony. That the results are Beethovenish need hardly be surprising.

In the context of what had preceded, the finale of the F-major Quartet could not follow on the Lento without some form of bridge. If Beethoven knew the meaning of *pons asinorum* ("asses' bridge"), which is unlikely, it could be used to describe precisely the kind of musical bridge he created here—a sixteen-measure structure of such solemnity and foreboding that the "asses" would expect something equally portentous to follow. Rather it is a true *scherz*, a *jeu d'esprit*, or W*itz*, worthy of the Gianni Schicchi celebrated by Dante (as well as Puccini) for having assumed the guise of another.[24] The quartet which treats this all as part of some profound philosophic discourse would make heavy going of Hugo Wolf's "Italian Serenade"—and some have done that, too.

6

IN A PERIOD OF STRESS during these final years, when Beethoven was struggling with the problems of the Ninth Symphony against disabilities of health, familial distractions, and financial woes, real or fancied, he wrote to Ries in London on November 15, 1822, with the news that his project was progressing and the words: "If I were in London what would I not write for the Philharmonic Society! For Beethoven can compose, God be thanked—though he can do nothing else in this world."[25]

Four years later, with his strength further depleted, and the incredible feat of having created not only the *Missa Solemnis* and the Ninth Symphony but, as an encore, five of the greatest quartets in history behind him, he could still say the same—if perhaps through clenched teeth. He was isolated on the farm of his brother Johann, up river (Danube) from Vienna, in a village called Gneixendorf, so small it cannot be found on a map, not far from Krems (which can).

He had come for a short visit, in late September 1826, on his nephew's behalf rather than his own. Karl's recovery from the attempted

---

[24] In the thirtieth canto of *The Inferno*, i.e., *The Divine Comedy*, Part I. He is associated with the Cyprian Myrhha, who also took the shape of another for purposes of personal gain.

[25] Anderson: *The Letters of Beethoven*, II, 978.

suicide was progressing, but still not accomplished. Some hair had been burnt off his head by the poorly aimed pistol shot, and until he was presentable, he could not claim his place in Stutterheim's regiment.[26] For the while Beethoven had occupation to distract him from the unattractive countryside. He finished work on the F-major Quartet. He addressed himself to the problem of a substitute finale for the B-flat Quartet, the real "schwer gefasste Entschluss" to take the place of the Grosse Fuge. He chose for the purpose a dance-like motive over a *moto perpetuo* figure. It could be interpreted as a bitter commentary on the unwillingness of the world to accept the ending to which he had given so much thought, and which he deemed thoroughly appropriate. However, the cellist Linke was anxious to perform the work with its new, less-taxing finale, and Beethoven extended himself to work it to a finish. It was sent on to Vienna by November 25. Thereafter the weather turned cold, there ensued the miserable journey back to the city, the disastrous chill, illness, inflammation, desperation, internal complications, decline, and death watch.

In the twilight of a long day of that twilight time, a friend who had visited with him often sat quietly on the bed waiting for Beethoven to waken from a nap. When he did, he showed him a note from Schuppanzigh saying a work of his performed the day before "did not please." Beethoven's comment was: "It will please them some day . . . I know that I am an artist."[27]

Such self-knowledge to one who had come from Bonn nearly thirty-five years before to "prove himself" in musical Vienna was sweeter than praise, more prized than applause, a richer reward than the medal from King Louis XVIII, all gold and weighing twenty-one louis d'or.

---

[26] Thayer-Forbes (1964), II, 996, describes him as "a bungler with firearms" as though half regretful the attempt had not succeeded (after all the difficulties he had caused his uncle).

[27] Ibid., p. 1044.

XV

The Sum of the Totals

I

WITHIN THE SPAN of one earthly existence, Ludwig van Beethoven forever transformed the art of music. He made music speak not only to men, but for man. He liberated it from servitude to caste or to class, the church or the court. He relieved it of a poetic status as "Music, heavenly Maid"[1] and established it as an utterance capable of conveying a philosophy, exerting a moral force, expounding a humane point of view, commanding respect as an instigator of social purpose and ethical action.

Such a conception of music's ethos, its ability to communicate beyond boundaries and languages, indeed to deal in other-worldly values, did not find an instantaneous or unanimous response among his fellow practitioners. Some were barred from participation by limitations of temperament, others by restriction to a national culture, and not a few by sheer lack of intellectual capacity. This was understandable in the nature of the philosophic influence he exerted on what is basically a medium of emotional expression.

But for those who found in him not merely a kindred spirit but a trailblazer toward their most cherished objectives—Schubert and Schumann, Berlioz and Wagner, Brahms, Bruckner, Richard Strauss, Mahler, Bartók and Schoenberg—the effect of Beethoven was transfixing, ennobling, and altogether irreplaceable.

How did this come about?

A series of totals has been spelled out in the preceding pages. They

---

[1] William Collins: *The Passions*, line 1.

could hardly have emanated from one with a more inconspicuous beginning. Beethoven was a musically susceptible offspring of a stock more distinguished for thoroughness than for creativity or imagination. Of the various careers to which his exposure predisposed him, Beethoven at first found the greatest attraction in performing at the keyboard and in creating music for himself to perform at the keyboard. As occasion, or occasions presented themselves, the urge took other forms. Until he was thirty, the impulse to use composition as a means to further his career as a performer tended to dominate.

The two contesting compulsions might have continued to battle each other through his lifetime had not an accident of fate intervened. The impaired hearing that was his greatest curse was also our greatest blessing. It not only drove him away from the easygoing social life to which he had been attracted in Vienna, and which his accomplishments made available to him. It drove him into a frenzy of activity, based on the belief that his lifespan might be as brief as, or briefer than, Mozart's. It multiplied productivity as it escalated expressivity beyond any rational expectation of what the talented youth of twenty-five might achieve by the time he was thirty-five.

The frenzy and its concommitants engendered a new sense of self, and also the need to accommodate the outpourings of that self in some referable form. What had been devised as a convenience became an indispensable adjunct not only to self-expression but also to self-preservation. The written record of works in progress which served him well enough in his early years (the "Kafka" Sketchbooks bear the evidence) were supplanted by much more exhaustive documentation of ideas as they came to him. Originally meant to serve only his own purposes, through a form of coded shorthand, they now serve our purposes not only as a guide to the understanding of the results but also to the method by which they were achieved. The urge to alter and improve both music as he found it and music as he imagined it, might have been thwarted or frustrated in the absence of such a resource. As the effect of his malady grew worse, he was driven ever more within himself. More so than almost any other composer, for whom music is primarily a means of self-expression, the creation of music became the wifeless, childless Beethoven's only means of self-fulfillment.

2

THE PRODUCTS of this concentration, urge to expressivity, and will to achieve were, by the time he reached forty, both amazing and unprecedented. A gush of impulse touched off years before had, under a lash of handicap and difficulty, erupted into: the *concerto sonata*, the *heroic symphony*, the *symphonic quartet*, and the *orchestral opera*.

No such works had existed before. No work in any of these categories could be undertaken in the future without regard for the changes, alterations, and expansions Beethoven had imposed upon all of them. One cannot characterize any of them as "improvements" on what had existed previously. Perfection is an absolute. Such perfection as Haydn had achieved in dozens of symphonies and quartets, or that Mozart had achieved in four operas (*Le Nozze di Figaro, Don Giovanni, Die Zauberflöte*, and *Così fan tutte*,) many of his symphonies, chamber music, divertimenti, etc., is beyond the cavil of a comparative. One can only say that, in his music, Beethoven ordained a new standard of values, organized a broader range of intellectual and emotional involvements, projected the realization of stresses and humors hitherto beyond the range of music to comprehend.

He had, indeed, left behind the expressive terrain marking the highest upward thrust of his predecessors, achieved an altitude of accomplishment which consumed even as it supplanted. Central to his achievement was conversion of forms into principles. Both Mozart and Haydn had expanded the relationship of elements that entered into "sonata form"—exposition, development, recapitulation—by the expansion of content, the addition of coda and codetta, etc. It remained for Beethoven, in the heat of creative effort that produced the Opus 57 Sonata, in F minor ("Appassionata"), or the Opus 59 Quartets ("Razumovsky"), to set aside such conventions as the "obligatory" recurrence of the exposition, the "conventional" repetitions of scherzo and trio, the "formal" divisions of sonatas, quartets, symphonies, and concertos into separate movements. From the finale of the Second Symphony on, cellos and basses were no longer bound to duplicate each other's traits and limitations through a marriage of convenience.

The kind of variations-through-embellishment that had sufficed, in most instances, for Haydn and Mozart as well as Bach, gave way— beginning with a sonata movement here, a quartet *satz* there—to the full-fledged variations-through-transformation first projected as a separate entity in the E-flat Variations, Opus 35. By the sort of misnomer that lends a kind of enduring innocence to earlier concepts of creativity, they continue to appear in print, or on records, with the title "Variations on a Theme from the *Eroica*," or "*Eroica* Variations." It would be closer to the truth—as set forth on page 164 *et seq.*—to describe Opus 55 as a "Symphony (*Eroica*) Based on the Variations in E-flat, Opus 35." The seeds of a chordal construction with a tonic dominant affinity had, of course, preceded its reaping—as seeds do.

In addition to destroying as it progressed, the momentum in Beethoven's creative urge consumed more than the rules of thumb deduced from the practices of his predecessors. It also, eventually, consumed the energy that fired such change. The decline in creativity that marks the years from 1811 (approximately) to 1816 can be associated with psychic states (the turn to forty), to emotional disturbances that destroyed his last hope for a really satisfactory sexual relationship, or even to the end of his career as a public performer.

In the aggregate, it was a period marked by the finalization of prior impulses, whether in the rounding out of his sequence of wholly instrumental symphonies with Nos. 7 and 8, or the completion of the enormous effort of 1814 which made a whole of *Fidelio*, rather than new beginnings or further transformations of musical designs as he had found them.

3

THE LANDFALL thus made on Cape Fidelio brings us to port on one stage of the long artistic journey. It is, in a way, a return to a point of beginning, a homeward leg bearing "cargo"—in the form of a musical idea—taken on many years before. That is, the matter from the early work of 1790 deemed seaworthy by Beethoven from the first launch of *Fidelio* in 1805, and never considered for displacement thereafter. Not many creators would have reposed such faith in expressions that could, on all reasonable grounds, have been termed juvenilia. Possibly none other than Beethoven would have expended the effort necessary to make it a coherent, consecutive—and what is more—congruent part of a whole covering twenty-four years of his creative life.

As such, *Fidelio* is the classic example, to this time in his career, of Beethoven's unending quest for the artistic equivalent of the alchemist's secret for transforming base metals into gold. In its final realization, it is a never-ending cause for wonder, and challenge to explanation. Like so much else in Beethoven's work, any endeavor to meet that challenge must rely in large part on personal evaluation of tantalizingly incomplete evidence.

In most discussions of Beethoven's mode of work, the emphasis is heavily on the tenacity, the pertinacity, and the patience with which Beethoven persevered in his search for the elusive objective. The intensity of the effort is akin to the late Christopher Morley's definition of good writing: "To stroke a cliché until it glows like an epigram." Of such effort, the evidence is total, unmistakable. The sketchbooks are full of it.

The more demanding question, still begging for adequate answer is: What was the prompting urge to that endeavor, the impulse behind the effort? I have yet to encounter a convincing answer, and I doubt that even were Beethoven restored among us, he could provide it. But that does not deter me from proposing my own explanation of the phenomenon.

My contention is that the force was contained in the musical microcosm itself, that it contained, for Beethoven—and for some later colleagues as well—a generative chemistry which contested for fulfillment in the same way that a virus clamors for domination of the body which is its host. Even as the salmon is driven to battle, for reasons it knows not, the rapids and currents that separate it from its spawning ground, so Beethoven was urged by a germination within him that was stronger than reason. Impalpable, non-identifiable, even more elusive than a random thought—because it cannot be translated into words—musical ideas found in Beethoven a uniquely fertile soil for growth and development.

If that hypothesis challenges credibility, let it be considered how many apples fell to earth from how many apple trees before Isaac Newton was prompted—even apocryphally—to ponder a law governing gravity. Or how many tea kettles boiled, with a chattering of covers, before George Stephenson speculated on the possibility that heating water to the boiling point might create a by-product—steam—with unprecedented propulsive power. Nor was Dr. Paul Ehrlich's celebrated compound called 606 because he had produced salversan after "only" 50 tries. The 605 previous efforts did not satisfy the criterium to which he aspired: a cure for syphilis.

It is conventional, even indispensable, for the scientist, the inventor, the research chemist to have a laboratory. But the notion that an artist could profit from the equivalent of such a facility has been offset by too many celebrated examples of inspiration to deal with the reality of the norm. The legend of Schubert writing "Who Is Sylvia?" on the back of a menu while waiting for a snack in a tavern, or the truth of Hugo Wolf enduring a dry spell of months before gushing forth with sixteen great songs in as many days[2] (when the right material coincided with the right

---

[2] *Grove's Dictionary of Music and Musicians*, 5th edn., see Beethoven article by Frank Walker, Vol. IX, p. 336.

chemical reaction to it) deals with romantic accident, which the lay-man loves to conceive as "art." But it bears hardly at all on the prosaic processes by which a substantial part of the musical literature has been produced.

So far as can be deduced from scanty evidence, the process with Mozart was wholly mental. He could perform the incredible feat of writing the *Linz* Symphony (No. 36, in C, K.425) for the Thuns in a visit of little more than a weekend, because, in all probability, he had the mechanics of such an apparatus fully fashioned in his mind. We know, for certain, from the manuscript score of the symphony directly preceding it (the *Haffner*, No. 35, in D, K.385) that Mozart employed his own kind of shorthand to facilitate such emergency requirements.

In the surge of creativity, he would write the top and bottom lines of the orchestral score (together with whatever else was fresh, compel-ling, and possibly forgettable) straight through. Then, at his leisure, he would go back and fill in the chordal structure, inner voices, etc.

How can one dogmatize about procedure after a lapse of nearly two centuries (the symphony was written in 1782)? The answer is contained in the visible evidence readily available since the *Haffner* manuscript was published in facsimile.[3] It shows the rapid, decisive strokes of the main lines of the work in a *darker* tint than the more leisurely, light-toned writing for the inner voices. In a discussion of this contrasting pen-manship with the late George Szell I hazarded the guess that the lighter strokes represented a hand other than Mozart's, possibly that of a copyist. "No," Szell corrected. "It is probably all in Mozart's handwriting. Don't forget, in those days they made ink by dropping a tablet in a little jar of water. As the ink was used up, more water was added. By the time Mozart had written out the main lines of the four movements and came back to put in the other voices, the ink had become very much diluted. That's why the part that was written in later is lighter in tone."

With Richard Strauss, the procedure was otherwise. When studying the problems of a stage work, such as an opera, he would immerse him-self in the text, meanwhile jotting down bits and pieces of thematic materials as they occurred to him. Eventually he would have a box, or a drawer, full of jottings. When he was ready for serious work, he would sift through the box or the drawer, select the most suitable, and then go about what, for him, was very much the *business* of composition. Of course, he added to the mechanical a masterly skill in transformation

[3] Wolfgang Amadeus Mozart, Symphony No. 35, in D (*Haffner*), K.385 (New York: Oxford University Press; 1968).

that, for example, converted a sentimental phrase to which Octavian-Mariandl sings "Nein, nein, nein, nein, Ich trink' kein wein" into the overarching line of the great trio that climaxes not only the third act of *Der Rosenkavalier* but the whole of the opera.

A long-lived as well as inordinately prolific composer, Strauss was not unversed in the capacity of the mind to do, by itself, things that the best will of its host, the body, could not force it to do. "If I am held up at a certain point in my composition at night," he has written, "and cannot see a profitable way of continuing in spite of much deliberation, I close the lid of the piano or the cover of the manuscript book and go to bed, and when I wake up in the morning—lo and behold! I have found the continuation." And, he adds, in some wonderment: "By what mental or physical process is this brought about?"[4]

Gustav Mahler's concept of a "second me" was articulated in the context of an interruption, by other duties, of the composition of his Fourth Symphony, in the fall of 1899. When he returned to work on it in the late spring of 1900, he was delighted to find that the "second me" had solved some of his most vexing problems while his conscious effort was directed elsewhere.[5]

There is, however, no visible record to indicate that any of the composers herein mentioned shared Beethoven's progressively closer involvement with his materials as he grew older. He was restricted, hemmed in, and eventually isolated from normal social contacts by his cruel disability. In the period that followed the beginning of the Conversation Books (1818), deafness drove him ever deeper within himself. Here, providentially, he found the richness of spirit and the strength of will to continue to generate musical ideas and to provide the fertile soil on which they could flourish.

4

SUCH CONCEPTS as "soil" and "fertility" have wider, more scientific connotations in these times than they did in Beethoven's. Much has been learned about rotation of crops, the virtues of permitting land periodically to lie fallow, the needs for replenishing materials normally found in the soil after usage, the care and feeding of second growths.

[4] Richard Strauss: *Recollections and Reflections,* ed. Willy Schuh (London: Boosey and Hawkes, Ltd.; 1953), p. 114.
[5] La Grange: *Mahler,* Vol. I, p. 580. The statement is contained in a letter to his musician-friend and perpetual correspondent, Natalie Bauer-Lechner.

So far as any evidence I am aware conveys, Beethoven knew nothing about such treatment of land. But the same sources confirm beyond doubt that he knew everything about replenishment of the spiritual terrain he cultivated. He had, in the aftermath of consuming the fertility in the rich loam that had served him well for more than twenty years, his fallow period. He had learned much about the virtue of dividing his energies among various types of writing from time to time, a creative equivalent of crop rotation. He plowed under, constantly, the materials that did not suit his conditions for harvest. If these became the seeds of second growths, the outcome was according to nature's own laws.

But he also did not forget to replenish the old soil from which he had drawn so much, by the addition of new, organic elements. Contrapuntal concerns became of increasing fascination to him as he grew older. Fugal patterns dominate a remarkable segment of the writing he did, after 1816, beginning with the Opus 102 Cello Sonatas. The closer-knit texture that could be woven from chromatic relationships was obviously much in his mind. His concept of variations took on new, broader dimensions. He reviewed Sebastian Bach, and came to revere the music of Handel.

At the time he began to sketch the second sonata of Opus 102 (see p. 225) he jotted down a fugal subject in D minor:

It is, without question, the motif from which he evolved the Scherzo of the Ninth Symphony. But, in a broader comprehension of the workings of this remarkable musical mind, it is more accurately described as a typically bare-boned "cell" of many things to come. Among such things to come—many months later—is a first movement with a descending motive that covers exactly an octave—in other words, it fills in the gap in the first two notes above.

Thus, the germination of the Ninth Symphony follows a generative process similar to that traceable in the *Eroica*, the "Waldstein" Sonata, and various other major works that have been dealt with in the preceding pages. It should be evident by now that creativity on the level of Beethoven's greatest works has little to do with beginning with a "motive" at point A and elaborating it, measure by measure, to a double bar at point Z four movements later. It has *everything* to do with elaborating an integrated structure, which is congruent in character and totally interrelated. It is possible to conceive the opening of the Ninth as a musical nebula, a kind of vaporous stirring of sonorities from which shapes of themes and ideas are precipitated. But it is thoroughly realistic to imagine Beethoven building, scheming, formulating such a nebulous opening in order to establish the preconditions from which a later objective—such as the Scherzo—would be a logical outgrowth. In one of his letters to Boito, Verdi said, "We must improve on truth," by which he meant, the artist must elaborate, extend, and make credible what exists in "true" human emotion. The scientist deals with a nebula as a true, physical fact. The artist, such as Beethoven, can improve on the "truth" by creating the effect of a nebula to serve his poetic purpose.

If he were asked to speculate on the origin of the fugue subject (see above) which became the Scherzo of the Ninth Symphony, Beethoven would doubtless have no ready answer. Indeed, it may not mean very much to make passing note of the resemblance, rhythmically, of that sketch to the opening of the *Fidelio* overture. Typically Beethoven, one might say of:

The resemblance comes to have considerably more meaning if it is recalled that the E-major (*Fidelio*) Overture was one of the last things to be written by Beethoven for the 1814 revision of *Fidelio* and was not, indeed, performed until June 26, 1814, some days after the première. Light as it is in tone—by the measure of the *Leonore* Overtures Nos. 1, 2, and 3, which it had supplanted—it is nevertheless notable for the energizing, wracking rhythmic impulse that Beethoven evolved from the opening pattern. That the impulse, timpani and all, persisted to become the generating force of the Ninth Symphony is merely to recognize that the fulfillment of one cycle of growth carried within it the seed for the next, second growth.

The time and trial which separated the Ninth's inception from its fulfillment eight years later has already been dealt with at length. But not in a conspectus of the ways in which all the resources amassed by Beethoven in his prior compositional career were marshaled to serve the ends to which he dedicated himself in this final, demanding period:

First, there was the *organization to productivity*, the ultimate refinement by which "random thought" (see p. 317) was converted into a creative methodology. In this plan of work, the sketchbooks serve as the repositories of change, the inventory of innovation in which, after trial and error on the order of Paul Ehrlich's, a solution to a problem was achieved. The difference is, however, that Beethoven did not designate the twelfth version of a particular passage in the C-sharp-minor Quartet (see p. 301) "Mark XII," as a manufacturer of today might label the perfected model of an initial design, nor label it, for the public record, "solution 12," as Ehrlich put "606" into the public mind. The process was Beethoven's own creative secret, the reward for effort expended on a solution that fulfilled his exacting standard, if only as applied to four "improvisatory" measures.

The sketchbooks also served the "retentive mind" of which Beethoven was justifiably proud. What better way of assuring that he "memorized" a musical theme, and thus would remember it forever (see p. 176), than by writing it down?

Then there was the role of the piano as catalyst, to generate new possibilities and involvements when compositions in which he did *not* use the piano were at an impasse. This, indeed, became the unspoken rationale of the work scheme from 1819, when the Ninth Symphony and *Missa Solemnis* were blocked by unresolved questions of content, discipline, and design he was unable to answer until 1822–23. In the interim he found an outlet for his immediate creative impulse in a series of piano works. Here the recently received Broadwood from England offered Beethoven new stimulation to realize the designs—fugue, counterpoint, variation—to which he was being drawn. Meanwhile, his equivalent of Mahler's "second me" was performing its function.

In these contexts, the *Diabelli* Variations, undertaken to "show what he could do" with a theme for which he had no great affection, became a form of Herculean diversion. They grew to dimensions no one, including the composer, could have predicted. One complication bred another, and another, till the rule of choice he had first projected in Opus 35 formed a frame that made a unity of expression out of a dazzling demonstration of compositional resource. In a way, this was Beethoven's ultimate sophistication—to cast into an imposing design a means of communication which had long enjoyed favor with other composers precisely because it required no design.

One could even argue that Beethoven continued to produce more sophisticated examples of whatever music engaged his attention as long as he lived and worked. What are the final quartets but an intellectualized form of Olympian games, in which the only competitor is Beethoven himself, the only criteria to be exceeded those of his own creation?

The organic outcome was the reward for devotion to order, elimination of the non-essential, and subservience of self to the ultimate objective.

APPENDIX

A Chronology of Beethoven's Afflictions
(Emotional as Well as Physical)

DATE	SOURCE*	PAGE**	CHARACTER	COMMENT
1792	T-F	134	"Pockmarked"	Affliction suffered before arrival in Vienna
1796–7	T-F	187–8	Typhus or some other grave infection	Summer months
1799	T-F	252–3	First traces of deafness	
1801 (June)	T-F	283–5	Confides his impaired hearing, details of "belly" being affected by medicines (almond); warm baths prescribed for diarrhea	Letter to Franz Gerhard Wegeler
1801 (November)	A	67	"Was I not always a sickly fellow?"	Says he would have traveled "half the world over" were it not for deafness
1802 (November)	A	77	"I was in the country for my health"	Letter to Breitkopf und Härtel

* "T-F" indicates Thayer-Forbes (1964); "A" indicates Anderson: *The Letters of Beethoven.*
** Volume I of Thayer-Forbes includes pages 1 to 605; volume II, pages 606 to 1,104 (index pages are 1,105–41). Volume I of Anderson includes pages 1 to 483; volume II, pages 487 to 984; volume III, pages 987 to 1,489.

Date	T-F	Page	Quote	Source
1802 (fall)	T-F	303–5	"Compelled to face the prospect of a *lasting malady* (whose cure will take years or, may be impossible)"	(Italics in the original Heiligenstadt Testament)
1805 (spring)	A	129	Complaint of "a heavy cold"	
1805 (spring)	A	131	"It is true that I have not been as diligent as I ought to have been—but a *private grief* robbed me for a long time of my usual intense energy . . . "***	Letter to Countess Josephine Deym
1805 (June)	A	139	"For the last week I have again been ailing"	
1805 (November)	A	142	"Since yesterday I have been suffering from *colic pains—my usual complaint* . . ."	
1807 (March)	A	164	"Not very well today"	Letter to Nikolaus Zmeskall von Domanovecz
1807 (May)	A	167	". . . I am not well"	
1807 (June)	A	169	"Yesterday and today I have not been very well, and I still have a terrible headache"	

*** This could be interpreted to refer to the syphilis Beethoven is believed, by some, to have contracted during his first years in Vienna. No written support for this belief has ever been discovered.

327

DATE	SOURCE	PAGE	CHARACTER	COMMENT
1807 (fall)	A	177	After a number of similar complaints: "My head is beginning to feel better"	
1808 (February)	A	185	"An attack of colic which seized me yesterday . . . prevents me from leaving the house . . ."	
1808 (March)	T-F	430	Operation for panaritium (felon, or fingertip infection/inflammation)	
1808 (summer)	A	193	"I have again been plagued by a wretched attack of colic"	
1808 (month unknown)	A	206	". . . suffering for a few days from a feverish attack . . . and now I am laid up in bed . . ."	
1809 (March)	A	222	". . . with my poor hearing I surely need to have someone always at hand"	
1809 (July)	A	234	"Since May 4th I have produced very little coherent work, at most a fragment here and there. The whole course of events [the	

Date	Source	Page	Note / Quotation
1809 (December)	T-F	473	French occupation of Vienna] has in my case affected body and soul"
1810 (January)	A	259	Continued after-effects of French occupation of Vienna: "fever" and "weakness" — "My illness sent me back to bed again for two whole weeks . . . we no longer have even decent bread"
1810 (February)	A	263	"My health is not yet quite restored. We are being supplied with bad food for which we have to play incredibly high prices. . . . It will probably be a long time before I am in a better state of health than I am now. But in any case I shall never recover the good health I used to enjoy"
1810 (May)	A	270	Letter to Wegeler — "I should be happy, perhaps one of the happiest of mortals, if that fiend had not settled in my ears . . ."
1810 (May)	A	275	"Had another violent attack of colic, but I am somewhat better today"
1810 (November)	A	300	"On account of my foot I cannot yet walk so far"

DATE	SOURCE	PAGE	CHARACTER	COMMENT
1810 (December)	A	301	"During the last few days I have had a headache and today it is very severe"	Letter to Archduke Rudolph
1811 (March)	A	316	"For over a fortnight now I have again been afflicted with a headache which is plaguing me. . . . During the festivities on behalf of the Princess of Baden I began to work rather hard; and one of the fruits of this diligence is a new pianoforte trio"	The trio is the B-flat Opus 97, now called the Archduke Trio
1811 (April)	A	317	"I have had to remain in bed, as I was struck down by a violent fever"	
1811 (June)	A	325	"On my doctor's orders I have to spend two full months at T[eplitz]"	
1811 (October)	A	343	"I was suddenly struck down by such a fever that I completely lost consciousness"	
1812 (February)	A	360	"My health has again been frequently exposed to some very fierce attacks; and the	

Date	Source	Page		
1812	A	368, 370	winter in Vienna destroys nearly all the good which the summer usually brings	
1812 (July)	A	373–6	Similar complaints during April, May "Immortal Beloved" letters, related to stay in Teplitz for treatment	
1812 (month unknown)	A	395	"Yesterday again and the day before yesterday and suddenly at the very time in the afternoon when I wanted to go to you, I was unwell . . ."	Letter to Archduke Rudolph
1813 (February)	A	407	Letter signed "LUDWIG VAN BEETHOVEN miserabilis": "I have been almost continuously ill . . ."	Letter to Zmeskall
1813			Similar complaints during the following months	
1814 (month unknown)	T-F	594–5	Dr. Alois Weissenbach, surgeon, music lover, and also deaf, visits Beethoven, who tells him of a "terrible typhus," and from "that time dates the decay of his nervous system and probably also his melancholy loss of hearing."	Weissenbach writes, in an account of his visit: "Beethoven's body has a strength and rudeness which is seldom the blessing of chosen spirits"

DATE	SOURCE	PAGE	CHARACTER	COMMENT
1815 (March)	A	505	"Unwell"	
1815 (summer)	A	519	"As soon as I feel better I shall visit you"	Letter to Archduke Rudolph
1815 (September)	A	526	"I am not well"	
1815 (November 20)	T-F	624	Beginning of emotional involvement with nephew Karl	
1816 (February)	A	567	"My condition once again deteriorated so that I was able to take a few walks only in the daytime . . ."	Letter to Archduke Rudolph
1816 (May)	A	576	"I have been ill and have had a great deal to do"	
1816 (November)	A	610	"Since the 14th of last month I have been continuously ill and have had to stay in bed and in my room . . ."	
1817 (February)	A	667	"My health has been undermined for a considerable time. *The condition of our country has been partly responsible for this;*	Letter to Franz Brentano

Date		No.	Description	Reference
1817 (June)	A	683	and so far no improvement is to be expected, nay rather, every day there is a further deterioration . . ." Discusses ailments of last six months' treatments: "...six powders daily and six bowls of tea"; "...it will be a long time ...before I am completely cured ..."	Letter to Countess Anna Maria Erdödy
1817 (August)	A	701	"I often despair and would like to die. For I can see no end to all my infirmities. . . . If the present state of affairs does not cease, next year I shall not be in London but probably in my grave . . ."	
1818	T-F	730	Deafness compels visitors' recourse to written questions in order to facilitate answers	Beginning of the Conversation Books
1818 (May)	A	764	"The doctor has promised me that by the middle of June I shall certainly be quite restored to health"	Letter to Archduke Rudolph
1819 (June)	A	813	"Caught a violent cold"	
1819 (June)	A	816	"I am in bed and cannot therefore embark on a lengthy disquisition on the subject of the oratorio"	Believed to have been written to the Gesellschaft der Musikfreunde, Vienna

DATE	SOURCE	PAGE	CHARACTER	COMMENT
1819 (September)	T-F	738	"The poor fellow is practically stone deaf"	Karl Friedrich Zelter, writing to Goethe
1819 (September)	A	844	"This year owing to enfeebled health my stay in the country has not been quite as beneficial as usual"	Letter of apology to Zelter, for failure to keep appointment
1819 (month unknown)	A	864	"All this while I have been a semi-invalid"	Letter to Archduke Rudolph
1820 (September)	A	901	"Not been feeling well"	Letter to Archduke Rudolph
1820 (September)	A	902	"Persistently poor health"	
1820 (month unknown)	A	908	"Owing to the sensitive condition of my abdomen it is quite impossible for me to go out without a strong protecting belt . . ."	
1821 (March)	A	915	"For six weeks I have been laid up with a violent attack of rheumatism"	

334

1821 (July)	A	**920**	"I had been been very poorly for a long time when finally *jaundice definitely* set in . . ."	Letter to Archduke Rudolph
1821 (November)	A	926	"Since last year and until now I have been constantly ill. . . . During the whole summer I was suffering from jaundice which persisted until the end of August. . . . At last good health seems to be returning to revive my spirits, so that I may again start a new life to be devoted to my art. This I have had to renounce for almost two years, both for lack of health and also on account of many other human sorrows . . ."	Letter to Brentano
1822 (February)	A	941	"Last night I again *succumbed to the earache* which I usually suffer from during *this season*"	
1822 (May)	A	944	"During the last four months I have again been constantly suffering from gout on my chest and have been able to do only very little work"	Letter to Nikolaus Simrock
1822 (September)	A	968	"You are receiving this letter from Baden, where I am taking the baths. For my illness, which has lasted two and a half years, is not yet completely cured"	Letter to Simrock

DATE	SOURCE	PAGE	CHARACTER	COMMENT
1822 (November)	A	976	"My health, I admit, has not been completely restored by the baths which I have been taking, but on the whole it has benefited from the cure"	Letter to Carl Friedrich Peters
1822 (May)	A	946	"God grant that the most natural bond, the bond between brothers, may not again be broken in an unnatural way. In any case my life will certainly not last very much longer . . ."	Letter to his brother Johann
1823 (July)	A	1,054	"Since Y.I.H's departure I have been ailing almost the whole time; and latterly I have been having bad pains in my eyes"	Letter to Archduke Rudolph
1823 (July)	A	1,060	"I myself have been constantly ailing for three and a half years"	Letter to Franz Stockhausen (a musician and father of the famous baritone Julius Stockhausen)
1823 (August)	A	1,080	"I came here with catarrh and a cold in my head, both serious complaints, seeing that,	Letter from Baden, to his nephew Karl

Date		No.	Quote	Source
1823 (September)	A	1,088	"as it is, the fundamental condition is still catarrh; and I fear that this trouble will soon cut through the thread of my life, or worse still, will *gradually* gnaw it through" "... I now feel better than I did. My eye complaint too is rapidly clearing up . . ."	Letter to Louis Spohr, in Cassel
1824 (January)	A	1,104	"Overwhelmed with work and still suffering from an eye complaint . . ."	
1824 (August)	A	1,135	"I am still living—but how?! the life of a snail. For the very unfavourable weather is constantly putting me back; and it is impossible when one is taking these baths to command one's *physical strength* as usual . . ."	Letter from Baden, to Archduke Rudolph
1824 (November)	A	1,150	"Being ill when I returned from Baden, I was prevented from visiting Your Imperial Highness as I desired; for I was forbidden to go out of doors . . ."	In Vienna, letter to Archduke Rudolph
1825 (April)	A	1,186	"I am not feeling well and I hope that you will not refuse to come to my help, for I am in great pain"	Letter to Dr. Anton Braunhofer

DATE	SOURCE	PAGE	CHARACTER	COMMENT
1825 (April–May)	T-F	944	Night work and poor diet are blamed by Schindler for Beethoven's new stomach distress	
1825 (April)	T-F	945	Braunhofer stipulates: "No wine, no coffee, no spices of any kind"	
1825 (May)	A	1,192	"I am about to go into the country and am just convalescing from an inflammation of my intestines . . ."	Letter to Bernhard Schotts Söhne, Mainz
1825 (May)	A	1,195	"I spit a good deal of blood, but probably only from my windpipe. But I have frequent nosebleedings, which I often had last winter as well . . ."	Letter to Braunhofer
1825 (May)	A	1,204	"We thank you for *the advice which was well given and well followed* by means of the *wheels* of your inventive genius; and we inform you that in consequence we now feel	Letter to Braunhofer

Date		No.		
1825 (June)	T	947	"very well. Our heart and soul are inclined to overflow and might therefore cause you, Sir, some inconvenience. Hence we are observing a reverent silence" Result of renewed health is resumption of work: Conversation Book of current usage (May–June) contains notation "Hymn of Thanksgiving to God of an Invalid on his Convalescence. Feeling of new strength and reawakened feeling"	The movement of the A-minor Quartet (Opus 132), which bears these words, was created at about this time
1825 (August)	A	1,238	"My stomach is in very bad shape and I have no doctor. . . . Since yesterday I have eaten nothing but soup and a couple of eggs and have drunk only water; my tongue is quite yellow . . ."	Letter to his nephew Karl
1825 (September 3)	A	1,245	"I must confess that in my case also the champagne went too much to my head and that again I had to experience the fact that such indulgence hampers rather than promotes my ability to work . . ."	Letter to Friedrich Kuhlau (after a social evening)
1826 (February)	A	1,278	"Please do visit me, for I have been plagued for some time with rheumatism or gout . . ."	Letter to Braunhofer

DATE	SOURCE	PAGE	CHARACTER	COMMENT
1826 (May)	A	1,286	"Constantly dogged by ill health . . ."	Letter to Schotts Söhne, Mainz
1826 (June)	T-F	978 n.	Ill-health	Letter to Prince Galitzin
1826 (July 30)	A	1,293	"A great misfortune has happened, a misfortune which Karl has accidentally brought upon himself. . . . Karl has a *bullet* in his head. . . . But come quickly, for God's sake, quickly"	Letter to Dr. Karl von Smetana
1826 (September–December)	T-F	1,006	Goes to visit brother Johann in Gneixendorf, taking Karl for recuperative purposes. Leaves Vienna on September 28 with Karl and Johann. His intention is to remain a week, but he stays through October and November, subsisting on a restricted diet of eggs, soup, etc. Diarrhea, edematous feet. Persists on the premise that the visit is beneficial to Karl	

| 1826 (December) | T-F 1,016–17 | He decides to leave Gneixendorf for Vienna on December 1. Bad weather, bad trip by carriage. Overnight stay at an inn, without heat in a shutterless room, on a frosty night—little sleep. He takes chill. Arrives in Vienna an invalid on December 3. Several doctors who are called in decline to participate, knowing his case history and fearing the worst. They do not want to preside over Beethoven's death. A doctor appears on December 5. His diagnosis is pneumonia, into dropsy. Beethoven makes some recovery after tapping |
| 1827 (January–March) | T-F 1,040–50 | Three more tappings between January and February 27, steady decline thereafter. His death: March 26, 1827 |

INDEX

NOTE

Page numbers in italics indicate
illustrations of musical notations.

A Note About the Author

IRVING KOLODIN was born in New York in 1908. He was a member of the music staff of the New York *Sun* from 1932 to 1949, and was music editor and music critic from 1945 until the paper was merged with the *World-Telegram*. Beginning in 1947 he was editor of the "Recordings" section of *The Saturday Review*, of which he became music editor and critic in 1949. He has retained that identity to the present day. In addition to his well-known books on the Metropolitan Opera, Mr. Kolodin has published several editions of a *Guide to Recorded Music*; *The Musical Life*; and the wide-ranging *Continuity of Music*. He has traveled broadly in this country, in Europe, and in South America to report on the musical scene, and has made three trips to Australia in recent years. Since 1968 he has been a member of the faculty of the Juilliard School, where he conducts graduate courses in the Criticism of Music and the Symphonies of Mahler. Mr. Kolodin lives in New York.

A Note on the Type

THE TEXT OF THIS BOOK is set in Electra, a typeface designed by William Addison Dwiggins for the Mergenthaler Linotype Company and first made available in 1935. Electra cannot be classified as either "modern" or "old style." It is not based on any historical model, and hence does not echo any particular period or style of type design. It avoids the extreme contrast between "thick" and "thin" elements that marks most modern faces, and is without eccentricities which catch the eye and interfere with reading. In general, Electra is a simple, readable typeface which attempts to give a feeling of fluidity, power, and speed.

Composed, printed, and bound by
The Haddon Craftsmen, Inc., Scranton, Pa.
Music scores by Maxwell Weaner
. Typography and binding design
by Anita Karl